T0192079

Undergraduate Topics in Computer Science

Undergraduate Topics in Computer Science (UTiCS) delivers high-quality instructional content for undergraduates studying in all areas of computing and information science. From core foundational and theoretical material to final-year topics and applications, UTiCS books take a fresh, concise, and modern approach and are ideal for self-study or for a one- or two-semester course. The texts are all authored by established experts in their fields, reviewed by an international advisory board, and contain numerous examples and problems. Many include fully worked solutions.

More information about this series at http://www.springer.com/series/7592

David R. Brooks

Programming in HTML and PHP

Coding for Scientists and Engineers

 Springer

David R. Brooks
Institute for Earth Science Research
  and Education
Eagleville, PA
USA

ISSN 1863-7310   ISSN 2197-1781   (electronic)
Undergraduate Topics in Computer Science
ISBN 978-3-319-56972-7   ISBN 978-3-319-56973-4   (eBook)
DOI 10.1007/978-3-319-56973-4

Library of Congress Control Number: 2017937517

Printed on acid-free paper

This Springer imprint is published by Springer Nature
The registered company is Springer International Publishing AG
The registered company address is: Gewerbestrasse 11, 6330 Cham, Switzerland

Preface

What is the Purpose of this Book?

There are many students and professionals in science and engineering, other than those specifically interested in fields such as computer science or computer engineering, who need to know how to solve computational problems on computers. There are basically two approaches to meeting the needs of such people. One is to rely on software applications such as spreadsheets, using built-in functions and perhaps user-defined macros, without requiring any explicit understanding of the principles on which programming languages are based.

A second approach is to learn a "traditional" programming language, for previous generations Fortran or Pascal, and more recently C, C++, or Java. These languages are important for certain kinds of work, but they may be viewed, possibly with good reason, as irrelevant by many students and professionals.

From a student's point of view, there is no painless solution to this dilemma, but in this book I assume that learning to solve computational problems in an online environment using HTML and PHP will at least appear to be a more relevant approach. HTML, **H**yper **T**ext **M**arkup **L**anguage is universally used as the foundation for online applications. HTML documents can be used as "data input forms" for PHP—originated by Rasmus Lerdorf in the mid 1990s as "Personal Home Page Tools," but long since expanded as a comprehensive programming language.

What separates PHP from an online development language such as JavaScript is its support for accessing externally stored data files, which greatly extends the range of science and engineering problems that can be addressed.

In some ways, an HTML/PHP environment is more difficult to learn than traditional and more "mature" (some might prefer "obsolete") text-based programming languages. C, for example, is a fairly small language with an unambiguous set of syntax rules and a primitive text-based input/output interface. You can view the limitations of C as either a blessing or a curse, depending on your needs. A major advantage of C is that programs written in ANSI Standard C[1] should work equally well on any computer that has a C compiler, making the language inherently platform-independent.

HTML, on the other hand, is an immature and developing programming languages (if we can agree to call HTML a "programming language") that functions within a constantly changing Web environment. It lacks a uniformly accepted set of syntax rules. There are dialects of HTML that will work only on particular computing platforms and the possibility exists for language "extensions" that may be even more platform-dependent. PHP is still an evolving language whose standards are set and maintained by a global user group—essentially by volunteers—but it adheres to broadly understood programming language concepts and has well-defined syntax rules.

Fortunately, it is possible to work with some core subsets of HTML which, along with PHP, can be used to solve some of the same kinds of computational problems that would be appropriate for a more traditional "scientific" programming language such as C or C++. My motivation for writing this book and its predecessors was to learn how to use HTML and PHP to create my own online applications, and I now use this environment for many tasks that I previously would have undertaken in Fortran or C. Based on my own experience I have concluded that, although it might not be accurate to define PHP as a "scientific" computing language, it is nonetheless entirely reasonable to use HTML/PHP as a framework for learning basic programming skills and creating a wide range of useful and robust science and engineering applications.

Although this book is intended for "scientists and engineers," as suggested by its title, the content is not technically complex. The examples and exercises do not require extensive science, engineering, or mathematics background and only rarely is mathematics beyond basic algebra needed. So, I believe this book could serve as a beginning programming text for undergraduates and even for high school students.

---

[1]ANSI = American National Standards Institute, a voluntary standardization system in the United States.

Learning by Example

It is well known that people learn new skills in different ways. Personally, I learn best by having a specific goal and then studying examples that are related to that goal. Once I understand those examples, I can incorporate them into my own work. I have used that learning model in this book, which contains many complete examples that can serve as starting points for your own work. (See the second quotation at the beginning of this preface).

This model works particularly well in an online environment. The amount of online information about HTML and PHP, including code samples, is so vast that it is tempting to conclude that nobody writes original code anymore. If you have trouble "learning by example," you will have trouble learning these languages, not just from this book, but in general because that is how most of the available information is presented.

It is an inescapable fact that a great deal of the source code behind Web pages involves nothing more (or less) than creative cutting, pasting, and tweaking of existing code. Aside from the issues of plagiarism and intellectual dishonesty that must be dealt with in an academic environment, there is also the practical matter of an effective learning strategy. You cannot learn to solve your own computational problems just by trying to paste together someone else's work. (Believe me, I've tried!) Until you develop your own independent skills, you will constantly be frustrated because you will never find *exactly* what you need to copy and you will be unable to synthesize what you need from what is available.

So, while you should expect to find yourself constantly recycling your own code based on what you learn from this book, you need to make sure that you really *learn how to use* these languages and don't just *learn to copy*!

If you are reading this book, you almost certainly are not and do not aspire to be a professional programmer. For a casual programmer from a scientific or technical background, it can be very time consuming to cut through the clutter of online information about these languages when the applications are not directly applicable to the needs of scientists and engineers. In my own work, what I need over and over again is some sample code that will jog my memory about how to approach recurring programming problems—how to pass information from an HTML document to a PHP application, how to extract information from a data file, how to display data-based graphics, etc. Throughout the book, I have tried to give examples that serve this need, including an entire chapter devoted to PHP graphics.

The Origin and Uses of this Book

In 2007, Springer published my book, *An Introduction to HTML and JavaScript for Scientists and Engineers*. This was followed in 2008 by *An Introduction to PHP for Scientists and Engineers: Beyond JavaScript* and, in 2011, by *Guide to HTML,*

JavaScript and PHP. Those books followed the sequence in which I learned to use HTML, JavaScript, and PHP in my own work. (See the first quotation at the beginning of this preface.) Although I still use JavaScript for some applications, I now rely mostly on an HTML/PHP environment in which an HTML document serves as the input interface to a separate PHP application that performs the required calculations and, as appropriate, generates graphics.

This book easily provides enough material for a one- or two-semester introductory programming course for science and engineering students because the possibilities for PHP-based applications are limitless. Because of the book's very specific focus on science and engineering applications, I believe the book is also particularly well suited for developing a working knowledge of HTML and PHP on your own if you are a student or professional in any technical field.

Acknowledgements

I am indebted to Wayne Wheeler, Senior Editor for Computer Science at Springer, and Simon Rees, Associate Editor for Computer Science at Springer for encouraging and supporting this project.

Eagleville, USA   David R. Brooks

Contents

Introducing HTML

1

This chapter provides an introduction to using HTML to create simple Web pages suitable for interfacing with PHP applications. Several examples show how to modify the appearance of a document by using HTML tags and their attributes.

1.1 Introducing the Tools

1.1.1 What Is an HTML Document?

HTML is an acronym for **H**yper**T**ext **M**arkup **L**anguage. HTML documents, the foundation of all content appearing on the World Wide Web (WWW), consist of two essential parts: information content and a set of instructions that tells your computer how to display that content. These instructions—the "markup," in editorial jargon—comprise the HTML "language." It is not a programming language in the traditional sense, but rather a set of instructions about how to display content in a Web browser. Ideally, online content should look the same regardless of the browser being used or the operating system on which the browser resides. This goal of complete platform independence is achieved only approximately in practice.

Every HTML document should contain a minimum of four elements:

```
<html> ... </html>
<head> ... </head>
<title> ... </title>
<body> ... </body>
```

These elements define the essential parts of an HTML document: the document itself, a heading section, a title section, and a body. All four elements should be included even if they don't enclose any content. Every HTML element is defined by one or two tags—usually a start tag and an end tag. Tags are always enclosed in angle brackets: <...>. End tags start with a slash (/). A few HTML elements have only one tag.

© Springer International Publishing AG 2017
D.R. Brooks, *Programming in HTML and PHP*, Undergraduate Topics in Computer Science, DOI 10.1007/978-3-319-56973-4_1

1

The four basic elements are organized as follows within an HTML document:

```
<html>
  <head>
    <title> ... </title>
  </head>
  <body>
    ...
  </body>
</html>
```

The html tag encloses all other tags and defines the boundaries of the HTML document. We will return to the other tags later. The indenting used to set off pairs of tags is optional, but it makes documents easier to create, read, and edit. This style is part of good programming practice in all languages.

HTML documents are usually used as to distribute information for access on the Web. However, for the purposes of this book, HTML documents will be used along with the PHP programming language to create an environment for solving a wide range of computing problems.

Good programming technique often involves separating the input/output (I/O) interface from the underlying calculations that do the work of a program. The HTML/PHP programming environment provides a conceptually elegant means of implementing this strategy. An HTML document provides the I/O interface and PHP handles the calculations. An advantage of HTML is that it provides a wealth of interface possibilities that far surpass those of older text-based languages.

1.1.2   How Do You Create HTML Documents?

Because HTML documents are just text documents, they can be created with any text editor. Even Windows' very basic Notepad application is a workable choice for simple tasks.[1] Once HTML files have been created, you can open them in your computer's browser, hopefully without regard to which browser you are using. As long as you give such documents an .htm or .html file name extension, they should automatically open in your browser when you double-click on the file name. Although Windows documents are no longer

---

[1]When you save a file in Notepad, the default extension is .txt, so you will have to specify .htm or .html as a file extension.

restricted to three-letter extensions, a convention dating back to the pre-Windows days of MS-DOS operating systems, the three-letter `.htm` extension is often used on Windows systems. The four-letter `.html` extension is commonly used on UNIX systems. However, either extension is perfectly acceptable.

There is one other consequence of using Windows computers for creating all the code examples in this text: Windows file names are case-insensitive, while on UNIX systems, all spellings, including file names and commands, are case-sensitive. In Windows, you can name a document `newDocument.htm`. Later, you can spell it `newdocument.htm`, `NEWDOCUMENT.HTM`, or any other combination of uppercase and lowercase letters and it won't matter. On a UNIX system, that file will be recognized only with the original spelling.

Although you can create text (and, therefore, HTML) documents with a full-featured word processor such as Microsoft Word, this is not recommended. When you save a word processor document it no longer contains just the text you have typed, but also all the layout and formatting information that goes with that document. You can choose to save a document as just text with an `.htm` extension, but it is easy to forget to do this.

Microsoft Word and other modern word-processing applications can also format any document as an HTML document. However, this is also not recommended. These converted documents may include a huge quantity of extraneous information and HTML instructions that make the resulting file much larger and more complex than it needs to be. (To see this for yourself, save a Word document as an HTML document and then look at the result in a text editor such as Notepad!)

RTF ("rich text format") documents are also unacceptable, as they still retain some formatting information that is inappropriate for an HTML document. Any document that contains "smart quotes" rather than "straight quotes" can also cause problems, because smart quotes may not be displayed properly by browsers. (This is much less of a problem on current browsers than it used to be.)

There are commercial Web development tools that allow you to create Web pages without actually knowing anything about HTML. These applications are not suitable for use with this book. The obvious reason is that the primary purpose of the book is to show you how to write your own HTML documents to be used as an interface to a PHP file. Also, these applications may create HTML files that are much larger and more complex than they need to be. Such applications are better suited for Web development projects that involve a lot of the other "bells and whistles" that make commercial Web pages attractive.

Creating an HTML document that does what you need it do inevitably involves switching back and forth between a text editor and a browser—making changes and observing the effects of those changes. A good editor should allow you to move back and forth quickly and easily between the source document and its display in a browser when you make changes. It is certainly possible, but not particularly convenient, to do this with a simple text editor such as Notepad.

There are many commercial software tools whose purpose is to facilitate writing and editing HTML documents by integrating document creation, editing, and viewing. As noted above, some of them are intended for large and complicated projects and may be "overkill" for use with this book. For many years, I have used Visicom Media's freeware AceHTML. This software is no longer available, but there are other freeware alternatives which provide automatic color-based text formatting, coding tools, and an integrated browser that makes it easy to create and edit HTML and PHP documents.

Although it *shouldn't* make any difference which browser you use, it is worth noting that all the HTML documents displayed in this text come from either AceHTML's internal browser or Mozilla's Firefox, which is the default browser on the author's Windows computers.

1.1.3   Some Typographic Conventions Used in This Book

HTML tags and other code are printed in a `monospaced (Courier) font` in document examples and whenever they are referred to in the text. Thus, `document` is interpreted as a reference to an HTML object, as opposed to its general use as a term identifying a body of text. Within descriptions of HTML and PHP document features, user-supplied text is denoted by *{italicized text in braces (curly brackets)}*; the curly brackets are usually *not* meant to be included in the user-supplied text.

AceHTML and other editors typically apply some combination of color coding, bold fonts, and italicized fonts to various language elements. When HTML and PHP code is copied from the editor and inserted into this book, bold and italic fonts are retained but the color coding is not.

The renderings of HTML documents and other output as displayed in a browser window have been captured and edited on a Windows computer by pressing the PrtScn (Print Screen) key and copying the resulting screen image into an image editing program.[2] Pressing Alt-PrtScn copies just the currently active window instead of the entire screen.

---

[2]For many years, I have used the freeware IrfanView program.

Because of the small format of this book, line breaks in HTML document examples, and later in PHP scripts, are often necessary and may sometimes cause problems. Although every effort has been made to use line breaks in a way that does not cause problems, it will sometimes be necessary to remove breaks and "rejoin" some lines when you reproduce these documents for your own use.

1.1.4 Finding More Information About HTML

It should be clear that this book is in no way intended as a reference source for HTML. Any attempt to provide complete coverage of HTML would thoroughly confound the purpose of the book and is far beyond the author's capabilities! You can easily find support online for those portions of HTML required for its use as an interface for PHP applications. Here are two standard reference sources for HTML programmers.

Thomas Powell, *HTML: The Complete Reference, Third Edition*, 2001, Osborne/McGraw-Hill, Berkeley, CA. ISBN 0-07-212951-4.

Thomas Powell and Dan Whitworth, *HTML Programmer's Reference, Second Edition*, 2001, Osborne/McGraw-Hill, Berkeley, CA. ISBN 0-07-213232-9.

These exhaustive treatments will tell more than you will ever need to know about using HTML!

1.2 Your First HTML Document

A typical first goal in learning any programming language is to display a simple message. With HTML, this is trivially simple: Just type the message in the body of the document, as shown in Document 1.1. (Appendix 1 contains an index to all documents in the text.) Save the file with the name shown.

Document 1.1 (`HelloWorldHTML.htm`)

```
<html>
   <head>
      <title>First HTML Document</title>
   </head>
<body>
Hello, world!
</body>
</html>
```

Hello, world!

Many examples presented in this text will include a browser's rendering of the screen output produced by the document. When a border appears around the output, as it does for the output from Document 1.1, the purpose is to distinguish the output from the rest of the text—the document doesn't generate that border. In the text, renderings are always in black and white or grayscale. Some documents will produce colored output, but you will have to try the code yourself to see these results.

Document 1.1 is certainly not very exciting. The point is that an HTML document simply displays the static content you provide. As you will learn in Chap. 2, HTML provides many facilities for changing the *appearance* of this content, but not the content itself.

HTML syntax is case-insensitive, which means that <html> is equivalent to <HTML> or even <hTmL>. Some HTML document authors favor uppercase spellings for tags because they stand out from the text content. However, XHTML (extensible HTML), the apparent successor to HTML, requires tags to be in lowercase letters.[3] Hence, this text will always use lowercase letters for tag names. Note that, despite previous warnings that file names and commands are case-sensitive in some systems, browsers should not be case-sensitive in their interpretation of HTML tags.

---

[3] Although this book adopts some XHTML style rules, the documents are written in HTML and are not intended to be fully XHTML-compliant.

1.3 Accessing HTML Documents on the Web

Documents intended for access by others on the World Wide Web are posted on a Web server, a computer system connected to the Internet. Colleges and universities typically provide Web servers for use by their faculty and students. Individuals not affiliated with an institution may have to purchase space on a commercial Web server, or they can set up their own server. In any case, access to Web pages is universal in the sense that any computer with an Internet connection and a browser can request to be connected to a website through its Internet address—its Uniform Resource Locator (URL).

Not all HTML documents have to be publicly accessible on the Web. They can be protected with logon identifications and passwords, or they can be available only locally through an intranet (as opposed to the Internet). The Internet is a global network of interconnected computers, whereas an intranet is a local network that may or may not also provide connections to the Internet. For example, a company can provide an intranet with no external access, exclusively for internal use by its own employees.

Note that when you view HTML documents in the browser on your local computer, they are not available on the Internet unless you have specifically set up a server, assigned it a URL, and placed HTML documents in a folder associated with that server. If you are associated with a university or other institution, you may be able to put internet content on its server. Typically, commercial providers of online services for individuals do not allow you to set up servers with a fixed URL. In that case, you have to purchase a domain name and set up a URL with an Internet Service Provider (ISP) which specializes in in Web hosting.

A university Internet address might look something like this:

```
http://www.myUniversity.edu/myName/index.htm
```

The URL for the author's organization looks like this:

```
http://www.instesre.org/
```

URLs usually start with the `http://` prefix, to indicate that the Hypertext Transfer Protocol (HTTP) is being used. There are some variations, such as `https`, indicating that the address that follows resides on a secure server, as required for financial transactions, for example. The rest of the address identifies a Web server and then a folder or directory on a computer system. The `.edu` extension identifies this site as belonging to an educational institution, in the same way as `.gov`, `.com`, and `.org` identify government, commercial, and organization sites. Sometimes names in URLs are case-sensitive, depending on the operating system installed on the computer system containing the Web page. Users of Windows computers should note the use of forward slashes rather than backslashes to separate folders (or directories).

The `index.htm` (or `index.html`) file contains the home page for a web site. By default, the `index.htm` file is automatically opened, if it exists, whenever this URL is accessed. That is, the address

```
http://www.myUniversity.edu/myName/
```

is equivalent to the address that includes the `index.htm` file name.

As they were being developed, the HTML documents discussed in this book resided neither on the Internet nor on an intranet. Instead, they were stored in a folder on a local computer and accessed simply by double-clicking on them.

You should create a separate folder on your computer as you work through the examples in this book and write your own documents. You *could* make documents you create yourself accessible on the Internet or an intranet by placing them on a Web server. For example, if you are taking a course based on this book, your instructor may require you to post homework assignments on a Web site.

1.4 Another Example

This example shows how to include an image in an HTML document.

Document 1.2 (`house.htm`)

```html
<html>
<head>
<title>Our New House</title>
<script language="javascript" type="text/javascript">
document.write("<font color='green'>This document was
  last modified on "+document.lastModified+"</font>");
</script>
</head>
<body>
<h1>Our New House</h1>
<p>
```

```
Here's the status of our new house. (We know you're
fascinated!)</p>
<!-- Link to your image goes here. -->
<img src="house.jpg" align="left" /><br />
</body>
</html>
```

Although this book doesn't deal with the JavaScript language, Document 1.2 does include one short but very useful JavaScript script:

```
<script language="javascript" type="text/javascript">
document.write("<font color='green'>This document was
  last modified on "+document.lastModified+"</font>");
</script>
```

This script displays the date on which the document was last modified. It is always a good idea to provide users of your documents (including yourself!) with some information about how recent the document is. As you have probably noticed, many websites do not include this information, so it is impossible to tell whether information on that site is current or not.

As mentioned previously, long lines of code are sometimes broken to fit in the pages of this text. The `document.write` statement extending over two lines is one such case. If you copy this text, as is, into an editor and save the document like that, the message won't be displayed. To make it work again, you have to reassemble the entire statement on just one long line.

There are several image formats that are widely used in HTML documents, including image bitmaps (`.bmp`), Graphics Interchange Format (`.gif`), and Joint Photographic Experts Group (`.jpg`).

The original .jpg file used in Document 1.2 has been compressed, and this process can result in jagged edges where edges should be straight. This effect is visible in the house framing and roof lines.

Within the img element, height and width attributes allow you to control the size of the image display (in pixels). However, this is not necessarily a good idea for photos like this because it is not equivalent to actually "re-

This document was last modified on 05/03/2006 13:12:30

Our New House

Here's the status of our new house. (We know you're fascinated!)

sizing" the image, as is possible with image-editing software.[4] Hence, it is important to use images that initially are sized appropriately. The house.jpg image was resized to 300 pixels high by 400 pixels wide, which retained the height-to-width ratio of the original (cropped) photo. If a very large high-resolution image file is displayed as a very small image, using the height and width attributes, the original large file must still be transmitted to the client computer. In view of the fact that high-resolution images can produce very large files (>10 Mb), it is still important to consider appropriate resolution and sizing for images included in HTML documents, even in an age of high-speed broadband Internet connections and large amounts of online storage space. (The size of the compressed grayscale house.jpg image printed here is about 93 Kb.)

Document 1.2 could be made into a default home page simply by changing its name to index.htm.

Here is a final admonition which hopefully does not sound too preachy: Intellectual honesty and fairness in the use of other people's material is important, no matter what the setting. The image displayed by Document 1.2 was taken by this book's author, of his own house under construction. In other words, the author "owns" this image. Whenever you post images or other material online, please be careful to respect intellectual property rights. Your default approach should be that online materials are copyrighted and cannot be used freely without permission. If you are in doubt about whether you have permission to use an image or other material, don't!

---

[4]IrfanView (www.irfanview.com) has been used for all image processing in this book.

HTML Document Basics

2

This chapter describes the characteristics of an HTML document, including some of the basic HTML elements and their attributes. The list of attributes is not complete, but is restricted to a subset larger than will usually be needed for working with PHP. The chapter includes a description of how to set colors in documents and a brief introduction to cascading style sheets.

2.1 Documents, Elements, Attributes, and Values

2.1.1 Documents and Their Essential Elements

As noted in Chap. 1, a basic HTML document consists of four sections defined by four sets of element tags, arranged as follows:

```
<html>
   <head>
      <title>… </title>
      …
   </head>
   <body>
      …
   </body>
</html>
```

Each of these four required elements has a start tag and an end tag. The `<title>…</title>` element is nested inside the `<head>…</head>` tag. This element, which search engines use to find documents on the Web, is required even if you don't include text for a title. Tags are always enclosed in angle brackets `<…>` and the end tag always includes a forward slash before the element name. The `body` element[1] supports attributes that can be used to control the overall appearance of an HTML document. Documents, elements, attributes, and values are organized in a specific hierarchy:

---

[1]Often, this book will use just the name of the element, like `body`, to refer to the element with its tags: `<body>…</body>`.

© Springer International Publishing AG 2017

D.R. Brooks, *Programming in HTML and PHP*, Undergraduate Topics in Computer Science, DOI 10.1007/978-3-319-56973-4_2

HTML document → elements → attributes → values

Elements exist within a document. Elements can have attributes and attributes (usually) have values. All elements are nested inside the `<html>...</html>` element. Some of the elements, such as `<title>...</title>`, are nested inside other elements. Some elements have only a single tag, in which case a forward slash precedes the closing angle bracket. For example, the `<br />` tag is used to start a new line.

Following is a brief description of the four elements that will be part of every HTML document. Attributes, if any, are listed for each element. Note, however, that not all possible attributes are listed. Thus, a listing of "none" may mean that there are attributes for this element, but that they are not used in this book. Consult an HTML reference manual for a complete list of attributes.

`<body> ... </body>`
The body element contains the HTML document content, along with whatever elements are required to format, access, and manipulate the content.
Attributes: background, bgcolor, text

`<head> ... </head>`
The head element contains information about the document. The head element must contain a title element and under XHTML rules, the title must be the first element after head.
Attributes: none

`<html> ... </html>`
The html element surrounds the entire document. All other HTML elements are nested within this element.
Attributes: none

`<title> ... </title>`
The title element contains the text that will be displayed in the browser's title bar. Every HTML document should have a title, included as the first element inside the head element.
Attributes: none

2.1.2   Some Other Important Elements

The four basic elements discussed above constitute no more than a blank template for an HTML document. Other elements are needed to display and control the appearance of content within the document. Here are some important elements that you will use over and over again in your HTML documents. They are listed in alphabetical order. The list of attributes is not necessarily complete, but includes only those which will be used in this book. Because several elements can share common attributes, attributes and their values are listed separately, following the list of elements.

`<a> ... </a>`
    The a (for "anchor") element provides links to an external resource or to an internal link within a document.
Attributes: href, name

`<b> ... </b>`
    The b element forces the included text to be displayed in a bold font. This is a "physical element" in the sense that it is associated specifically with displaying text in a bold font.
Attributes: none

`<br />`
    The br element inserts a break (line feed) in the text. Multiple breaks can be used to insert multiple blank lines between sections of text. The break element has no end tag because it encloses no content. Under XHTML rules, a closing slash (after a space) must be included: `<br />`. The slash is rarely seen in older HTML documents, so its use will be encouraged but not required.
Attributes: none

`<center> ... </center>`
    The center element causes displayed text to be centered on the computer screen.
Attributes: none

`<font> ... </font>`
    The font element controls the appearance of text. The two most commonly used attributes control the size and color of the text.
Attributes: size, color, face

`<hr />`
    The horizontal rule element draws a shaded horizontal line across the screen. It does not have an end tag. A closing slash (after a space) is required in XHTML. A noshade attribute displays the rule as a solid color, rather than shaded.
Attributes: align, color, noshade, size, width

`<h$n$> ... </h$n$>`
    Up to six levels of headings (for n ranging from 1 to 6) can be defined, with decreasing font sizes as n increases from 1 to 6.

Attributes: align

`<i> ... </i>`

i is a "physical element" that forces the included text to be displayed in italics. The actual appearance may depend on the browser and computer used.

Attributes: none

`<img />`

The img element provides a link to an image to be displayed within a document. The image is stored in a separate file, perhaps even at another Web address, the location of which is provided by the src attribute.

Attributes: align, border, height, src, vspace, width

`<p> ... </p>`

The p element marks the beginning and end of a paragraph of text content. Note that HTML does not automatically indent paragraphs. Rather, it separates paragraphs with an empty line, with all the text aligned left. It is common to see only the start tag used in HTML documents, without the corresponding end tag. However, the use of the end tag is enforced by XHTML and this is the style that should be followed.

Attributes: none

`<pre> ... </pre>`

The default behavior of HTML is to collapse multiple spaces, line feeds, and tabs to a single space. This destroys some of the text formatting that you may wish to preserve in a document, such as tabs at the beginning of paragraphs.

The pre element forces HTML to recognize multiple spaces, line feeds, and tabs embedded in text. The default action for pre is to use a monospaced font such as Courier. This may not always be appropriate. But, because line feeds and other text placement conventions are recognized, pre is very useful for embedding programming code examples within an HTML document.

Attributes: none

Note that most of the elements described here require both start and end tags. The general rule is that any element enclosing content requires both a start and end tag. The `<br />` and `<hr />` elements, for example, do not enclose content, so no end tag is needed.

Description of attributes:

These descriptions may not include all possible values. For a complete listing, consult an HTML reference manual. Values of attributes should be enclosed in single or double straight quotes, although HTML doesn't enforce this requirement.

```
align = "…"
```
Values: `"left"`, `"right"`, or `"center"`
  Aligns text horizontally.

```
background = "…"
```
Value: the URL of a gif- or jpeg-format graphics file

Setting the background attribute displays the specified image as the background, behind a displayed HTML document page. Depending on the image size (in pixels), background images may automatically be "tiled," resulting in a repeating image that can be visually distracting. It is never required to use background images, and they should be used with care.

```
bgcolor = "…"
```
Values: Background colors can be set either by name or by specifying the intensity of red, green, and blue color components. This topic is addressed in section **2.4 Selecting and Using Colors**.

```
border="…"
```
Value: The width, in pixels, of a border surrounding an image

```
color = "…"
```
Values: Text colors can be set either by name or by directly specifying the intensity of red, green, and blue color components. See section **2.4 Selecting and Using Colors.**

```
face = "…"
```
Values: Font typefaces can be set either generically, with `cursive`, `monospace`, `sans-serif`, or `serif`, or with specific font names supported by the user's computer. The generic names should always produce something that looks reasonable on any computer, but specific font names that are not available on the user's computer may produce unexpected results.

```
height = "…"
```
Value: The displayed height of an image in pixels (`width="80"`, for example) or, when followed by a `%` sign (`width="80%"`, for example), as a percent of total screen height. The displayed height overrides the actual height of the image file—the number of rows in the image.

```
href = "…"
```
Value: The URL of an external or internal Web resource, or the name of an internal document reference.

`hspace = "…"`
Value: The horizontal space, in pixels, between an image and the surrounding text.
`name = "…"`
Value: The name assigned to an internal document reference through an "a" element.

`size = "…"`
Values: An unsigned integer from 1 to 7 or a signed number from +1 to +6 or -1 to -6.

An unsigned integer is an absolute font size, which may be system-dependent. The default value is 3. A signed integer is a font size relative to the current font size, larger for positive values and smaller for negative values.

For the `hr` element, `size` is the vertical height of the horizontal rule, in pixels.

`src = "…"`
Value: As an attribute for an `img` tag, the URL of a graphics file. For local use, images and their HTML document are usually stored in the same folder.

`text = "…"`
Values: The `text` attribute, used with the `body` element, selects the color of text in a document, which prevails unless overridden by a `font` attribute.

`vspace = "…"`
Value: The vertical space, in pixels, between an image and the surrounding text.

`width = "…"`
Values: The width of an image or horizontal rule, in pixels or as a percent of total screen width, in percent. For example, `width="80"` is interpreted as a width of 80 pixels, but `width="80%"` is a width equal to 80 percent of the total screen width. The displayed width overrides the actual width of the image file—the number of columns in the image.

Document 2.1 shows how to use some of these elements.

Document 2.1 (tagExamples.htm)

```
<html>
<head>
<title>Tag Examples</title>
</head>
<body bgcolor="white">
<h1>Here is a Level 1 Heading</h1>
<h2>Here is a Level 2 Heading</h2>
<hr />
<pre>
    Here is some <b><i>preformatted text</i></b> that has
    been created with the pre element. Note that it retains
the
paragraph tab
included
in the <b><i>original         document</b></i>. Also, it does
not "collapse" line feeds
and
        white                spaces. Often, it is easier to use
preformatted text than it
is to use markup to get the same effect. Note, however, that
the default
rendering of
preformatted text is to use a monospaced Courier font. This
is often a good choice for
displaying code in an HTML document, but perhaps not a good
choice for other kinds of text content.
</pre><p><center>
<img src="checkmark.gif" align="left" />Here, a small
graphic (the check box) has been inserted into
the document using the "img" element. This text is outside
the preformatted
region, so the default font is different. If you look at the
original document, you can also see that
white          spaces and line   feeds are now collapsed.
</p><p>
Note too, that the text is now centered. The way the text is
displayed will
depend on how you
have the display window set in your browser. It may change
when you go from full screen to a window, for example.
</center></p><p>
Centering is now turned off. The default text alignment is
to the left of your screen.
You can change the size and color of text <font size="7"
color="blue"> by using the &lt;font&gt;</font>
<font color="purple">element.</font>
</body>
</html>
```

The small checkbox graphic has been created with Windows' Paint program. The actual text displayed in your browser is larger than this, but the output image has been reduced in size (perhaps to the extent of not being readable) to fit on the page. Also, because of the line feeds imposed on the text of this code example by the page width, the output looks a little different from what you might expect. So, you need to try this document on your own browser.

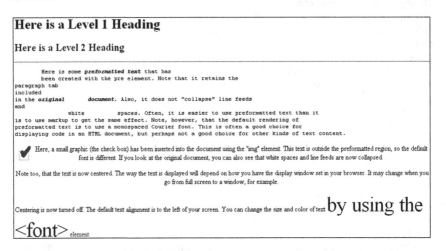

Document 2.1 answers an interesting question: How can HTML display characters that already have a special meaning in the HTML language, or which do not appear on the keyboard? The angle brackets (< and >) are two such characters because they are part of HTML tags. They can be displayed with the < and > escape sequences (for the "less than" and "greater than" symbols from mathematics). There are many standardized escape sequences for special symbols. A list of some of them is given in Appendix 2.

2.2   HTML Syntax and Style

A general characteristic of programming languages is that they have very strict syntax rules. HTML is different in that regard, as it is not highly standardized. The positive spin on this situation is to call HTML an "open standard," which means that self-described bearers of the standard can treat the language as they see fit, subject only to usefulness and market acceptance. HTML has an established syntax, but it is very forgiving about how that syntax is used. For example, when a browser encounters HTML code that it does not understand, typically it just ignores it rather than crashing, as a "real" program would do.

Fortunately, market forces—the desire to have as many people as possible accept your browser's interpretation of HTML documents—have forced uniformity on a large subset of HTML. This text will adopt some HTML style conventions and syntax that will be as platform-independent as possible. Although these "rules" might seem troublesome if you are not used to writing stylistically consistent HTML documents, they should actually help beginners by providing a more stable and predictable working environment. The only thing worse than having syntax and style rules is having rules that nobody follows.

Here are some style rules that will be used in this text. Under the circumstances of HTML, they are more accurately referred to as "guidelines." Some of them will make more sense later on, as you create more complicated documents.

1. Spell the names of HTML elements in lowercase letters.

Unlike some other languages, the HTML language is not sensitive to case. Thus, `<html>`, `<HTML>`, and `<hTmL>` are equivalent. However, the XHTML standard requires element names to be spelled with lowercase letters. In the earlier days of HTML, many programmers adopted the style of using uppercase letters for element names because they stood out in a document. You will often still see this style in Web documents. Nonetheless, this book will consistently use lowercase letters for element names.

2. Use the pre element to enforce text layout whenever it is reasonable to use a monospaced font (such as `Courier`).

HTML always collapses multiple "white space" characters—spaces, tabs, and line breaks—into a single space when text is displayed. The easiest way to retain white space characters is to use the `pre` element. Other approaches may be needed if proportional fonts are required. Also, tabbed text may still not line up, as different browsers have different default settings for tabs.

3. Nest elements properly.

Improperly nested elements can cause interpretation problems for your browser. Even when browsers do not complain about improperly nested elements, HTML is easier to learn, read, and edit when these guidelines are followed.

Recall this markup in Document 2.1:

```
Here is some <b><i>preformatted text</i></b>
```

If you write this as:

```
Here is some
<b>
    <i>
        ...{text}
    </i>
</b>
```

it is easy to see that the i element is properly nested inside the b element. If this is changed to

```
<b><i> ...{text} </b></i>
```

with the order of the </b> and </i> tags reversed, your browser probably won't complain, but it is not good programming style.

4. Enclose the values of attributes in single or double quotes.

In Document 2.1, bgcolor="white" is an attribute of <body>. Browsers generally will accept bgcolor=white, but the XHTML standard enforces the use of quoted attribute values. This text will be consistent about using double quotes unless attribute values appear inside a string that is already surrounded with double quotes. Then attribute values will be single-quoted.

5. Use comments to explain what you are doing.

Good programmers always provide comments in their code for their own benefit as well as for the benefit of others who might use their code. This applies to HTML documents as well as to "real" programs. The syntax for HTML comments, which can appear anywhere in a document, including across multiple lines, is:

```
<!-- {Insert text here...} -->
```

2.3 Creating and Organizing a Website

Creating, organizing, and maintaining a website is a major topic, a thorough investigation of which would go far beyond the reach of this text. There is an entire industry devoted to hosting and creating websites, including helping a user obtain a domain name, providing storage space, developing content, and tracking access. For the purposes of this book, the goal is extremely simple: create web pages to solve some computational problems.

The first step toward creating a website is establishing its location. In an academic environment, a college, university, or department computer may provide space for web pages. A URL might look something like this:

`http://www.myuniversity.edu/~username`

where the "~" symbol indicates a directory where web pages are stored. Together with a user name, this URL directs a browser to the home Web directory for that user. As noted in Chap. 1, HTML documents are not automatically Internet-accessible, and for the purposes of this book your web pages may be accessible only locally on your own computer.

In this home directory there should be at least one file, called `index.htm` (or `index.html`). UNIX systems favor the `.html` extension, but Windows users may prefer the three-character `.htm` extension because it is more consistent with Windows file extension conventions. This is the file that will be opened automatically in response to entering the above URL. That is, the `index.htm` file is the "home page" for the Website. This home page file could be named something different, but then its name would have to be added to the URL:

`http://www.myuniversity.edu/~username/HomePage.htm`

An `index.htm` file can contain both its own content as well as links to other content (hyperlinks), including other pages on the user's Website and to external URLs. Here are four important kinds of links:

1. Links to other sites on the World Wide Web.
   This is the essential tool for globally linking web pages.

Syntax: `<a href="`*{URL of web page}*`">`
       {description of linked web page}`</`a`>`

The URL may refer to a completely different Website, or it may be a link to local documents in the current folder or a subfolder within that folder.

2. Links to images.
   The `img` element is used to load images for display or to use as a page background.

Syntax: `<img src="`*{URL plus image name}*`" align="..."`
    `height="..." width="..." />`

The image may exist locally or it may be at a different Website. The `align`, `height`, and `width` attributes, which can be used to position and size an image, are optional. However, for high-resolution images, it is almost always necessary to specify the height and width as a percentage of the full page or as a number of pixels in order to reduce the image to a manageable size in the context of the rest of the page. Actually resizing the image with a photo editing program will solve this problem.

You can also make a "clickable image" to direct the user to another link:

Syntax: `<a href="{URL of web page}">`
`<img src="{URL plus image name}" align="..."`
`height="..." width="..." /></a>`

3. Links to email addresses.

An email link is an essential feature that allows users to communicate with the author of a web page.

Syntax: `<a href="mailto:{email address}">`
`{description of recipient}</a>`

The *{description of recipient}* is usually the email address or the recipient's name. The actual sending of an email will be handled by the default mailer on the sender's computer.

4. Internal links within a document.

Within a large document, it is often convenient to be able to move from place to place within the document, using internal links.

Syntax: `<a href="#{internal link name}">`
`{description of target position}</a>`

...

`<a name="{internal link name}">{target text}</a>`

The "#" symbol is required when specifying the value of the `href` attribute, to differentiate this internal link from a link to another (external) document.

The careless specification of linked documents can make websites very difficult to maintain and modify. As noted above, every website should have a "home" directory containing an `index.htm` file. In order to make a site easy to transport from one computer to another, all other content should be contained either in the home directory or in folders created within that directory. References to folders that are not related in this way should be avoided, as they will typically need to be renamed if the site is moved to a different computer. Although it is allowed as a matter of syntax to give a complete (absolute) URL for a local web page, this should be avoided in favor of a reference relative to the current folder.

This matter is important enough to warrant a complete example. Document 2.2a–c shows a simple website with a home folder on a Windows desktop called `home` and two subfolders within the `home` folder named `homework` and `personal`. Each subfolder contains a single HTML document, `homework.htm` in `homework` and `resume.htm` in `personal`.

Document 2.2a (`index.htm`)

```
<html>
<head>
<title>My Page</title>
</head>
<body>
<!-- These absolute links are a bad idea! -->
Here are links to
<a href="C:/Documents and Settings/David/desktop/
/Book/homework.htm">homework</a> and
<a href="C:/Documents and Settings/
   David/desktop/Book/resume.htm">
personal documents.</a>
</body>
</html>
```

Document 2.2b (`resume.htm`)

```
<html>
<head>
<title>Resume</title>
</head>
<body>
Here is my r&eacute;sum&eacute;.
</body>
</html>
```

Document 2.2c (`homework.htm`)

```
<html><head>
<title>Homework</title>
</head>
<body>
Here are my homework problems.
</body>
</html>
```

Note that Document 2.2a uses forward slashes to separate the directories and file names. This is consistent with UNIX syntax, but Windows/DOS systems use backward slashes. Forward slashes are the HTML standard, and they should always be used even though backward slashes may also work. Another point of interest is that UNIX directory paths and filenames are case-sensitive, but Windows paths and filenames are not. This could cause problems if you develop a web page on a Windows computer and then move it to a UNIX-based system. As a matter of style, you should be consistent about case in directory and file names even when it appears not to matter.

Note how the "é"s in résumé, which are not keyboard characters, are produced by using the escape sequence é—see Appendix 2.

In Document 2.2a, the absolute references to a folder on a particular Windows computer desktop are a bad idea because this reference will need to be changed if the index.htm file is moved to a different place on the same computer, or to a different computer—for example, to a University department computer with a different directory/folder structure. Document 2.2d shows the preferred solution. Now the paths to homework.htm and resume.htm are given relative to the home folder, wherever the index2.htm file resides. (Remember that this file, no longer named index.htm, will not be recognized as a default home page, but you can rename it.) This document assumes that folders homework and personal exist in the home folder. This relative URL should work without modification when the website is moved to a different computer. If the website is moved, only a single reference, to the index2.htm file, needs to be changed.

Document 2.2d (index2.htm, a new version of index.htm)

```
<html>
<head>
<title>My Page</title>
</head>
<body>
<!-- Use these relative links instead! -->
Here are links to
<a href="homework/homework.htm">
homework</a> and
<a href="personal/resume.htm">
personal documents.</a>
</body>
</html>
```

Paying proper attention to using relative URLs from the very beginning when designing a website will save a lot of time in the future!

2.4   Selecting and Using Colors

As previously noted, several attributes, such as `bgcolor`, are used to set colors of text or backgrounds. Colors may be identified by name or by a six-character hexadecimal numeric code that, historically, specified the strength of the signal emitted from the red, green, and blue electron "guns" that excited the corresponding phosphors on a cathode ray tube color monitor screen. This convention has been retained even though other display technologies are used now. The hex code[2] is in the format *#RRGGBB* where each color value can range from 00 (turned off) to FF (maximum intensity).

There are many color names in use on the Web, but only 16 are completely standardized, representing the 16 colors recognized by the Windows VGA color palette. These colors are listed in Table 2.1. The problem with additional color names is that there is no enforced standard for how browsers should interpret them. Two examples: magenta probably should be, but doesn't have to be, the same as fuchsia; ivory is a nonstandard color that should be rendered as a yellowish off-white. The colors in Table 2.1 are standardized in the sense that all browsers should associate these 16 names with the same hexadecimal code. Of course, variations can still occur because monitors themselves will respond somewhat differently to the same name or hex code; blue on my computer monitor may look somewhat different than blue on your monitor.

Table 2.1 16 standard HTML color names and hex codes

Color Name	Hexadecimal Code
aqua	#00FFFF
black	#000000
blue	#0000FF
fuchsia	#FF00FF
gray	#808080
green	#008000
lime	#00FF00
maroon	#800000
navy	#000080
olive	#808000
purple	#800080
red	#FF0000
silver	#C0C0C0
teal	#008080
white	#FFFFFF
yellow	#FFFF00

Note that the standardized colors use a limited range of hex codes. With the exception of silver (nothing more than a lighter gray), the RGB gun colors are either off (00), on (FF), or halfway on (80).

What should you do about choosing colors? Favor standardized colors, and if you wish to make an exception, try it in as many browser environments as possible. Be careful to choose background and text colors so that text will always be visible against its background. The safest approach for

---

[2]Hex code = hexadecimal code, a base-16 numbering system using integers 0–9 and letters A–F to represent values ten to fifteen.

setting colors in the `body` element is to specify both background and text colors. This will ensure that default colors set in a user's browser will not result in unreadable text.

If you're not sure whether a color name is supported and what it looks like on your monitor, you have nothing to lose by trying it. If you set `bgcolor="lightblue"`, you will either like the result or not. If a color name isn't recognized by your browser, the result will be unpredictable, but not catastrophic. There are (of course!) numerous websites that will help you work with colors, including getting the desired result with hex codes.

2.5 Using Cascading Style Sheets

As you create more web pages, you may wish to impose a consistent look for all your pages, or for groups of related pages. It is tedious to insert elements for all the characteristics you may wish to replicate—font size, font color, background color, etc. Style sheets make it much easier to replicate layout information in multiple sheets. A complete discussion of style sheets is far beyond the scope of this book, as there are many different kinds of style sheets, many ways to make use of them, and many browser-specific nuances. This book will use cascading style sheets (CSS), which are widely accepted as a default kind of style sheet, but will present only a *small* subset of all the possibilities! By way of introduction, Document 2.3 shows how to use a `style` element to establish the default appearance of the body of an HTML document.

Document 2.3 (`style1.htm`)

```
<html>
<head>
<title>Style Sheets</title>
<style title="David's default" type="text/css">
    body.bright {background: red; font: 16pt serif;
          color: blue; font-style: italic; font-weight: bold}
</style>
</head>
<body class="bright">
Here is the body.
</body>
</html>
```

Here is the body.

The `style` element has an optional `title` attribute and a `type` attribute set equal to `"text/css"`, where the `css` stands for cascading style sheet. Inside the `style` element, dot notation is used to assign a class name, bright, to the body element: body.bright. Inside curly brackets attributes are assigned values, with each attribute and its value being separated by a semicolon. Then, the <body> tag assigns the class name bright as the value of the class attribute. As a result, the document background color is red, with the font set to a blue, bold, italicized 16-point serif font.

Any HTML tag that encloses content can be assigned a class value defined in a style element. For this simple example, with styles applying only to a single body element, the class name is optional. With no class name and no class attribute in <body>, the style rules will automatically be applied to the entire HTML document.

In general, several different style rules can apply to the same HTML element. For example, several style rules could be established for paragraphs (<p> ... </p>), each of which would have its own class name.

In summary, style specifications follow a hierarchy:

style element → other HTML elements{.class name} →
properties → value(s)

where the {.class name} is optional.

How did CSS get that name? Because the properties set for an element cascade down, or are "inherited," by other elements contained within that element unless those elements are assigned their own style properties. So, for example, properties set for the body element are inherited by the p and h1 elements, because these are contained within the body element. Properties set for the head element are inherited by content appearing in the title element.

CSS can be used to modify the appearance of any HTML element that encloses content. Here are some properties that can be specified in style sheets.

Background properties

background-color
When used in a body element, background-color sets the background color for an entire document. It can also be used to highlight a paragraph, for example, when used with a p element.

background-image
This property is used with a URL to select an image file (gif or jpeg) that will appear as a background. Typically, this is used with a body element, but it can also be used with other elements, such as p. For other background properties that can be used to control the appearance of a background image, consult an HTML reference text.

`background`

This allows you to set all background properties in a single rule.

Color property

The `color` property sets the default color for text, using the descriptions discussed in Sect. 2.4.

Font properties

`font-family`

Font support is not completely standardized. However, browsers that support style sheets should support at least the generic font families given in Table 2.2.

Example: `font-family: Arial, sans-serif;`

`font-size`

This property allows you to set the actual or relative size of text. You can use relative values, such as `large`, `small`, `larger`, `smaller` (relative to a default size); a percentage, such as `200%` of the default size; or an actual point size such as `16pt`.

Table 2.2 Some font families

Generic Name	Example
cursive	Script MT Bold
monospace	Courier
sans-serif	Arial
serif	Times New Roman

Some sources advise against using absolute point sizes because a point size that is perfectly readable on one system might be uncomfortably small on another. But, for our purposes, specifying the point size is a reasonable choice.

Example: `font-size: 24pt;`

`font-style`

This property allows you to specify `normal`, `italic`, or `oblique` fonts.

Example: `font-style: italic;`

`font-weight`

This property allows you to select the font weight. You can use values in the range from `100` (extra light) to `900` (extra bold), or words: `extra-light`, `light`, `demi-light`, `medium`, `demi-bold`, `bold`, and `extra-bold`. Some choices may not have a noticeable effect on some fonts in some browsers.

Example: `font-weight: 900;`

`font`

This property allows you to set all font properties with one style rule.

Example: `font: italic 18pt Helvetica, sans-serif;`

How will your browser interpret a font name? For the generic name `serif`, it will pick the primary serif font it supports—probably Times or Times Roman. Browsers will probably also recognize specific font names such as Times or Helvetica (a sans-serif font). If you specify a font name not supported by your browser, it will simply ignore your choice and use its default font for text. It is possible to list several fonts, in which case your browser will select the first one it supports. For example, consider this style specification:

`font-family: Arial, Helvetica, sans-serif;`

Your browser will use an Arial font if it supports that, Helvetica if it doesn't support Arial but does support Helvetica, or, finally, whatever sans-serif font it does support by default. By giving your browser choices, with the generic serif or non-serif name as the last choice, you can be reasonably sure that text will be displayed approximately as you wish it to appear.

Text properties

Of the many text properties, here are just three that may be useful.

`text-align`

This is used in block elements such as `p`. It is similar in effect to the HTML `align` attribute. The choices are `left`, `right`, `center`, and `justify`. With large font sizes, `justify` may produce odd-looking results.

Example: `text-align: center;`

`text-indent`

Recall that paragraphs created with the p element do not indent the first word in the paragraph. (HTML inserts a blank line and left-justifies the text.) This property allows you to set indentation using typesetting notation or actual measurements. An actual English or metric measurement—inches inches (`in`), millimeters (`mm`), or centimeters (`cm`) —may be easiest and will always give predictable results.

Example: `text-indent: 0.5in;`

`white-space`

The value of this property is that you can prevent spaces from being ignored. (Remember that the default HTML behavior is to collapse multiple spaces and other non-printable characters into a single blank space.) Some older browsers may not support this property. You can use the HTML `pre` element by itself, instead, but this causes text to be displayed in a mono-spaced font such as Courier. The example given here retains white space regardless of the typeface being used.

Example: `white-space: pre;`

Styles aren't restricted just to the body element. For example, paragraphs (`<p>` ... `</p>`) and headings (`<h`*n* `>` ... `</h`*n*`>`) can also have styles associated with them. You can also set styles in selected portions of text, using the `span` element, and in blocks of text using the `div` element.

`<div>` ... `</div>`
Attributes: `align`, `style`

`<span>` ... `</span>`
Attributes: `align`, `style`
Values for align: `"left"` (default), `"right"`, `"center"`

You can create style sheets as separate files and then use them whenever you wish to use a particular style on a web page. This makes it easy to impose a uniform appearance on multiple web pages. Document 2.4a and 2.4b show a simple example.

Document 2.4a (`body.css`)

```
body { background:silver; color:white; font:24pt Times}
h1 { color:red; font:18pt Impact;}
h2 { color:blue; font:16pt Courier;}
```

Document 2.4b (`style2.htm`)

```
<html>
<head>
<title>Style Sheet Example</title>
<link  href="body.css" rel="stylesheet"
   type="text/css" />
</head>
<body>

   < h1 > Heading 1 </h1>
   < h2 > Heading 2 </h2>
   Here is some text.
</body>
</html>
```

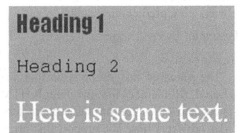

This example shows how to create a file, `body.css`, containing style elements that can be applied to any document by using the `link` element, as in Document 2.4b. The `.css` extension is standard, but not required. (You could use `.txt`, for example, although there is no reason to confuse matters by doing that.) This example is very simple, but the concept is powerful because it makes it easy to create a standard style for all your documents which can be invoked with the `link` element. The `Impact` font chosen for `h1` headings may not be supported by all browsers. If not, a default font will be used in its place.

The attributes of `link` include href, which contains the URL of the style sheet file, the `rel="stylesheet"` (relationship) attribute, which describes how to use the file (as a style sheet), and the `type`, which should be `"text/css"`, just as it would be defined if you created a `style` element directly in the head element. In this example, `body.css` is in the same folder as `style2.htm`. If you keep your style sheets in a separate folder, you will of course need to reference that folder.

This discussion has barely scratched the surface of style sheets. Style sheets can make your web pages more visually appealing and can greatly simplify your work on large Web projects. Some developers advocate replacing *all* individual formatting elements, such as `font` and its attributes, with style sheet specifications. Despite the fact that the use of individual formatting elements is "deprecated" in favor of using CSS, there is little likelihood that support for individual elements will disappear from browsers in the foreseeable future. For the kinds of applications discussed in this book, cascading style sheets may sometimes be convenient, but they are not required.

2.6   Another Example

Documents 2.5a and 2.5b show how to use a style sheet file to specify different background and text colors for different sections of text.

Document 2.5a (`rwb.css`)

```
p.red {background:red;color:blue;font:20pt Times}
div.white {background:white;color:red;font:20pt Times}
span.blue {background:blue;color:white;font:20pt Times}
```

Document 2.5b (rwb.htm)

```
<html>
<head>
<title>A Red, White, and Blue Document</title>
<link href="rwb.css" rel="stylesheet" type="text/css" />
</head>
<body>
<img src="stars.jpg" height="150" width="250" />
<p class="red">
This text should be blue on a red background.
</p><p><div class="white" style="font-style: italic;">
This text should be red on a white background.
</div></p>
<p><span class="blue">This text should be white on a blue
background.</span>
</p>
</body>
</html>
```

This text should be blue on a red background

This text should be red on a white background

This text should be white on a blue background

The stars, which are supposed to be red, silver, and blue, have been drawn using Windows' Paint program.

HTML Tables, Forms, Lists, and Frames

3

This chapter shows how to use HTML tables, forms, lists, and frames to organize documents and provide a framework for interfacing with PHP applications.

3.1 The `table` Element

3.1.1 Table Formatting

HTML table and form elements are the two most important ways to organize the content of a web page. Forms are critical because they provide the interface with PHP. Sometimes it is helpful to organize information in a form through the use of one or more tables. With that approach in mind, first consider tables.

Because HTML ignores text formatting, such as white space and line feeds (the Enter key), it can be difficult to control the placement of content on a web page. The addition of images only compounds this problem. An easy way to gain some control is to create a table, using the table element. Then the relative locations of text and graphics can be established by entering them into cells of the table. Within the start and end tags, `<table>` ... `</table>`, rows and cells are defined with the `tr` ("table row") and `td` ("table data") elements. These elements are nested as follows:

```
<table>
  <tr>
    <td>...</td> {as many columns as you need...}
    ...
  </tr>
    {as many rows as you need...}
    ...
</table>
```

© Springer International Publishing AG 2017
D.R. Brooks, *Programming in HTML and PHP*, Undergraduate Topics in Computer Science, DOI 10.1007/978-3-319-56973-4_3

The <tr>...</tr> tags define the rows and the <td>...</td> tags
define cells in columns within those rows. You can define as many rows and
columns as you need to organize information in a familiar spreadsheet-like
row-and-column format. Document 3.1 shows how to use a table to organize
and display some results from residential radon testing.

Document 3.1 (radonTable.htm)

```html
<html>
<head>
<title>Radon Table</title>
</head>
<body>
<h1>Results of radon testing</h1>
<p>
The table below shows some radon levels measured in
residences.<br /> For values greater than or equal to 4
pCi/L, action should be taken<br /> to reduce the
concentration of radon gas. For values greater than or<br />
equal to 3 pCi/L, retesting is recommended.
</p>
<table>
  <tr bgcolor="silver">
    <td>Location</td><td>Value, pCi/L</td>
  <td>Comments</td></tr>
  <tr>
    <td>DB's house, basement</td><td>15.6</td>
    <td bgcolor="pink">Action should be taken!</td></tr>
  <tr>
    <td>ID's house, 2nd floor bedroom</td><td>3.7</td>
    <td bgcolor="yellow">Should be retested.</td></tr>
  <tr>
    <td> FJ's house, 1st floor living room</td><td> 0.9</td>
    <td bgcolor="lightgreen">No action required.</td></tr>
  <tr>
    <td> MB's house, 2nd floor bedroom</td><td>2.9</td>
    <td bgcolor="lightgreen">No action required.</td></tr>
</table>
</body>
</html>
```

In a color rendition of this page, the first value will have a pink
background, the second a yellow background, and the others a light green
background.

Results of radon testing

The table below shows some radon levels measured in residences. For values greater than or equal to 4 pCi/L, action should
be taken to reduce the concentration of radon gas. For values greater than or equal to 3 pCi/L, retesting is recommended.

Location	Value, pCi/L	Comments
DB's house, basement	15.6	Action should be taken!
ID's house, 2nd floor bedroom	3.7	Should be retested.
FJ's house, 1st floor living room	0.9	No action required.
MB's house, 2nd floor bedroom	2.9	No action required.

The syntax for tables includes several possibilities in addition to `tr` and `td` for customizing appearance. These include the `caption` element, which associates a caption with the table, and the `th` element, which is used to create a "header" row in a table by automatically displaying text in bold font. (The `th` element can be used anywhere in a table in place of `td`.) The `caption`, `td`, `th`, and `tr` elements are used only inside the start and end tags of a `table` element: `<table>...</table>`. With these elements, a more comprehensive table layout looks like this:

```
<table>
  <caption> ... </caption>
  <tr>
  <!-- Use of th in place of td is optional. -->
    <th> ... </th>
    ...
  </tr>
  <tr>
  <td> ... </td>
    ...
  </tr>
    ...
</table>
```

Here is a summary of some table-related elements and their attributes. All the elements except `table` itself should appear only inside a `table` element.

`<caption> ... </caption>`
Displays the specified text as a caption for a table. Earlier versions of HTML support only `"top"` (the default value) or `"bottom"` for the value of the `align` attribute. Some browsers may allow `"center"` as a value for `align`, which might often be the alignment of choice for a table caption.

Attributes: `align`

```
<table> … </table>
```
Contains table-related and other elements.
Attributes: `border, bordercolor, cellpadding, cellspacing, width`

```
<tbody> … </tbody>
```
Groups rows within the body of a table so each group can be given different attributes and styles.
Attributes: `align, char, charoff, valign`

```
<td> … </td>
```
Defines data cells in the rows of a table. Does not contain other table-related elements.
Attributes: `align, bgcolor, char, charoff, colspan, nowrap, rowspan, width`

```
<th> … </th>
```
The `th` element works just like the `td` element except it automatically displays text in bold font, serving as headings for table columns. Does not contain other elements.
Attributes: `align, bgcolor, char, charoff, colspan, nowrap, rowspan, valign, width`

```
<tr> … </tr>
```
Defines rows in a table. Contains `td` or `th` elements.
Attributes: `align, bgcolor, valign`

Description of attributes:

```
align = "…"
```
Values: `"left", "right",` or `"center"`
   Aligns text horizontally. When `align` is specified in a `tr` element, its value will be overridden if it is specified again within a `td` element in that row.

```
bgcolor = "…"
```
Values: color names or hexadecimal values `"#RRGGBB"`
   Sets the background color for a cell or row. When `bgcolor` is specified in a `tr` element, its value will be overridden if it is specified again within a `td` element in that row.

`border = "..."`

Values: an integer number of pixels

Adds a border to the table and its cells. A value is optional. If it is included, a colored (or gray, by default) border is added around the outer boundary of the table.

`bordercolor = "..."`

Values: color names or hexadecimal values `"#RRGGBB"`

Sets the color of a table border.

`cellpadding = "..."`

Values: an integer number of pixels

Defines vertical spacing between cells in a table.

`cellspacing = "..."`

Values: an integer number of pixels

Defines horizontal spacing between cells in a table.

`colspan = "..."`

Values: an integer

Defines how many columns a cell will span.

`nowrap`

Prevents text from being automatically wrapped within a cell. It does not have a value.

`rowspan = "..."`

Values: an integer

Defines how many rows a cell will span.

`valign = "..."`

Values: `"top"`, `"middle"`, or `"bottom"`

Aligns text vertically. When `valign` is specified in a `tr` element, its value will be overridden if it is specified again within a `td` element in that row.

`width = "..."`

Values: a number or a percentage

Specifies table or cell width in pixels (`width="140"`) or as a percentage of the window or table header width (`width="80%"`).

The attributes associated with these tags all have default values or are just ignored if you don't use them. You can create a table without using any attributes and then add attributes as needed. When creating tables, it is often useful to include the `border` attribute, which can be removed when you are happy with how the table looks. In Document 3.1, the only specified attribute is the background color in some cells. An easy way to familiarize yourself with the effects of specifying table attributes and their values is to experiment with Document 3.1.

Document 3.1 is not very useful except for showing how to create tables. The radon values and the colors associated with them are all "hard coded" values. There is no provision for changing the radon values, and even if you could do that, you couldn't use HTML to change the background colors in response to the radon values. However, if the radon values and perhaps the site names are entered into `input` elements, PHP can be used to generate a table with background colors calculated based on the radon values entered. (See Document 4.1.)

3.1.2   Subdividing Tables into Sections

The `tbody` element allows a table to be divided into two or more groups of rows. Each group of rows enclosed by a `<tbody> ... </tbody>` tag can have its own attributes and can have different pre-defined `class` attribute values. Document 3.2 shows a simple example in which rows in a table are grouped by background color.

Document 3.2 (`tbody.htm`)

```
<html>
<head>
  <title>Using the tbody element</title>
  <style>
    th {background-color:black; color:white;}
    tbody.cold {text-align:center;
      font-weight:bold; background-color:gray;}
    tbody.cool {text-align:center;
      font-weight:bold; background-color:silver;}
    tbody.hot {text-align:center;
      font-weight:bold; background-color:ivory;}
  </style>
</head>
<body>
<table border>
  <tr><th>Month</th><th>Average<br />Temperature
```

```
        <br />&deg;F</td></tr>
<tbody  class="cold">
  <tr><td >January</td><td>30.4</td></tr>
  <tr><td>February</td><td>33.0</td></tr>
  <tr><td>March</td><td>42.4</td></tr>
</tbody>
<tbody class="cool">
  <tr><td>April</td><td>52.4</td></tr>
  <tr><td>May</td><td>62.9</td></tr>
</tbody>
<tbody class="hot">
  <tr><td>June</td><td>71.8</td></tr>
  <tr><td>July</td><td>76.7</td></tr>
  <tr><td>August</td><td>75.5</td></tr>
</tbody>
<tbody class="cool">
  <tr><td>September</td><td>68.2</td></tr>
  <tr><td>October</td><td>56.4</td></tr>
</tbody>
<tbody class="cold">
  <tr><td>November</td><td>46.4</td></tr>
  <tr><td>December</td><td>35.8</td></tr>
</body>
</html>
```

January–March and November–December use the "cold" class, April–May and September–October use "cool," and June–August use "hot." Each class has a different background color. (For this grayscale rendering of the output, gray, silver, and ivory have been chosen instead of something more colorful.)

Document 3.2 is another example of an HTML document which displays content, but which offers no way to interpret or manipulate that content.

Month	Average Temperature °F
January	30.4
February	33.0
March	42.4
April	52.4
May	62.9
June	71.8
July	76.7
August	75.5
September	68.2
October	56.4
November	46.4
December	35.8

3.1.3   Merging Cells Across Rows and Columns

If you are familiar with creating tables in a word processing application, you know that it is easy to create more complicated table layouts by merging cells across rows and columns. You can also do this with HTML tables, using the `colspan` and `rowspan` attributes. Document 3.3 shows a table that displays cloud names, altitudes, and whether they produce precipitation or not.

Document 3.3 (`cloudType.htm`)

```
<html>
<head>
<title>Cloud Type Chart</title>
</head>
<body>
<table border="2">
<caption>Cloud Type Chart</caption>
<tr>
  <th align="center">Altitude</th>
  <th colspan="2">Cloud Name</th></tr>
<tr><td align="center" rowspan="3">High</td>
    <td colspan="2">Cirrus</td></tr>
    <tr><td colspan="2">Cirrocumulus</td></tr>
    <tr><td colspan="2">Cirrostratus</td></tr></tr>
<tr><td align="center" rowspan="2">Middle</td>
    <td colspan="2">Altocumulus</td></tr>
    <tr><td colspan="2">Altostratus</td></tr></tr>
<tr><td align="center" rowspan="5">Low</td>
    <td>Cumulus</td>
    <td>nonprecipitating</td></tr>
<tr><td>Altocumulus</td>
    <td>nonprecipitating</td></tr>
<tr><td>Stratocumulus</td>
    <td>nonprecipitating</td></tr>
    <tr><td>Cumulonimbus</td>
    <td align="center"
bgcolor="silver">precipitating</td></tr>

    <tr><td>Nimbostratus</td> <td align="center"
bgcolor="silver">precipitating</td></tr></tr>
</table>
</body></html>
```

It is more tedious to merge cells across rows in columns in an HTML table than it is in a word processor. You need to plan your table in advance, and even then you should be prepared for some trial-and-error editing!

Cloud Type Chart		
Altitude	**Cloud Name**	
High	Cirrus	
	Cirrocumulus	
	Cirrostratus	
Middle	Altocumulus	
	Altostratus	
Low	Cumulus	nonprecipitating
	Altocumulus	nonprecipitating
	Stratocumulus	nonprecipitating
	Cumulonimbus	precipitating
	Nimbostratus	precipitating

3.2   The `form` and `input` Elements

One of the most important applications of HTML documents is to provide the web page equivalent of a paper data input form. In some cases, a form just helps to organize user input to a web page. For this book, the purpose of a form is to facilitate interaction between an HTML document and PHP code for processing user input.

HTML forms are defined by the `form` element, using start and end tags: `<form>` ... `</form>` tags. The attributes of the `form` element are:

```
action = "…"
```
Value: a programmer-supplied URL that identifies a processing script, PHP file name, or `mailto:` followed by an email address. For example, `action="mailto:my_mail@my_univ.edu"`.

```
enctype="…"
```
Value: `enctype="text/plain"` is the usual value, but it is not needed when `method="post"` is used with PHP applications.

```
method = "…"
```
Values: `"get"`, `"post"`

Controls how data from a form is sent to the URL, PHP file, or email address identified in the `action` attribute. In this book, the `"post"` value is used because it is the easiest way to transmit form data in an easily usable format.

`name = "..."`
Value: a programmer-selected name that is used to identify the form.

The `name` attribute is needed only if a document contains more than one form.

Forms contain one or more input fields identified by `<input />` tags. Because the `input` element does not enclose content, it has no end tag, so it requires a closing slash for XHTML compliance. The most important attribute of `input` is its `type`. There are several field types that have well-defined default behaviors in HTML. The possible values are listed in Table 3.1.

Table 3.1   Values for the `input` element's `type` attribute

Field type	Description
`type = "button"`	Provides a programmer-defined action to be associated with the field through the use of an event handler such as `onclick`
`type = "checkbox"`	Allows selection of one or more values from a set of possible values
`type = "hidden"`	Allows the definition of text fields that can be accessed by a PHP script but are not displayed in a document
`type = "password"`	Allows entry of character data but displays only asterisks
`type = "radio"`	Allows selection of one and only one value from a set of possible values
`type = "reset"`	Used to reset all form fields to their default values
`type = "submit"`	Processes form contents according to `method` and `action`
`type = "text"`	Allows entry of character data

There is no field type specifically for numerical values. In some circumstances, this can be an issue, but as will be seen later, it presents no problem for sending values from an `input` element to a PHP application.

Here is a list of attributes for the input element.

`checked`
Value: none
   Applies to `type="radio"` and `type="checkbox"` only.

`maxlength="..."`
Value: Maximum number of characters that can be entered in the field. This value can be greater than the value given for the `size` attribute.

`name="..."`
Value: A programmer-supplied name for the field. The name should follow the variable-naming conventions for PHP in order to facilitate its use in PHP scripts.

`readonly`
Value: none
   Prevents field values in `type="text"` or `text="password"` from being changed.

`size="..."`
Value: width of the displayed field, in characters.

`type="..."`
Values: See Table 3.1.

`value="..."`
Value: a programmer-supplied default value that will be displayed in the field. This value can be overridden by user input unless the `readonly` attribute is also specified.

The `form` element typically contains a combination of text and input fields. The text can be used to explain to the user of the form what kind of input is expected. Document 3.4 gives a simple example that uses several input field types:

Document 3.4 (`location.htm`)

```
<html>
<head>
<title>Data Reporting Site Information</title>
</head>
<body>
```

```
<form>
    Please enter your last name:
    <inputtype="text" name="last_name" size="20"
      maxlength="20" /><br />
    Please enter your latitude:
    <input type="text" name="lat" value="40" size="7"
      maxlength="7" />
      N <input type="radio" name="NS" value="N" checked />
      or S <input type="radio" name="NS" value="S" /><br />
    Please enter your longitude:
    <input type="text" name="lon" value="75" size="8"
      maxlength="8" />
      E <input type="radio" name="EW" value="E" /> or W
    <input type="radio" name="EW" value="W" checked /><br />
    Please enter your elevation:
    <input type="text" name="elevation" size="8" maxlength="8"
      /> meters<br />
    Please indicate the seasons during which your site reports
      data:<br />
    Winter: <input type="checkbox" name="seasons"
      value="Winter" />
    Spring: <input type="checkbox" name="seasons"
      value="Spring" />
    Summer: <input type="checkbox" name="seasons"
      value="Summer" />
    Fall: <input type="checkbox" name="seasons"
      value="Fall" />
</form>
</body>
</html>
```

| Please enter your last name: [   ] |
| Please enter your latitude: [40   ] N ● or S ○ |
| Please enter your longitude: [75   ] E ○ or W ● |
| Please enter your elevation: [   ] meters |
| Please indicate the seasons during which your site reports data: Winter: ☐ Spring: ☐ Summer: ☐ Fall: ☐ |

Note that some of the text fields are blank because no default value attribute has been specified. These require user input, and there is no way to establish ahead of time what this input might be. However, it may still be worthwhile in some cases to provide a default value if that would help the user to understand what is required. When the allowed input choices can be limited ahead of time by the creator of the document, it is appropriate to use radio buttons and checkboxes. You can create as many different combinations of these kinds of field as your application needs.

Each group of `radio` and `checkbox` buttons has its own unique field name and, within each group, each button should have its own value. In Document 3.4, there are two `radio` button groups, named NS and EW. It is important to specify a value for each button, because the value of the checked button will be captured when the contents of the form are submitted to a PHP application. Default values for the radio field can be specified by using the `checked` attribute. When you access the document, the button with the `checked` attribute will be "on." You can change it by clicking on another of the buttons in the group.

The same basic rules apply to `checkbox` fields. You can have more than one group of checkboxes, each with its unique name. The only difference is that you can select as many boxes as you like within each group, rather than just one value with `radio` fields.

3.3 Creating Pull-Down Lists

A common feature on web pages that use forms is a pull-down list. The `select` and `option` tags provide another way to limit the input choices a user can make on a form. The implementation described here is similar to a group of radio buttons in the sense that only one item can be selected from a list. This can simplify a document interface and eliminate the need for some input checking that might otherwise need to be done if a user is free to type whatever she/he likes in an input field. For example, creating a pull-down list of the months of the year eliminates the need for a user to type (and perhaps to mistype) the name of a month, as shown in Document 3.5.

Document 3.5 (`select. htm`)

```html
<html>
<head>
<title>Pull-Down List</title>
</head>
<body><form>
Select a month from this menu:
 <select name="testing">
   <option value="1" selected>January</option>
   <option value="2">February</option>
   <option value="3">March</option>
   <option value="4">April</option>
   <option value="5">May</option>
   <option value="6">June</option>
```

```
    <option value="7">July</option>
    <option value="8">August</option>
    <option value="9">September</option>
    <option value="10">October</option>
    <option value="11">November</option>
    <option value="12">December</option>
  </select>
</form></body>
</html>
```

Including `size="12"` ensures that all the months will be visible. Without this attribute, HTML can add a scroll bar to the list.

For the output shown, the user has chosen the month of April, which is now highlighted. The values of the `value` attribute can be, but do not have to be, the same as the text displayed for each option. In this case, the month values are numbers between 1 and 12, rather than the names of the months. Assigning the `selected` attribute to the first option means that "January" will be highlighted when the pull-down box is first displayed. For longer lists, the default action is for HTML to include a scroll bar alongside the list.

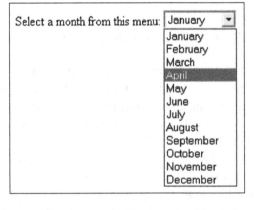

Adding the `multiple` attribute to the `<select>` tag allows more than one selection to be made by holding down the Control key on Windows computers or the Command key on Mac Computers.

Although it is easy to create pull-down lists as well as groups of radio buttons and checkboxes, it is not yet obvious how to make use of the selections a user makes. As will be shown in subsequent chapters, PHP provides the required capabilities.

3.4   Combining Tables and Forms

In terms of organizing an HTML document which will be linked to a PHP application, it is often helpful to create one or more tables in which the cell contents are fields in a form. Document 3.6 gives an example.

Document 3.6 (siteDefinition.htm)

```html
<html>
<head>
<title>Observation Site Descriptions</title>
</head>
<body>
<form>
<table border="2"cellpadding="5" cellspacing="2"
  align="center">
  <caption><font size="+2">Observation Site
  Descritions</font></caption>
  <tr bgcolor="lightblue">
    <th>Site #</th><th>Site Name</th><th>Latitude</th>
    <th>Longitude</td><th>Elevation</th>
  </tr>
  <tr bgcolor="palegreen">
    <td>Site 1</td>
    <td><input type="text" name="Name1" size="10"
      maxlength="10" value="Name1" /></td>
    <td><input type="text" name="Latitude1" size="10"
      maxlength="10"
      value="Latitude1" /></td>
    <td><input type="text" name="Longitude1" size="10"
      maxlength="10" value="Longitude1" /></td>
    <td><input type="text" name="Elevation1" size="10"
      maxlength="10" value="Elevation1" /></td>
  </tr>
  <tr bgcolor="ivory">
    <td>Site 2</td>
    <td><input type="text" name="Name2" size="10"
      maxlength="10" value="Name2" /></td>
    <td><input type="text" name="Latitude2" size="10"
      maxlength="10" value="Latitude2" /></td>
    <td><input type="text" name="Longitude2" size="10"
      maxlength="10" value="Longitude2" /></td>
    <td><input type="text" name="Elevation2" size="10"
      maxlength="10" value="Elevation2" /></td>
  </tr>
  <tr bgcolor="palegreen">
    <td>Site 3</td>
    <td><input type="text" name="Name3" size="10"
      maxlength="10" value="Name3" /></td>
    <td><input type="text" name="Latitude3" size="10"
```

```html
          maxlength="10" value="Latitude3" /></td>
      <td><input type="text" name="Longitude3" size="10"
          maxlength="10" value="Longitude3" /></td>
      <td><input type="text" name="Elevation3" size="10"
          maxlength="10" value="Elevation3" /></td>
    </tr>
    <tr bgcolor="ivory">
      <td>Site 4</td>
      <td><input type="text" name="Name4" size="10"
          maxlength="10" value="Name4" /></td>
      <td><input type="text" name="Latitude4" size="10"
          maxlength="10" value="Latitude4" /></td>
      <td><input type="text" name="Longitude4" size="10"
          maxlength="10" value="Longitude4" /></td>
      <td><input type="text" name="Elevation4" size="10"
          maxlength="10" value="Elevation4" /></td>
    </tr>
    <tr bgcolor="palegreen">
      <td>Site 5</td>
      <td><input type="text" name="Name5" size="10"
          maxlength="10" value="Name5" /></td>
      <td><input type="text" name="Latitude5" size="10"
          maxlength="10" value="Latitude5" /></td>
      <td><input type="text" name="Longitude5" size="10"
          maxlength="10" value="Longitude5" /></td>
     <td><input type="text" name="Elevation5" size="10"
          maxlength="10" value="Elevation5" /></td>
    </tr>
  </table>
</form>
</body>
</html>
```

Observation Site Descritions				
Site #	Site Name	Latitude	Longitude	Elevation
Site 1	Name1	Latitude1	Longitude1	Elevation1
Site 2	Name2	Latitude2	Longitude2	Elevation2
Site 3	Name3	Latitude3	Longitude3	Elevation3
Site 4	Name4	Latitude4	Longitude4	Elevation4
Site 5	Name5	Latitude5	Longitude5	Elevation5

The output is shown with the original default field names, before a user starts to add new values.

Although it may seem like a lot of work to create Document 3.6, the task is greatly simplified by copying and pasting information for the rows. When you access this page, the Tab key moves from field to field but skips the first column, which is just fixed text. The user of the page can change the default values of all the input text boxes.

3.5 HTML List Elements

As shown earlier in this chapter, the table and form elements are used as tools for organizing content in an HTML document. List elements provide another way to impose formatting on related content. Table 3.2 gives a brief summary of three kinds of lists.

Table 3.2 HTML list elements

Description	HTML tags	Use
Definition (or glossary)	`<dl> ... </dl>`	For a list that includes names and extensive descriptions
Ordered	`<ol> ... </ol>`	When a list of things needs to be numbered
Unordered	`<ul> ... </ul>`	For a list of "bulleted" items
List item	`<li> ... </li>`	Create list entry for `<ul>` or `<ol>`
Glossary head	`<dt> ... </dt>`	Create glossary heading for `<dl>`
Glossary term	`<dd> ... </dd>`	Create glossary term description for `<dl>`

Document 3.7 shows how to use these list tags.

Document 3.7 (lists.htm)

```
<html>
<head>
 <title>Using HTML Lists</title>
</head>
<body>
This page demonstrates the use of unordered, ordered, and
definition lists.
<ul>
    <li> Use unordered lists for "bulleted" items.</li>
    <li> Use ordered lists for numbered items. </li>
```

```
<li> Use definition lists for lists of items to be defined.
</li>
</ul>
Here are three ways to organize content in an HTML document:
<ol>
   <li>Use a table. </li>
   <li>Use a list. </li>
   <li>Use <font face="courier">&lt;pre&gt; ...
&lt;/pre&gt;</font> tags. </li>
</ol>
This is a way to produce a neatly formatted glossary list.
<dl>
   <dt><b>definition list</b>
    (<font face="courier">&lt;dl&gt;</font>)</dt>
   <dd>Use this to display a list of glossary items and their
definitions. </dd>
   <dt><b>ordered list</b>
    (<font face="courier">&lt;ol&gt;</font>) </dt>
   <dd>Use this to display a numbered list. </dd>
   <dt><b>unordered list</b>
     (<font face="courier">&lt;ul&gt;</font>)</dt>
   <dd>Use this to display a list of bulleted items. </dd>
</dl>
</body>
</html>
```

The use of these tags imposes a preset format for displaying list items. Blank lines are inserted before and after the list, with no <br /> or <p> ... <p> tags required to separate the lists from other text in the document. For ordered and unordered lists, the list items themselves are indented. For the definition list, the items are not indented, but the "definitions" are. The contents of a list item can include text formatting elements. For example, in Document 3.7, the items in the definition list use the b element to display the item name in a bold font. A list item can be an image, <img src="..." />, or a URL reference, <a href="...">.

Note the use of < and > to display the < and > characters in the document. (If you just type these characters, they will not be displayed on the screen because HTML will try to associate them with tags and will simply ignore them when it can't figure out what you meant.)

This page demonstrates the use of unordered, ordered, and definition lists.

- Use unordered lists for "bulleted" items.
- Use ordered lists for numbered items.
- Use definition lists for lists of items to be defined.

Here are three ways to organize content in an HTML document:

1. Use a table.
2. Use a list.
3. Use `<pre>` ... `</pre>` tags.

This is a way to produce a neatly formatted glossary list.

definition list (`<dl>`)
> Use this to display a list of glossary items and their definitions.

ordered list (`<ol>`)
> Use this to display a numbered list.

unordered list (`<ul>`)
> Use this to display a list of bulleted items.

There are some attributes associated with list elements that provide a little more control over the appearance of lists.

`start="n"`
Value: The integer n specifies the starting value of an ordered list. The default value is `start="1"`.

`type = "…"`
Values: For unordered lists: `"disc"` (the default value), `"square"`, `"circle"`

For ordered lists: `"A"` (uppercase letters), `"a"` (lowercase letters), `"I"` (uppercase Roman letters, `"i"` (lowercase Roman letters), `"1"` (numbers, the default value)

`value = "n"`
Value: The integer n specifies a numerical value for an item in an ordered list which overrides the default value. Subsequent list items will be renumbered starting at this value.

Finally, it is possible to combine list types to create more complicated list structures. Document 3.8 shows how list tags can be used to create the table of contents for a book.

Document 3.8 ((bookContents.htm)

```
<html>
<title>Table of Contents for My Book</title>
<body>
<h2>Table of Contents for My Book</h2>
<ol>
<b><li>Chapter One</b></li>
  <ol type="I">
    <li>Section 1.1</li>
      <ol type="i">
        <li>First Topic</li>
        <li>Second Topic</li>
          <ul type="circle">
            <li><i> subtopic 1</i></li>
            <li><i> subtopic 2</i></li>
          </ul>
      </ol>
    <li>Section 1.2</li>
    <li>Section 1.3</li>
  </ol>
<b><li>Chapter Two</b></li>
  <ol type="I">
    <li>Section 2.1</li>
   <ol type="i">
    <li>First Topic</li>
    <li>Second Topic</li>
      <ul type="circle">
        <li><i> subtopic 1</i></li>
        <li><i> subtopic 2</i></li>
      </ul>
  </ol>
    <li>Section 2.2</li>
    <li>Section 2.3</li>
  </ol>
<b><li>Chapter Three</b></li>
  <ol type="I">
    <li>Section 3.1</li>
      <ol type="i">
        <li>First Topic</li>
        <li>Second Topic</li>
          <ul type="circle">
```

```
            <li><i> subtopic 1</i></li>
            <li><i> subtopic 2</i></li>
            <li><i> subtopic 3</i></li>
          </ul>
        </ol>
    <li>Section 3.2</li>
    <li>Section 3.3</li>
      <ol type="i">
        <li>First Topic</li>
        <li>Second Topic</li>
      </ol>
    <li>Section 3.4</li>
  </ol>
</ol>
</body>
</html>
```

Note that if this list were used for an online book, for example, each list item could include a link to a URL or a hypertext link to another location within the same document.

Table of Contents for My Book

1. Chapter One
   I. Section 1.1
      i. First Topic
      ii. Second Topic
         ○ *subtopic 1*
         ○ *subtopic 2*
   II. Section 1.2
   III. Section 1.3
2. Chapter Two
   I. Section 2.1
      i. First Topic
      ii. Second Topic
         ○ *subtopic 1*
         ○ *subtopic 2*
   II. Section 2.2
   III. Section 2.3
3. Chapter Three
   I. Section 3.1
      i. First Topic
      ii. Second Topic
         ○ *subtopic 1*
         ○ *subtopic 2*
         ○ *subtopic 3*
   II. Section 3.2
   III. Section 3.3
      i. First Topic
      ii. Second Topic
   IV. Section 3.4

3.6   HTML Frames

Another way of organizing content in HTML documents is through the use of frames to divide a window into several separately addressable blocks of content. Frames are built using two elements, frame and frameset.

<frame > ... </frame>
Attributes: bordercolor,   frameborder,   marginheight, marginwidth, name, scrolling (yes, no, or auto), src
   Provides a nameable window region, as defined by the frameset element, with a link to the content of that region. A value for the src attribute must be given, but the other attributes are optional. The default value for the scrolling attribute is auto, which automatically provides a scroll bar if needed to display all of a window's content.

<frameset> ... </frameset>
Attributes: border,   bordercolor,   cols,   frameborder, framespacing, rows
   Provides specifications for dividing a webpage window into two or more separately linkable sub-windows. All attributes are optional except cols and rows, which must have values of n pixels, n% of the available window, or * to fill the remaining window space.

   Consider the following screen display. It is divided into three sections. The upper left-hand corner contains a clickable image. The lower left-hand corner contains links to other HTML documents. The right-hand column will be used to display those documents. When this page is first accessed, a "home page" document should be displayed.
   Document 3.9a shows the first step in creating this page.

Document 3.9a (frameMain.htm)

```
<html>
<head>
<title>A simple frameset document</title>
</head>
<frameset cols="30%, 70%" frameborder="1">
    <frameset rows="60%, 40%">
            <frame src="frame1.htm" scrolling="no" />
            <frame src="frame2.htm" />
    </frameset>
    <frame name="homeFrame" src="homeFrame.htm" />
```

```
</frameset>
</html>
```

The `frameset` element is used to define the frames. In this case, the window is divided into two columns. The left-hand column occupies 30% of the page and the right-hand column occupies the remaining 70%. (In the graphic displayed below, the proportions look different because the screen display has been cropped to save space.) The line

```
<frameset cols="30%, 70%" frameborder="1">
```

could also be written

```
<frameset cols="30%, *" frameborder="1">
```

where the asterisk is interpreted as "fill the remaining portion of the screen with the right-hand column." If the frame size is given as a number without the % sign, it is interpreted as pixels rather than a percentage of the full window. Setting this frame size to `cols="200,*"` will produce a left-side frame that is always 200 pixels wide, regardless of the screen width and resolution.

The left-hand column is further divided into two sub-windows. The top window occupies the top 60% and the bottom window occupies the remaining 40%. Each window is associated with a separate HTML document, `frame1.htm` and `frame2.htm`. These windows *could* be given names, but they don't have to have names. The right-hand column is associated with another HTML document, `homeFrame.htm`. This "home frame" will be the destination for content that will be linked from the frame in the lower left-hand corner. This frame needs a name to serve as a "target" for the other documents that will be displayed here. The name can be anything, but `homeFrame` is a self-explanatory and therefore reasonable choice.

Documents 3.9b through 3.9d show the HTML code for each of the three frames.

Document 3.9b (`homeFrame.htm`)

```
<html>
<head>
<title>My Home Frame</title>
</head>
<body bgcolor="lightgreen">
<h1><blink><font color="maroon"><b><i>Home page display
goes here.</i></b></font></blink></h1>
```

```
</body>
</html>
```

Document 3.9c (frame1.htm)

```
<html>
<head>
<title>Title Frame</title>
</head>
<body bgcolor="pink">
<font size="+6" color="navy"><center><b><i>Frames
<br />Demo<br />
<a href="frameDescription.htm" /><img src="frame.gif"
  border="2"></i></b></center></a>
</font>
</body>
</html>
```

Document 3.9d (frame2.htm)

```
<html>
<head>
<title>Gossip Column</title>
</head>
<body bgcolor="lightblue">
<font size="+3">
Links to other stuff...<br />
<a href="gossip.htm" target="homeFrame" /> Gossip Column</a>
<br />
<a href="photoGallery.htm" target="homeFrame" />
  Picture Gallery</a><br />
<a href="homeFrame.htm" target="homeFrame" />home</a><br />
</font>
</body>
</html>
```

Document 3.9e is the HTML document referenced in Document 3.9c.

Document 3.9e (frameDescription.htm)

```
<html>
<head>
<title>How this image was created.</title>
</head>
<body>
This image was created in Windows' Paint program.
<a href="frame1.htm" />Click here to return.</a>
</body>
</html>
```

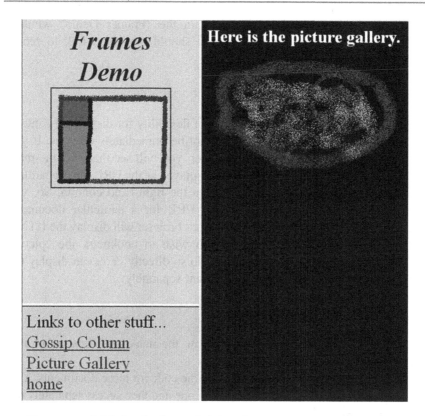

Document 3.9d, for the lower left-hand corner, contains links to several other documents, each of which can be displayed in the right-hand window. This is done by using the `target` attribute, which links to `homeFrame`, the `name` value given in Document 3.9a:

```
<a href="gossip.htm" target="homeFrame">Gossip Column</a>
```

It is up to you to provide the `gossip.htm` and `photoGallery.htm` documents. Document 3.9d also includes a link back to the home page document. The image shown here is the result of clicking on the "Picture Gallery" link to a document on the author's computer; the page image has been cropped to save space.

Document 3.9b contains the code for the home frame that is displayed when the page is first accessed. (The `blink` element, which causes text to blink on and off, will be ignored by some browsers.) Document 3.9c, for the upper left-hand frame, contains the clickable image, `frame.gif`, with a border drawn around it. Clicking on the image opens a link to descriptive file, `frameDescription.htm` (see Document 3.9e), to be provided by you. This document will be displayed in the "Frames Demo" window (not opened in a new window), and it should contain a link to return to frame1.htm:

```
<a href="frame1.htm">Click here to return.</a>
```

HTML frames provide a great deal of flexibility for displaying content, but there is one consequence that may not be immediately obvious. If you try these examples on your own computer, you will see that *only* the main frame document (frameMain.htm) is displayed as the URL link, regardless of which document is being displayed in the right-hand column. So, you cannot directly copy or bookmark the URL for a particular document. Accessing the "view source" option on your browser will display the HTML code only for frameMain.htm. If you wish to bookmark the "picture gallery" page, for example, you cannot do so directly. You can display the page separately by accessing the document separately:

```
http:// ... /photoGallery.htm
```

but doing that assumes you already know the name and location of this document.

This situation does not really hide all the code for these documents. You can look at the frameMain.htm HTML code and then access separately the homeFrame.htm, frame1.htm, and frame2.htm documents to examine their HTML code.

3.7 More Examples

3.7.1 Selecting Cloud Types from a List of Possibilities

Create a document that allows users to select observed cloud types from a list of possibilities. More than one cloud type can exist simultaneously. The categories are:

high altitude: Cirrus, Cirrocumulus, Cirrostratus
mid altitude: Altostratus, Altocumulus
low altitude: Stratus, Stratocumulus, Cumulus
precipitation-producing: Nimbostratus, Cumulonimbus

A good way to organize this information is to use a table within a form. The form fields should be of type checkbox rather than radio because cause multiple selections are possible. Compare this problem with Document 3.3, in which a table was used to display just the cloud types.

Document 3.10 (cloud1.htm)

```html
<html>
<head>
<title>Cloud Observations</title>
</head>
<body bgcolor="#aaddff">
<h1>Cloud Observations</h1>
<b> Cloud Observations </b>
(Select as many cloud types as observed.)
<br />
<form>
<table>
  <tr>
    <td><b>High</b> </td>
     <td>
      <input type="checkbox" name="high"
        value="Cirrus" /> Cirrus</td>
    <td>
      <input type="checkbox" name="high"
        value="Cirrocumulus" /> Cirrocumulus </td>
    <td>
       <input type="checkbox" name="high"
        value="Cirrostratus" /> Cirrostratus </td></tr>
  <tr>
    <td colspan="4"><hr noshade color="black" />
     </td></tr>
   <tr>
    <td> <b>Middle</b> </td>
     <td>
      <input type="checkbox" name=" mid"
        value="Altostratus" /> Altostratus </td>
    <td>
      <input type="checkbox" name="mid"
        value="Altocumulus" /> Altocumulus</td></tr>
   <tr>
    <td colspan="4"><hr noshade color="black" />
     </td></tr>
   <tr>
    <td> <b>Low</b></td>
    <td>
    <input type="checkbox" name="low" value="Stratus" />
      Stratus</td>
    <td>
```

```
        <input type="checkbox" name="low"
          value="Stratocumulus" /> Stratocumulus</td>
      <td>
      <input type="checkbox" name="low" value="Cumulus" />
        Cumulus </td></tr>
   <tr>
      <td colspan="4"><hr noshade color="black" />
        </td></tr>
   <tr>
      <td> <b>Rain-Producing </b> </td>
      <td>
         <input type="checkbox" name="rain"
           value="Nimbostratus" /> Nimbostratus</td>
      <td>
         <input type="checkbox" name="rain"
           value="Cumulonimbus" /> Cumulonimbus </td></tr>
</table>
</form>
</body>
</html>
```

In Document 3.10, checkboxes for the cloud types are organized into four groups, for high-, mid-, and low-altitude clouds, plus rain-producing clouds. Within each

Cloud Observations

Cloud Observations (Select as many cloud types as observed.)

High	☐ Cirrus	☐ Cirrocumulus	☐ Cirrostratus
Middle	☐ Altostratus	☐ Altocumulus	
Low	☐ Stratus	☐ Stratocumulus	☐ Cumulus
Rain-Producing	☐ Nimbostratus	☐ Cumulonimbus	

group, each checkbox has a name associated with it.

Note that the names given to each checkbox in Document 3.10 are the same as the text entered in the corresponding cell. This is only because these names and text are reasonable descriptions of the cell contents. In general, the text in the cell does not need to be the same as, or even related to, the value of the name attribute of the checkbox.

In general, there's not much point in being able to make choices in checkboxes unless there is a way to respond to the choices. As will be shown later, it is easy to transfer these choices to a PHP application.

3.7.2   A "Split Window" Application

Create an application that maintains one or more "header lines" across the top of a web page window while scrolling through a long text document.

Consider this file:

```
DRB Worcester PA
40.178 -75.3325
4030 5200
Mon day  yr   hr min sec EST            PYR-1   PYR-2   T
7   1    2008 0  0   0   1              0.00031 0.00031 20.198
7   1    2008 0  1   0   1.000694444 0.00031 0.00031 20.174
7   1    2008 0  2   0   1.001388889 0.00031 0.00031 20.174
...
```

The file contains 1440 lines of data (24 hours times 60 minutes per hour for July 1, 2008) with the date and time, the day and time converted to a fractional Eastern Standard Time day (EST), data from two instruments, PYR-1 and PYR-2, and air temperature in degrees Celsius. The instruments measure incoming solar radiation.

For a file of this size, it might be convenient to be able to display these data under a fixed header that identifies the columns, in the same way that spreadsheets allow creation of a "split window." Documents 3.11a and 3.11b show a very simple solution to this problem, using HTML frames.

Document 3.11a (pyranometerMain.htm)

```
<html>
<head>
<title>Display pyranometer data</title>
</head>
<frameset rows="10%, *">
        <frame src="header.htm" scrolling="no" />
     <frame src="pyranometer.dat" />
</frameset>
</html>
```

Document 3.11b (header.htm)

```
<html>
<head>
  <title></title>
</head>
<body>
<font face="courier" >
This is the header.<br />
mon    day     yr    hr  
  min    sec     EST    
      PYR-1  PYR-2  T<br />
</font>
</body></html>
```

This is the header.									
mon	day	yr	hr	min	sec	EST	PYR-1	PYR-2	T

DRB Worcester PA									
40.178	-75.3325								
4030	5200	-999							
mon	day	yr	hr	min	sec	EST	PYR-1	PYR-2	T
7	1	2008	0	0	0	1	0.00031	0.00031	20.198
7	1	2008	0	1	0	1.000694444	0.00031	0.00031	20.174
7	1	2008	0	2	0	1.001388889	0.00031	0.00031	20.174
7	1	2008	0	3	0	1.002083333	0.00031	0.00031	20.174
7	1	2008	0	4	0	1.002777778	0.00031	0.00031	20.174
7	1	2008	0	5	0	1.003472222	0.00031	0.00031	20.174
7	1	2008	0	6	0	1.004166667	0.00031	0.00031	20.15
7	1	2008	0	7	0	1.004861111	0.00031	0.00031	20.126
7	1	2008	0	8	0	1.005555556	0.00031	0.00031	20.079
7	1	2008	0	9	0	1.00625	0.00031	0.00031	20.055
7	1	2008	0	10	0	1.006944444	0.00031	0.00031	20.031
7	1	2008	0	11	0	1.007638889	0.00031	0.00031	20.031
7	1	2008	0	12	0	1.008333333	0.00031	0.00031	20.007
7	1	2008	0	13	0	1.009027778	0.00031	0.00031	19.984
7	1	2008	0	14	0	1.009722222	0.00031	0.00031	19.984
7	1	2008	0	15	0	1.010416667	0.00031	0.00031	19.984
7	1	2008	0	16	0	1.011111111	0.00031	0.00031	19.984
7	1	2008	0	17	0	1.011805556	0.00031	0.00031	19.96
7	1	2008	0	18	0	1.0125	0.00031	0.00031	19.936
7	1	2008	0	19	0	1.013194444	0.00031	0.00031	19.888
7	1	2008	0	20	0	1.013888889	0.00031	0.00031	19.841
7	1	2008	0	21	0	1.014583333	0.00031	0.00031	19.793
7	1	2008	0	22	0	1.015277778	0.00031	0.00031	19.793
7	1	2008	0	23	0	1.015972222	0.00031	0.00031	19.793
7	1	2008	0	24	0	1.016666667	0.00031	0.00031	19.746
7	1	2008	0	25	0	1.017361111	0.00031	0.00031	19.746
7	1	2008	0	26	0	1.018055556	0.00031	0.00031	19.698
7	1	2008	0	27	0	1.01875	0.00031	0.00031	19.698
7	1	2008	0	28	0	1.019444444	0.00031	0.00031	19.651
7	1	2008	0	29	0	1.020138889	0.00031	0.00031	19.627
7	1	2008	0	30	0	1.020833333	0.00031	0.00031	19.603

The   escape sequence allows the insertion of "white space" between text to align headers. The `frameset rows` attribute allocates the top 10% of the page to the header and the output file, `pyranometer.dat`, is displayed in the remainder of the page. For a display that is too long to fit in one window, HTML automatically creates a scroll bar down the right-hand side of the window. A border has been retained under the top frame, just to make clear how the page is divided, but it is optional; to remove the border, set the `frameset` attribute `border="0"`.

A simple modification of the `frameset` code in Document 3.11a would allow listing a number of different files in a left-hand column, each of which could be displayed in the home page frame simply by clicking on the file name. To do this, the direct link to `pyranometer.dat` in Document 3.11a would be replaced with another name specified as the value of a `target` attribute in the reference to each document to be displayed:

```
<a href="…" target="…" … />
```

The `pyranometer.dat` file is just a tab-delimited text file, not an HTML document. Although it is of some interest to be able to display a large text file in HTML, it would be more useful to be able to use that file for something. HTML documents cannot process external data files and that is the purpose of interfacing HTML with PHP, which will be the topic of the rest of this book.

Creating a PHP Environment

4

This chapter provides an introduction to setting up a PHP environment for solving computational problems. An example introduces PHP's ability to read external files.

4.1 A Simple HTML/PHP Application

As shown in previous chapters, HTML documents can be used to display content and manipulate the appearance of that content, but they cannot manipulate the content itself. Even with the addition of scripting languages such as JavaScript, an HTML document cannot manipulate information residing outside that document, regardless of whether the file containing that information resides locally or remotely.

For scientific and other computing tasks, a programming language must support not only the required kinds of calculations and logical structures, but also the ability to manipulate external data. PHP, a server-based language, provides a solution for remote or local programming solutions (as opposed to a language installed as a standalone application on a local computer).

As will be shown later in this chapter, a PHP application can stand alone for performing computational tasks, but its most useful feature is that it can easily accept user inputs transferred from an HTML document. The PHP application can then process those data and display output. The display capabilities can even make use of HTML elements to format output. For example, PHP can generate HTML-like tables. Finally, and significantly, the PHP language includes commands for generating the graphical output that is essential for displaying and understanding data.

As a simple example of how PHP works together with an HTML document, recall the table of radon values created by Document 3.1. In that document, a table was built with "hard coded" radon values and appropriate colors to indicate the desired actions. This is not a very useful application! The goal now is to create an application that allows a user to enter radon values for four locations and then creates a table whose cells are color coded according to the radon values at each location.

© Springer International Publishing AG 2017
D.R. Brooks, *Programming in HTML and PHP*, Undergraduate Topics in Computer Science, DOI 10.1007/978-3-319-56973-4_4

The solution to this problem is to use two documents—an HTML document into which a user enters radon values and a PHP application that processes those values.

Document 4.1a (`radonTable1.htm`)

```html
<html>
<head>
<title>Radon Table</title>
</head>
<body>
<h1>Results of radon testing</h1>
<p>
The table below shows some radon levels measured in
residences.<br />
For values greater than or equal to 4 pCi/L,
action should be taken<br /> to reduce the concentration of
radon gas.
For values greater than or<br />
equal to 3 pCi/L, retesting is recommended.
</p>
<form method="post" action="radonTable1.php">
<table border>
   <tr bgcolor="silver">
      <th>Location</th><th>Value, pCi/L</th>
</tr>
   <tr>
      <td><input type="text" name="site1_name"
value="basement" /></td><td><input type="text" size="10"
name="site1"/></td>
   <tr>
      <td><input type="text" name="site2_name"
value="1st floor" /></td><td><input type="text" size="10"
name="site2"/></td>
   <tr>
      <td><input type="text" name="site3_name"
value="2nd floor" /></td><td><input type="text" size="10"
name="site3"/></td>
   <tr>
      <td><input type="text" name="site4_name"
value="master_bedroom" /></td><td><input
type="text"size="10" name="site4"/></td>
</table>
<input type="submit" value="Click to generate table..." />
</form>
</body>
</html>
```

Document 4.1b (radonTable1.php)

```php
<?php
// Transfer the values.
$site1=$_POST["site1"];
$site2=$_POST["site2"];
$site3=$_POST["site3"];
$site4=$_POST["site4"];
$site1_name=$_POST["site1_name"];
$site2_name=$_POST["site2_name"];
$site3_name=$_POST["site3_name"];
$site4_name=$_POST["site4_name"];
// Select colors for a color-coded table.
$bg1=pickColor($site1);
$bg2=pickColor($site2);
$bg3=pickColor($site3);
$bg4=pickColor($site4);
echo "<h1>Results of radon testing</h1><p>";
echo "The table below shows some radon levels measured in
residences.<br />";
echo "For values greater than or equal to 4 pCi/L, action
should be taken<br />";
echo "to reduce the concentration of radon gas. For values
greater than or<br />";
echo "equal to 3 pCi/L, retesting is recommended.</p>";
// Create the color-coded table.
echo "<table border><tr><th>Site
name</th><th>Value</th></tr>";
echo "<tr bgcolor=$bg1>
<td>$site1_name</td><td>$site1</td></tr>";
echo "<tr bgcolor=$bg2>
<td>$site2_name</td><td>$site2</td></tr>";
echo "<tr bgcolor=$bg3>
<td>$site3_name</td><td>$site3</td></tr>";
echo "<tr bgcolor=$bg4>
<td>$site4_name</td><td>$site4</td></tr>";
echo "</table>";
function pickColor($value) {
   if ($value>=4) $bg="pink";
   elseif ($value>=3) $bg="yellow";
   else $bg="lightgreen";
   return $bg;
}
?>
```

Document 4.1a contains nothing new except for the line

<form method="**post**" action="**radonTable1.php**">

that includes two attributes of the form element: method and action. This single line is all that is required to send the value of *every* input field inside a form element to the PHP application radonTable1.php!

Document 4.1b contains a lot of new information, with syntax details that will be explained later in more detail. For now, consider these lines:

```
$site1=$_POST["site1"];
$site2=$_POST["site2"];
$site3=$_POST["site3"];
$site4=$_POST["site4"];
$site1_name=$_POST["site1_name"];
$site2_name=$_POST["site2_name"];
$site3_name=$_POST["site3_name"];
$site4_name=$_POST["site4_name"];
```

These statements "receive" the values entered into the corresponding input fields from Document 4.1a, sent as a result of clicking on the "submit" button. These values are stored in variable names defined in the PHP application, indicated by the $ in front of each name. In this case, the variable names are the same as the names defined in the input fields, but they don't have to be. You can give the PHP variables any names you like, but it often makes sense to use the same names in both documents.

Recall that, previously, it was noted that values entered in input fields are treated by HTML as "text" values; HTML does not "know" anything about numerical values. In this case, the first four variables, the radon values, are supposed to be numbers, while the last four, the site names, are text values. But, no problem! PHP will *automatically* interpret text that looks like a number as a numerical value. (If you pass a value to PHP that is supposed to be a number, but isn't entered as something that looks like a number, PHP will not be able to figure that out.[1])

Next, the lines

```
$bg1=pickColor($site1);
$bg2=pickColor($site2);
$bg3=pickColor($site3);
$bg4=pickColor($site4);
```

---

[1]For example, entering an amount of money with a $, like $17.30, will not work.

call a user-defined function (much more about that in Chap. 7) that calculates the appropriate color value for each radon value.

Finally, a series of PHP `echo` commands generate the output. Optionally, the explanatory text from the HTML document, along with its formatting, is duplicated. A table is created in which the background colors are chosen based on the values of $bg1, $bg2, $bg3, and $bg4. Note that in a command like

```
echo "<tr bgcolor=$bg1>
```

the text string "value" of the variable $bg1 is "pasted in" to the command; it is not obvious that this should work so easily!

4.2 Setting Up an HTML/PHP Environment

4.2.1 Install or Gain Access to a PHP-Enabled Server

There is a very significant difference between HTML documents and PHP applications. HTML documents are self-contained documents that can be opened and "executed" in a Web browser on your local computer or accessed online from any location where those documents are stored. In contrast, PHP applications require access to a server on which a PHP interpreter has been installed.[2] The server must be configured to allow PHP scripts to be processed and all PHP applications must be saved on the server in an appropriate location.

Because of the potential for carelessly written or malicious code to wreak havoc on any computer allowing remote access to its contents (in this case, through an HTML document passing information to a PHP application), appropriate safeguards must be established to limit the ability to read and write data from or to specific locations on the server. Because of these potential problems, some servers do not allow the use of *any* server-side applications.

Even if the client browser and server reside on the same physical computer, a server and PHP interpreter must still be installed and configured, and precautions should still be taken to protect the computer's contents. All the PHP work described in this book is done with the widely used Apache server, which is available through free downloads in versions for Windows (WAMP), Macintosh (MAMP), and Linux (LAMP) computers.

---

[2]PHP is an interpreted, as opposed to a compiled, language in the sense that stand-alone executable binary files are not generated.

On the author's Windows computers, a default installation of the WAMP local server automatically provides all the required capability to run PHP applications, including graphics-based applications. For all the code in this book, PHP version 5.6 has been used.

It should not be difficult to create an environment for building HTML/PHP applications. Although it is certainly possible to use PHP on a remote server, it will be much easier to learn how to use this language if you install a server on your own computer. This is the situation assumed for all the PHP code examples in the rest of this book. By default, the Apache server includes a PHP environment when it is installed.

It is, of course, possible that problems will arise with installing a PHP-enabled server. Fortunately, there are many online sources of help. For using PHP on a remote server, you don't have to do the setup yourself, but you still need to know how to access the server. The details vary from system to system, and you may need to get help from your system administrator.

4.2.2   Use an Editor to Create PHP Scripts

Just like HTML documents, PHP scripts are text files that can be created with any text editor. The AceHTML freeware editor used to produce all the code in this book[3] provides convenient editing and color-coded syntax formatting capabilities for creating and editing PHP code just as it does for creating HTML documents.

At first, it may not be obvious that you cannot execute PHP scripts directly from an editor's browser window, as you can with HTML documents. You can create and edit PHP scripts with an editor, but you must then execute them on a server regardless of whether you are using a remote server or a server residing on your own computer. For example, on a Windows computer with a default WAMP installation, PHP files are probably saved in the C:\wamp\www folder and executed by entering localhost\{PHP file name} in a browser window. It shouldn't make any difference which browser you using because any browser will display your HTML document and the execution of PHP scripts doesn't depend on your browser.

The required folders for using PHP are automatically created when an Apace server is installed. For convenience, you can also store the corresponding HTML documents in the same folder. For example, Documents

---

[3]Visicom Media's AceHTML freeware editor is no longer available, but a "Pro" version is available for purchase. There are several other freeware programming editors available online that are suitable for the purposes of this book.

4.1a and 4.1b could both be stored in the `C:\wamp\www` folder on a Windows computer.

In summary, to execute a PHP application, create it in a code or text editor, save it in `www` (for a WAMP installation) then switch to a browser to execute it at `localhost` on a local server or do whatever is required to execute it on a remote server. If the PHP application is accessed locally through an HTML document, then you will open that document in your browser at `localhost\`*{HTML document name}.* Whenever you make changes, save them and refresh the PHP or HTML document in your browser.

When you create applications in any language, it is important to develop a consistent approach that minimizes the time spent correcting the errors you will inevitably make. This is especially important when using PHP, which requires switching back and forth between your editor and (for a local server) your `localhost`.

It is rarely a good idea to create an entire application all at once. A much better plan is to proceed step-by-step, adding small sections of code and testing each addition to make sure the results are what you expect. When you pass information from an HTML document to a PHP application, it is *always* a good idea to display the values passed to the PHP application *before* writing more PHP code.

The error messages you receive when you make mistakes in your code will almost never be as helpful as you would like, although experience and practice will improve your ability to interpret these messages. They may tell you where an error has been encountered but not what (or even exactly where) the error actually is. You might like to see a message like "You forgot to put a semicolon at the end of line 17." But that will *not* happen! PHP interpreters will never tell you what you really need to know—exactly what you did wrong and how to fix it. And of course, no syntax checker will protect you against the worst errors of all—code that works perfectly well but is logically flawed and gives the wrong answers!

The Apache server installation automatically creates a log file containing all PHP error messages, `wamp\php_error.log` on a Windows computer. It appends new error messages to the existing log so, over time, this file can become *very* large. You can delete this file at any time and it will be recreated the next time an error is encountered. For some kinds of errors, the file can become large from just trying to execute a single PHP script.

To test your PHP/server environment, start with this minimal PHP script. Name it `helloWorld.php` and save it in `wamp\www` (or the

equivalent location on your system). Every PHP script is enclosed inside a
<?php ... ?> tag.

Document 4.2 (helloWorld.php)

```php
<?php
  echo "Hello, world!";
?>
```

Open a browser and type localhost\helloWorld.php (or whatever is
the appropriate URL for your system). You should see the text, "Hello,
world!" displayed in your browser window.

Your computer is probably configured to automatically associate
HTML files with an .htm or .html file name extension with a browser. So,
if you double-click on a file with such an extension, it will open in your
browser.[4] But, if you double-click on a file with a .php extension, the result
is uncertain unless you have specifically associated the .php extension with
some other application, such as a code editor. If you haven't made such an
association, your computer may ask you to find an application for opening
such files. (You could use Notepad on a Windows computer, for example.) In
any case, you cannot "execute" this file by double-clicking on it. Instead, you must
enter its URL in a browser, as noted above.

You can also save and execute this file:

Document 4.3 (PHPInfo.php)

```php
<?php
  echo phpinfo();
?>
```

This file will display a great deal of information about how PHP is
configured on your server. (If you view the source code for this document,
you can also learn a lot about formatting output from PHP.)

The echo language construct in Documents 4.2 displays the specified
text string enclosed in quote marks, "Hello, world!", and Document 4.3
displays the (very long!) string output returned by phpinfo().

---

[4]If you have more than one browser on your computer, it will be the default browser or one you
have designated as the default.

Even more simply, you can just type `http://localhost/` (for a WAMP server). There *should* be an `index.php` file that will, by default, display some information about your server and PHP configuration.

The first thing to notice about Documents 4.2 and 4.3 is that the PHP files are not associated with an HTML document; they serve as stand-alone applications.

If you get error messages, or if nothing happens when you try to execute the scripts in this chapter, then something is wrong with your server/PHP installation. It is hopeless to try to offer system-specific advice for resolving this kind of problem, but the most likely sources of trouble at this level, assuming that you have installed both a server and PHP, is that some server configuration options have been overlooked or have been given inappropriate settings, that you haven't stored your PHP application in an appropriate folder on a local computer, or that you do not understand the procedure for running PHP applications on a remote server. You may need to consult with your system administrator (if you have one) to resolve these problems.

4.2.3 Pass Information from HTML to a PHP Application

Although PHP applications can stand by themselves, as shown in the previous examples, it is more often the case that you will want to build HTML/PHP applications. In general, with any programming language, it is a good idea to start solving a problem by specifying what input is available and required to solve the problem. The HTML/PHP environment facilitates this approach by using an HTML document to collect user input and a PHP script to do the computation. This approach was used in Documents 4.1a and 4.1b.

By design, because this is the essential reason for its existence, PHP makes transferring information from an HTML document *very* easy. It requires only that `input` elements for values to be passed to a PHP application be enclosed inside a `form` element. The data transfer is handled with the `action` and `method` attributes:

```
<form action="{URL of PHP file}" method="post">
...
<input type="submit" value="{Put submit button text here.}" />
</form>
```

For an example, see Document 4.1 at the beginning of this chapter. Often, it is most useful to give the HTML document and its corresponding PHP file the same name, but this is not required.

This code in this book will always use `method="post"`, although it is also possible to use `method="get"` in some circumstances. A PHP application stored on a remote server needs to be identified through its complete URL and not just by a directory/folder reference on the server. But, for the examples in this book, the assumption is that an HTML document and its corresponding PHP application always reside in the same folder/directory on the same local server. For local use on a Windows computer using a WAMP installation, this location should be `C:\wamp\www` with an automatically assigned URL of `localhost`. This co-location of files is done just for convenience in a local server environment. When you use PHP on a remote server, you will store the HTML interface document on your local computer or download it from a server, and the URL for the PHP file will be different, of course.

What makes the process of calling a PHP application from an HTML document so painless is the fact that the contents of *all* form `input` fields in the calling document are *automatically* available to the target PHP file, without any additional programming effort on your part! To reinforce how the HTML/PHP environment works, look again at Documents 4.1a and 4.1b. Information about four locations are given names in HTML `input` elements and values are assigned—you can use the default values or replace them with new values. Pressing the `submit` button passes all the values (the radon numbers and their site names) to the PHP application. The numerical radon values are automatically interpreted correctly and stored as numerical values and the site names are stored as text strings.

4.2.4 Access Information Stored in Server-Based Files

Although not every HTML/PHP application requires access to external data files, it is a common requirement for many computing problems. As an example, consider the file used in the "split window" HTML document discussed in Chap. 3, Document 3.11. That file, `pyranometer.dat`, contains incoming solar radiation data (insolation) collected with two pyranometers at one-minute intervals. The file might reside on your computer, but it could also reside on a remote server. At each minute, the voltage recorded by each pyranometer is stored. The top of the file includes some information about the site and calibration constants, with units of $(W/m^2)/V$, for the two pyranometers. The solar radiation is the recorded voltage times the calibration constant for each instrument.

> Problem: Read the `pyranometer.dat` file. Create as output a comma-separated file containing the year, month, day, hour, and minute, and the two pyranometer outputs converted to units of W/m^2.

As was shown in Document 3.11, the contents of the `pyranometer.dat` file can be displayed in a scrollable `frame` of an HTML document. However, the document could not actually access or manipulate the contents of that file. Although the solution to this problem *could* work through an HTML interface linked to a PHP application, it is not necessary. All the information required to solve the problem is included in the input data file.

Approach this problem one step at a time. There is a lot of new PHP syntax to absorb in this code but, once you have understood it, it will be easy to access and process the contents of any text file. First, create and save a new PHP script in an editor.

```
<?php ... ?>
```

Then add code to access the file, read the first three lines in the `pyranometer.dat` file, and display them. The file is easy to work with because it is a plain text file, rather than some kind of binary file.

```php
<?php
// Open pyranometer.dat file as "read only."
$in=fopen("pyranometer.dat",'r');
// Read three header lines.
$site=fgets($in); // Read the whole line.
fscanf($in, "%f %f",$Lat,$Lon); // read these values
individually.
fscanf($in, "%f %f",$C1,$C2);
$headers=fgets($in); // Read the whole line.
echo $site."<br />";
echo $Lat.", ".$Lon."<br />";
echo $headers."<br />";
?>
```

The file resource handle `$in` (it can be any name you like) in the `$in=fopen("pyranometer.dat",'r');` statement creates a link between the physical file stored on a server and the "logical" name by which that file will be known in a PHP script. This code assumes that the requested file actually exists, which shouldn't be a problem for applications you are creating yourself. If you like, you can add code that looks for the file before doing anything else:

```
$in = fopen("pyranometer.dat", "r") or
    exit("Can't open file.");
```

Once a file is opened, the value of the file handle variable is the location in memory of the first byte of the physical file. If the file doesn't exist, the `exit()` function prints a message and terminates the application. (Note the syntax of this code, which is a "shorthand" PHP version of an `if...else...` statement, to be described later.

The parameters for the `fopen()` function are the file name and a character that specifies the operations that are allowed to be performed on the file. You can assign a separate variable to the file to be opened. It's not necessary for this application, but it would be if you were passing the name of a file through an HTML document.

```
$inFile = "pyranometer.dat";
$in = fopen($inFile, 'r') or exit("Can't open file.");
```

A value of `'r'` (or `"r"`) indicates that the file will be opened as a read-only file. This means that the PHP script can extract information from the requested file but it cannot change its contents in any way—almost always a good thing!

Text files are subject to an important restriction: they are sequential access files whose contents can only be read sequentially, starting at the beginning. Even if a program does not need all the information at the beginning of a text file, it must still be read and then, perhaps, ignored.

Once the `pyranometer.dat` file is open, the first task it to read the three "header" lines at the beginning of the file, one line at a time. There are two basic ways to read a line in such a file: (1) read the entire line into a string variable; (2) read individual values on the line one at a time, based on the data type of the values.

The statement `$site=fgets($in);` reads one line from the file into the variable `$site`.

The statements

```
fscanf($in, "%f %f",$Lat,$Lon); // Read values separately.
fscanf($in, "%f %f",$C1,$C2);
```

read individual values from the file and interpret them based on the format specification string which is supplied. A complete list of format specifiers will be given in Chap. 5. In this, case the `%f` specifier indicates that the values to be read from the file are real ("floating point") numbers, as opposed to integers. Despite the fact that the values to be associated with

$C1 and $C2, 4030 and 5200, are whole numbers that look like integers, the
format specification indicates that they will be treated like real numbers.

Next, read the data one line at a time. The %u specifier interprets values
in the file as integers. Then, assign the contents to variables, and write the
values separated by commas. Stop when the end-of-file is reached and close
the file.

```
...
while (!feof($in)) {
   fscanf($in, "%u %u %u %u %u %u %f %f %f %f",
     $mon,$day,$yr,$hr,$min,$sec,$day_frac,$P1,$P2,$T);
   echo $mon. ",". $day. ",". $yr. ",". $hr. ",". $min. ",". $sec. ",".
     $day_frac. ",". $P1. ",". $P2. ",". $T. "<br />";
...
}
```

The while (...) {...} "conditional execution" construct is an essential
component of many programming languages. (These kinds of code elements
will be discussed in Chap. 5.) It performs statements repeatedly as long as
certain conditions are met. In this case, it reads lines from the data file as
long as an end-of-file character is not encountered. You can't see this
mark in a text file, but it is always there and feof($in) looks for it. The
while (!feof($in)) statement is interpreted as "As long as I don't see an
end-of-file mark, I will keep reading and processing data from the specified
file." (The ! is the "not" operator, as in "not at the end-of-file mark.")[5]

Except for white space, the contents of the data file must *exactly* match
what the format specifier string tells your code to expect. If, for example, the
data records in the pyranometer.dat file were separated by commas
instead of "white space," which can consist of spaces or tabs, the format
specification string would have to be rewritten as

```
"%u,%u,%u,%u,%u,%u,%f,%f,%f,%f"
```

Document 4.4 completes the code development by multiplying the
pyranometer outputs by their calibration constants and writing the results to
a new comma-separated data file with a .csv extension. It is good
programming practice to close the files when you are done with them,
although PHP will do this for you when the application terminates. Once it
has been saved, double clicking on the output file will automatically open it
in Excel or other spreadsheets.

---

[5]More about logical operators in Chap. 5!

Document 4.4 (pyranometerData.php)

```php
<?php
// Open pyranometer.dat file as "read only."
$in=fopen("pyranometer.dat", 'r');
// Read three header lines.
$site=fgets($in); // Read the whole line.
fscanf($in, "%f %f", $Lat, $Lon); // read these values
individually...
fscanf($in, "%f %f", $C1, $C2); // ...with specified format.
$headers=fgets($in); // Read the whole line.
echo $site. "<br />";
echo $Lat. ", ".$Lon. "<br />";
echo $headers. "<br />";
// Open new "write only" output file and write header lines.
$out=fopen("pyranometer.csv", 'w');
fprintf($out, "%s", $site);
fprintf($out, "%f, %f\n", $Lat, $Lon);
fprintf($out, "%f, %f\n", $C1, $C2);
fprintf($out, "%s\n",
    "mon,day,yr,hr,min,sec,day_frac,PYR-1,PYR-2");
// Read data lines to end-of-file.
while (!feof($in)) {
    fscanf($in, "%u %u %u %u %u %u %f %f %f %f",
        $mon, $day, $yr, $hr, $min, $sec, $day_frac, $P1, $P2, $T);
    echo $mon, ",".$day. ",".$yr. ",".$hr. ",".$min. ",".$sec. ",".
        $day_frac. ",".$P1. ",".$P2. ",".$T. "<br />";
    fprintf($out, "%u, %u, %u, %u, %u, %u, %f, %f, %f\n",
        $mon, $day, $yr, $hr, $min, $sec, $day_frac, $P1* $C1, $P2* $C2);
}
// Close input and output files.
fclose($in);
fclose($out);
?>
```

Figure 4.1 shows the first few lines of the .csv file opened in Excel and a graph of the data. (It was clear through mid-morning. After that, cumulus clouds were passing through. If the two pyranometers are near each other, perhaps one of them needs to be re-calibrated!) It was decided not to include the temperature values in this output file.

When you create a file with PHP, you can give it any name you want, including any file name extension you like—PHP doesn't care—but you will often want to create comma-separated files for which .csv is the standard extension. PHP *does* care where you store files. On a remote server, you need to find out where it is allowed to save files you create. On a Windows computer running Apache, files can be saved in the \wamp\www folder.

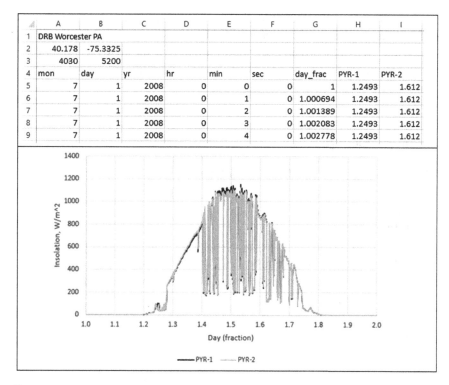

⊿	A	B	C	D	E	F	G	H	I
1	DRB Worcester PA								
2	40.178	-75.3325							
3	4030	5200							
4	mon	day	yr	hr	min	sec	day_frac	PYR-1	PYR-2
5	7	1	2008	0	0	0	1	1.2493	1.612
6	7	1	2008	0	1	0	1.000694	1.2493	1.612
7	7	1	2008	0	2	0	1.001389	1.2493	1.612
8	7	1	2008	0	3	0	1.002083	1.2493	1.612
9	7	1	2008	0	4	0	1.002778	1.2493	1.612

Fig. 4.1 Output from Document 4.4, with Excel graph of results

In Document 4.4, the output file is opened with write-only permission, 'w'. If that file doesn't already exist, it will be created. If it already exists, all the existing contents of the file will be destroyed and only the results from executing this PHP script will be written in the file. Basically, "write" permission wipes the slate clean each time an output file is created. This may or may not be what you intend, so be careful!

The other option for creating files is to open the $out file with append permission, 'a'. If the file doesn't already exist, it will be created. If the file already exists, new data will be appended to the end of the file.

It is important to understand that the output files created by a PHP application are not in any sense "special." They are just text files formatted according to the format specifications you provide. Such files can be used by other software and applications, including spreadsheets and other PHP scripts, as needed.

Finally, it is important to understand that text files are always sequential access files. This means that files can be read starting only from the beginning. If you wish to skip some information in the file, you still have to read that information even though you don't want to use it. When creating output files, the same sequential access restrictions apply. Writing always starts at the beginning of a write-only file and at the current end of an append file. It is not possible to "jump around" a file to write new information in random locations, any more than it is possible to read information from random locations from an input file.

4.3 More Examples

4.3.1 Solving the Quadratic Equation

For the quadratic equation $ax^2 + bx + c = 0$,
find the real roots:
$r_1 = [-b + (b^2 - 4ac)^{1/2}]/(2a)$ $r_2 = [-b - (b^2 - 4ac)^{1/2}]/(2a)$
The "a" coefficient must not be 0. If the discriminant
$b^2 - 4ac = 0$, there is only one root. If the discriminant is less than 0, there are no real roots.

Document 4.5a (quadrat.htm)

```
<head>
<title>Solving the Quadratic Equation</title>
</head>
<body>
<form method="post" action="quadrat.php">
Enter coefficients for ax<sup>2</sup> + bx + c = 0:
<br />
a = <input type="text" value="1" name="a" />
  (must not be 0)<br />
b = <input type="text" value="2" name="b" /><br />
c = <input type="text" value="-8" name="c" /><br /><br />
<input type="submit" value="click to get roots..." />
</form>
</body>
</html>
```

Enter coefficients for $ax^2 + bx + c = 0$:

a = 1   (must not be 0)

b = 2

c = -8

click to get roots...

Note the use of the <sup> tag in Document 4.5a, for creating a superscript. There is a corresponding <sub> tag for creating a subscript.

Document 4.5b (quadrat.php)

```php
<?php
$a = $_POST["a"];
$b = $_POST["b"];
$c = $_POST["c"];
$d = $b*$b - 4*$a*$c;
if ($d == 0) {
  $r1 = $b/(2*$a);
  $r2 = "undefined";
}
else if ($d < 0) {
  $r1 = "undefined";
  $r2 = "undefined";
}
else {
  $r1 = (-$b + sqrt($b*$b - 4*$a*$c))/2/$a;;
  $r2 = (-$b - sqrt($b*$b - 4*$a*$c))/2/$a;;
}
echo "r1 = " . $r1 . ", r2 = " . $r2;
?>
```

$$r1 = 2, r2 = -4$$

If the coefficient c is changed from −8 to 8, the equation has no real roots:

$$r1 = \text{undefined}, r2 = \text{undefined}$$

Note that in this example, the PHP variable names are the same as the form field names in the corresponding HTML document. These are reasonable names for coefficients of a quadratic equation, but they could be given other names if there were some reason to do that. The PHP application needs to know only the field names by which these values were identified in the calling HTML document, because those names must be available to extract values from $_POST[]. For the kinds of problems presented in this book, in which an HTML document is typically paired with a PHP application, it is often a reasonable style choice to use the same names for variables in the PHP code as were used in the HTML document.

4.3.2 Future Value with Compounded Interest

Given an amount of money A, an annual interest rate r percent, and a number of years, y, calculate the future value of that amount, F, assuming interest compounded annually:

$$F = A \cdot (1 + r/100)^y$$

So far in this chapter, HTML documents have been kept separate from their related PHP applications, with the understanding that an HTML document will provide an input interface for a PHP application. The PHP application can be stored on a local server—often, in the same directory—or on some remote server. For some simple problems, it may be convenient to combine an HTML document and its associated PHP code into a single PHP script. Document 4.6 shows how to do this.

Document 4.6 (compoundInterest.php)

```html
<html>
<head>
<title>Calculate Compound Interest</title>
</head>
<body>
<h3>Calculate Compound Interest</h3>
<form action="<?php $_SERVER['PHP_SELF'] ; ?>" method="post">
Initial amount (no commas), $: <input type="text"
    name="initial" value="10000" size="6" /><br />
Annual interest rate, %: <input type="text" name="rate"
size="4"
    value="4.5" /><br />
How many years? : <input type="text" name="years"
    value="10" size="3" /><br />
<input type="submit" name="submit"
    value="Generate compound interest table." />
</form>
<?php
   $initial=$_POST["initial"] ;
   $rate=$_POST["rate"] ;
   $years=$_POST["years"] ;
   echo $initial." ".$rate." ".$years."<br />";
   for ($i=1; $i<=$years; $i++) {
     $amount=$initial*pow(1+$rate/100,$i) ;
     echo $i." $".number_format($amount,2)."<br />";
   }
?>
</body>
</html>
```

The action specified in the `<form>` tag,

$$\$\_SERVER['PHP\_SELF']$$

is a call to the PHP section of the same document.

The possible advantage of writing a combined HTML/PHP application is that, during code development, you can bypass the need to pass information through an HTML document every time you make changes to PHP code. The possible disadvantage is that there are no provisions for user input that may be needed to test your code.

Calculate Compound Interest

Initial amount (no commas), \$: 10000
Annual interest rate, %: 4.5
How many years?: 10

Generate compound interest table.

10000 4.5 10
1 $10,450.00
2 $10,920.25
3 $11,411.66
4 $11,925.19
5 $12,461.82
6 $13,022.60
7 $13,608.62
8 $14,221.01
9 $14,860.95
10 $15,529.69

Introduction to PHP

5

This chapter introduces syntax and some capabilities of the PHP language.

5.1 What Should a Programming Language Do?

PHP is a structured programming language, which means that it provides a way to solve computational problems by breaking them into discrete steps that can be carried out in a "top to bottom" fashion, one step at a time. All structured languages share certain essential features.

1. Manage input and output.
   To be useful, any language must provide an input/output (I/O) interface with a user. When a computer program is executed or a script is interpreted, the user may be asked to provide input either as the program is being executed or within the program itself. The language instructs the user's computer to perform tasks based on that input. The language then instructs the computer to display the results. Older languages such as C will accept keyboard input and display text output on a computer monitor. HTML and PHP work together to provide a much richer I/O environment.

2. Permit values to be manipulated in a symbolic way, independent of the way a particular computer stores that information internally.
   The essential thrust of high-level programming languages is to provide a name-based symbolic interface between a computer and a programmer. When quantities can be given names instead of memory addresses, they can then be accessed and manipulated through those names rather than requiring a programmer to keep track of where values are stored in a computer's memory. (This may seem obvious, but it was not so in the early days of "machine language" programming that required a programmer to keep track of where information was stored.)

© Springer International Publishing AG 2017   85
D.R. Brooks, *Programming in HTML and PHP*, Undergraduate Topics
in Computer Science, DOI 10.1007/978-3-319-56973-4_5

3. Perform arithmetic operations on numbers.

A general-purpose programming language must include a range of arithmetic operations on numbers. Although PHP may not have the "number-crunching" features required for serious scientific computing, it does support several numerical data types and many arithmetic operations and functions including, for example, trigonometric, logarithmic, and exponential functions. So, it is useful for a wide range of numerical calculations of interest in science and engineering.

4. Perform operations on characters and strings of characters.

A great deal of the work computers are asked to do involves manipulating characters and strings of characters rather than numbers. For example, a program may be asked to compare a name provided as input against a predefined set of names or find a name in a list. PHP supports the manipulation of characters and strings of characters, including interpreting strings of characters as numbers and vice versa. The latter capability is important because information in HTML documents is inherently treated as text; HTML does not "know" anything about numbers.

5. Make decisions based on comparing values.

Computers can't make decisions by "thinking" about multiple possibilities in a human-like way. However, they can compare values and act on the results of those comparisons. Typically, a program will compare values and then execute instructions based on the results of those comparisons. In particular, such decisions are often embedded in branching structures that execute one set of instructions to the exclusion of others, based on a comparison of values.

6. Perform repetitive calculations.

Loop structures allow computers to perform repetitive calculations. These calculations may be terminated after they have been executed a specified number of times, or they may be executed only until or while some set of conditions is satisfied.

5.2 Some Essential Terminology

It is essential to agree upon the meaning and use of programming language terminology in order to discuss programming concepts, especially because the programming-specific meaning of some terms must be distinguished from their everyday conversational use. Table 5.1 gives some essential terms and their definitions.

Table 5.1 Definition of some essential programming language terms

Term	Definitions and examples

Expression	A group of tokens that can be evaluated as part of a statement to yield a result
	`$y + $z`
	`"This is a string."`

Identifier	The name associated with a variable, object, or function any allowed name, *e.g.*, `$x`, `$getArea`, `$my_name`, without embedded spaces
Keyword	A word that is part of a language and has a specific meaning. Keywords cannot be used as identifiers `function, for`

Literal	A value (as opposed to an identifier) embedded in a script
	`3.14159`
	`"Here's a string."`

Operator	A symbol that represents a mathematical or other operation `=, +, -, *, /, %`
Program	Loosely, a series of statements or a compiled equivalent. In PHP, a "program" is better referred to as a script. Scripts are interpreted one line at a time, not compiled
Reserved word	A word that is or might become part of a language. Reserved words should not be used as identifiers `int, true`
Script	A series of statements written in PHP or some other interpreted languages

Statement	A command that changes the status of a program as it executes, by defining variables, changing the value of a variable, or modifying the order in which other statements are executed
	`$x = $y + $z;`
	`$area=M_PI*$radius*$radius;`

Token	An indivisible lexical unit defined within a programming language all variables, keywords, operators, and literals
Variable	A location in memory that holds data and is represented by a unique identifier. (see "identifier")

These terms define the building blocks of a PHP script, starting with tokens—the basic "indivisible" components of a programming language:

tokens (identifiers, keywords, literals, operators) → expressions → statements → script

Individual tokens form expressions. Expressions form statements. A script consists of a collection of statements.

5.3   Structure of PHP Scripts

5.3.1   Statements and Statement Blocks

Instructions in PHP are conveyed through a series of statements. Statements are built from expressions consisting of tokens. To begin a statement, simply start typing something that follows the syntax rules. When it's time to terminate a programming language statement, end it by typing a semicolon. The semicolon acts as a unique terminating character to mark the end of a statement. Through the use of a terminating character, multiple statements separated by semicolons can appear on the same line.

A set of PHP statements is called a script. Presumably, the goal of a script is to do something useful. So, the implication of calling something a "script" is that it contains all the instructions required to complete a specific task. Even the simplest text editor can be used to create a script, which is nothing more than a text document. But, as was the case for creating HTML documents, it will be easier to create PHP scripts with an editor intended for this purpose.

PHP is a free-format language. This means that statements can appear anywhere on a line and, as noted above, you can even put multiple statements on a single line. However, with few exceptions, you cannot continue a statement from one line to the next. This free-format flexibility is *supposed* to encourage the writing of code that is logically organized and easy to read. Good programmers always adopt a consistent approach to the layout of their code. Hopefully, the examples in this book will point the way to producing easily readable code.

Often, several code statements are grouped together in a statement block. These blocks begin and end with curly brackets:

```
{
    {statements go here}
}
```

Later in this chapter, there will be several examples of how to use statement blocks.

5.3.2   Comments

Comments are an essential part of good programming style, no matter what the language. Comments are inserted into code by using certain combinations of characters that will always be interpreted unambiguously as marking the beginning or end of a comment. PHP supports two kinds of comments: single- and multiple-line comments. You can use either or both of these comment formats within the same script. However, you cannot have "nested" multiple-line comments:

```
// This is a single-line comment. # also works.
/* This
   is a
      multiple-line
         comment.
*/
/* This code
/* will generate a syntax error! */
*/
```

Because a PHP interpreter ignores comments when it executes statements, comments can occur on separate lines or on the same line as a statement. Comments started with a double slash cannot be placed at the beginning of a statement because PHP has no way of knowing where the comment ends and the code begins. This code will work because there is an (invisible) "return" character at the end of the line that is interpreted as the end of the comment:

```
// The gravitational constant is
$g=9.8; // m/s^2
```

This will not work:

```
// The gravitational constant is $g=9.8; // m/s^2
```

but this will:

```
/* The gravitational constant is */ $g=9.8; //m/s^2
```

It is easy to overlook the importance of including comments in your code. Intelligently commented code is easier to understand, both for you when you return to it at a later date and for others who need to examine your code. If you don't develop the habit of including comments in all your code, eventually you will be sorry!

5.3.3 Data Types, Variables, and Literals

A concept central to all high-level programming languages is that discrete information-holding units called variables can be associated with specific locations in computer memory. Variables serve as "containers" for data. A data container is established by giving it a symbolic name and associating it with a data type. This process is called data declaration. Once variables have been established with meaningful names, you can write code to manipulate information symbolically by using the identifier names, thereby freeing you from having to think directly about where information is actually stored in your computer's memory. (As a practical matter, you can't figure out exactly where this information is stored even if you think you need to know.) This symbolic approach makes it possible to write scripts that will work without modification on any computer with a server that supports PHP.

Some languages require explicit data declaration. This means that a statement is required to assign a data type to a variable before it is given a value. Other languages, such as PHP, rely on implicit data declaration. This means that the data type of variables is determined based on the kind of values assigned to them. Such languages are referred to as "weakly typed" languages.

Different kinds of variables require different amount of storage location in your computer's memory. Also, the kinds of operations which can be performed on variables depends on their data type. Hence, the data declaration process, whether explicit or implicit, is required to enable a programming environment to manage its memory resources and enable appropriate operations.

PHP variables are always preceded by a $. Variable names can be of any length you like. Names can contain only alpha-numeric characters (A–x, 0–9) and the underscore symbol. A name can start with a letter or the underscore character, but not with a digit.

PHP supports four primitive data types:

boolean *(bool)*   integer *(int)*
float *(float)*   string *(string)*

Boolean data can have values of true or false. The maximum size of an integer that can be represented is system dependent, but they are often represented with a 32-bit word, with one bit allocated for a sign. This gives a maximum integer range of $\pm 2,147,483,647$. If presented with an integer larger than the allowed maximum, PHP will convert it to a floating point number, possibly with some loss of precision. The precision of floating point (real) numbers is also system dependent but is often approximately 14 digits. In other programming languages you will sometimes find references to a "double" data type. In C, for example, the precision of "float" and "double" real-number values is different, but there is no such distinction in PHP, which supports only a single floating point number representation. Strings, enclosed in straight double quotes, are composed of 8-bit characters (giving 256 possible characters), with no limit imposed on string length. Characters are enclosed in straight single quotes.

PHP supports arrays as a compound data type, used to aggregate a mixture of data types under a single name. (More about arrays in Chap. 6.) Array components (elements) can be any of the primitive data types, as well as other arrays.

When a collection of data with various types is specified, such as the elements of a mixed-type array, they can be identified for convenience as *(mixed)*, but this word represents only a "pseudo" data type, not an actual data type specification. In the definitions of math functions given later (see Table 7.3), inputs and outputs are sometimes identified as having a *(number)* data type. This is also a pseudo data type that can be either an integer or a floating-point number, depending on context.

Another pseudo data type is *(resource)*. This refers to any external resource, such as a data file, which is accessible from a PHP application. You can also use "hard-coded" numbers, text strings, or Boolean values in PHP scripts. In programming terminology these are referred to as literals.

In the statement `$pi=3.14159;`, 3.14159 is a number literal. In the statement `$name="David";`, `"David"` is a string literal. The advantage of using literals is that their value is self-evident.

In general, it is good programming style to limit the use of the same literal value in many places in your code. For example, rather than using the literal 3.14159 whenever you need the value of π, you should assign a value to the quantity π by using a data declaration statement `$pi=3.14159;`. Now you can insert the value of π anywhere in your program just by referring to its identifier. Suppose you declare `$B=5.195;` and use this variable name in several places in your code. If, later on, you decide you need to change the value of `$B` to `5.196`, you can make this change just once, in the data declaration statement, and the change will automatically apply everywhere the B identifier is used.

5.3.4 Arithmetic Operators

Operators are also tokens. PHP operators, shown in Table 5.2, include arithmetic operators for addition, subtraction, multiplication, division, and the modulus operator for returning the remainder from division. These are all binary operators, which means that they require two operands, one to the left of the operator and one to the right. The addition and subtraction operators can also function as unary operators, with a single operand to the right of the operator; for example, -$x.

The addition, subtraction, and multiplication operators work as expected. The division operator returns an integer value unless one or both of the two operands are real numbers. That is, 7/3 returns a value of 2. 7./3, 7/3., or 7./3. return a value of 2.333333 because the decimal point forces a number to be treated as a real number rather than an integer.

The modulus operator works with either integer or real number operands, but the operands are converted to integers (by stripping off the decimal part) before performing the operation. 9.7%2 and 9%2 both return a value of 1.

Table 5.2 PHP arithmetic operators

Operator	Symbol	Examples	Precedence
Addition	+	3 + 4	2
Subtraction	−	$z − 10	2
String concatenation	.	$s=$s1.$s2;	2
Multiplication	*	$A*$b	1
Division	/	$z/3.333	1
Modulus (remainder)	%	17%3 (= 2), 16.6%2.7 (=0)	1

In common with other programming languages, when PHP interprets an expression, it scans the expression from left to right one or more times. Operations implied by the presence of operators are evaluated according to precedence rules. Fortunately, these rules are the same ones that apply in algebraic expressions. Suppose a = 3, b = 4, and c = 5. What is the value of x in the algebraic expression x = a + bc? Based on precedence rules, multiplication and division operations are carried out before addition and subtraction. So, x = 3 + 4·5 = 3 + 20 = 23. That is, a multiplication operation has precedence over an addition operation, so the addition operation is delayed until after the multiplication is performed, even though the addition operator is to the left of the multiplication operator. Parentheses are required to alter the precedence rules: x = (3 + 4)·5 = 35.

So, in this code:

```
$a=3,$b=4,$c=5;
$x=$a+$b*$c;
$y=($a+$b)*$c;
```

the variable $x has a value of 23. In the fourth statement, parentheses are used to override the natural order in which operations are evaluated, so y has a value of 35. The expression is evaluated from the innermost set of parentheses outward, so the $a+$b operation is performed before the multiplication by $c.

5.3.5 The Assignment Operator

The PHP assignment operator is the symbol =. Thus, the PHP statement x=a +b; looks very much like the algebraic equation x=a+b. However, they are not at all the same thing! In programming, the assignment operator has a completely different meaning from the symbolic equality implied by the algebraic use of the = sign. In algebra, the equation x=a+b defines a symbolic relationship among a, b, and x; given the values of a and b, you can determine the value of x. Given the values of x and a, you can solve for the value of b: b=x–a. Note also that a+b=x is algebraically equivalent to x=a+b. But, in programming,

> The meaning of the assignment operator is: "Evaluate the expression on the right side of the assignment operator and assign the result to the identifier on the left side of the assignment operator."

For the statement $x=$a+$b;, the specific meaning is "If $a and $b have been given numerical values, calculate their sum and assign the result to the identifier $x."

With this definition of the assignment operator, it is clear that the PHP statement $a+$b=$x; makes no sense, and will generate a syntax error. Why? Because:

> Only a variable identifier name can appear on the left side of the assignment operator.

Finally, note that the algebraic expression x=x+1 makes no sense at all because it is not possible for x to be equal itself plus 1. However, the PHP statement $x=$x+1; makes perfect sense. It means "Add 1 to the current value of x and then replace the value of x with this new value." So, as a result of executing these statements:

$x=5.5; $x=$x+1;

$x will have a value of 6.5.

It is sometimes difficult for beginning programmers to remember that an assignment statement is not the same thing as an algebraic equation. Although PHP (and other programming languages) allow you to perform mathematical operations with variable identifiers, these languages do not understand the concepts of algebra. When it sees an assignment operator, all it knows how to do is evaluate the expression on the right side of the operator and assign that result to the identifier on the left side of the expression. In doing the expression evaluation, it assumes that every identifier has already been assigned an actual, and not just a symbolic, value.

As a result of how the assignment operator works, a general rule about assignment statements is:

> An identifier should never appear on the right side of an assignment operator unless it has previously been assigned an appropriate value.

Identifiers that do not follow this rule are called uninitialized variables. Numerical variables are assigned a value of 0 by default, but you should never violate the rule based on this assumption.

Table 5.3 shows some shorthand operators for combining arithmetic operations and assignments. They are popular among programmers because they are easy to write quickly, but their use is never required.

Table 5.3 Shorthand arithmetic/assignment operators

Operator	Implementation	Interpretation
+=	$x+=$y;	$x=$x+$y;
-=	$x-=$y;	$x=$x-$y;
.=	$s=$s.$t;	$s.=$t;
*=	$x*=$y;	$x=$x*$y;
/=	$x/=$y;	$x=$x/$y;
%=	$x%=$y;	$x=$x%$y;
++	$x++; or ++$x;	$x=$x+1;
--	$y--; or --$y;	$x=$x-1;

The increment operator (++) adds 1 to the value of the variable to which it is applied, and the decrement operator (−−) subtracts 1. These operators are commonly used in looping structures, as discussed later in this chapter.

As shown in Table 5.3, you can apply the increment or decrement operators either before the variable name (pre-increment or pre-decrement) or after (post-increment or post-decrement). This choice can lead to some unexpected results. Consider Document 5.1.

Document 5.1 (`incrementDecrement.php`)

```php
<?php
    $x=3;
    $y=($x++)+3;
    echo "post-increment: y=".$y."<br />";
    echo "x=".$x."<br />";
    $x=3;
    $y=(++$x)+3;
    echo "pre-increment: y=".$y."<br />";
    echo "x=".$x."<br />";
?>
```

In the post-increment case, the value of x is incremented *after* the expression is evaluated to provide a value for y. In the pre-increment case, the value of x is incremented *before* the value of y is calculated. A similar result would occur for the

```
post-increment: y=6
x=4
pre-increment: y=7
x=4
```

decrement operator. For the most part, you should avoid combining the increment/decrement operators with other operations in a single expression. Also, do not apply both pre- and post-operators at the same time (that is, do not write ++x++; or −−x−−;) and do not apply these operators to the same variable more than once in an expression.

5.3.6 Relational and Logical Operators

PHP supports a large number of relational and logical operators, some of which are listed in Table 5.4, in order of precedence. As will be shown later, it is good programming practice, especially in relational and logical expressions, to use parentheses to clarify the order in which operations should be performed, rather than depending solely on precedence rules.

Table 5.4 Relational and logical operators, in decreasing order of precedence

Operator	Description
<, <=, >, >=	Relational comparisons
==, !=, ===, !==, <>, <=>	Relational comparisons
!	Not true
&&[1]	Logical AND
||[1]	Logical OR
and	Logical AND
xor	Logical EXCLUSIVE OR
or	Logical OR

[1]Note the availability of two AND (&& and and) and two OR (\|\| and or) operators, at different precedence levels. (and and or have lower precedence than && and \|\|.)

5.4 Conditional Execution

As noted at the beginning of this chapter, a programming language should be able to make decisions based on comparing values.

Conditional (or branching) structures are based on a translation into programming syntax of plain language statements such as: "If x is greater than y, then let z=10, otherwise let z=0" or "If today is Tuesday, I should be in class." Translating such statements into relational and logical tests makes it possible to build decision-making capabilities into a programming language.

PHP supports if... then... else... conditional execution. The "then" action is implied. Multiple "else" branches can be included. PHP syntax is close to plain language statements, but of course it follows strict syntax rules. Here is a generic code outline:

```
if ({an expression. If true, statements are executed})
{
    {statements here}
}
// optionally
else if ({an expression. If true, statements are executed})
{
    {statements here}
}
// optionally, more else if statements

// optionally
else
{
    {statements here}
}
```

You can have as many "else if" statements as you need. For `else if`, writing `elseif`, is also acceptable. Usually, the statements to be executed in a `true` branch of an `if`... statement are enclosed in curly brackets. If there is only one statement, the brackets are optional. Some programmers always use curly brackets even when they're not required.

If you consider an `if` structure as defining branches in a road that eventually rejoin at a main road, the minimum choice is a road with no branches, where you may or may not bypass part of the road. The other option is to take one of several possible branches before rejoining with the main road.

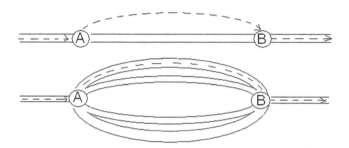

With multiple possible branches, it is important to understand that

> **Only the *first* branch of an `if`... statement for which the expression evaluates as `true` will be taken.**

To use the road analogy, once you select a branch in the road, you take only that branch and no other. To make this clear, consider Document 5.2.

Document 5.2 (`letterGrade.php`)

```php
<?php
$grade=87;
if ($grade >= 90) echo "A<br />";
elseif ($grade >= 80) echo "B<br />";
elseif ($grade >= 70) echo "C<br />";
elseif ($grade >= 60) echo "D<br />";
else echo "F<br />";
?>
```

A grade of 87 is less than 90, so the first branch is ignored. The second branch is true, so a "B" is displayed. 87 is also greater than 70 and 60, but these and the final "else" branches are ignored.

When comparisons get more complicated, you must be careful about how you form logical/relational expressions. Suppose you want your code to respond to the statement: "If today is Tuesday or Thursday, I should be in class." The proper implementation is:

```
if (($today == "Tuesday") || ($today == "Thursday"))
```

If this expression is rewritten as

```
($today == "Tuesday" || "Thursday") // don't do it!
```

it has a value of `true` if `today` is `"Tuesday"` but a value of `"Thursday"` (rather than `false`) if `today` has previously been given a value of `"Monday"`. This is almost certainly *not* what you intended!

An alternate version of the original expression, without the two inner sets of parentheses, is:

```
// OK, but not how I would do it!
($today == "Tuesday" || $today == "Thursday")
```

This will be interpreted correctly, but it depends on the fact that the equality operator has precedence over the OR operator. In cases like this, the author believes the use of the "extra" parentheses in the first example above is better programming style. It makes clear the order in which you wish the operations to be performed and also makes it unnecessary to memorize the precedence rules for relational and logical operators.[1]

Finally, consider this code fragment:

```
if(($today = "Tuesday") || ($today = "Thursday")) …
```

Because the == operator is replaced with the = operator. This code does *not* compare the current value of `$today` with `"Tuesday"` or `"Thursday"`. All it does is set the value of `$today` to `"Tuesday"`! Do not forget that the = operator does *not* mean "equals"; it is an assignment operator, with a completely different interpretation. In this context, the == operator is required to convey the sense of "is equal to."

---

[1] It is nonetheless true that many programmers *do* regularly take advantage of the precedence rules in their code.

> Using an assignment operator (=) when you intend to use an equality operator (==) is a common programming mistake that is very hard to find because it does not generate a syntax error. Be careful!

PHP also supports a "switch" construct for case-controlled conditional execution.

```
switch ($i) {
  case 0:
    echo "i equals 0.";
    break;
  case 1:
    echo "i equals 1.";
    break;
  case 2:
    echo "i equals 2.";
    break;
  default:
    echo "i does not equal 0, 1, or 2.";
}
```

The order of the `case` values does not matter. Unlike the `if...` construct, in which only the first "true" path is executed, the `break;` statement is needed to exit the construct after the first case match is encountered. Otherwise, all subsequent statements within the construct are executed. There are certainly circumstances under which this might be the desired result, in which case the `break;` statements wouldn't be needed, although the order of the `case` values probably *would* matter.

Multiple case values can be associated with the same action, as shown in Document 5.3.

Document 5.3 (`daysInMonth.php`)

```
<?php
$month=5; // Try different values.
switch ($month) {
  case 1:
  case 3:
  case 5:
  case 7:
  case 8:
  case 10:
```

```
  case 12:
     echo "There are 31 days in this month.<br />"; break;
  case 4:
  case 6:
  case 9:
  case 11:
     echo "There are 30 days in this month.<br />"; break;
  case 2:
     echo "There are either 28 or 29 days in this month.
<br />"; break;
   default:
     echo "I do not understand your month entry.";
}
?>
```

PHP case values can be strings:

```
switch ($fruit){
case "apple":
    echo "This is an apple.";
    break;
  case "orange":
    echo "This is an orange.";
    break;
  case "banana":
    echo "This is a banana.";
    break;
  default:
    echo "This is not an allowed fruit treat.";
}
```

Comparisons against the value to be tested are case-sensitive. So, if $fruit is assigned as $fruit = "Banana"; prior to the switch construct, (instead of $fruit = "banana";) the default message is printed. If this is a problem, it can be overcome by using the strtolower() or strtoupper() functions.

5.5 Loop Structures

The ability to perform repetitive calculations is important in computer algorithms. This is enabled through the use of loop structures. Loops can be written to execute the same code statements a prescribed number of times, or they can be written so that loop execution (or termination) is based on conditions that change while statements in the loop are being executed. The former situation uses count-controlled loops and the latter uses conditional loops.

5.5.1 Count-controlled Loops

Count-controlled loops are managed with the `for` keyword. The general syntax of a count-controlled loop is:

```
for ($counter= {expression giving on initial value of counter};
  {expression giving high (or low) value of counter};
  {expression controlling incrementing (or decrementing) of counter}) {
    {one or more statements to be executed inside loop}
}
```

The `for` keyword is followed by three statements inside parentheses. The first statement sets the initial value of a counter. You can give the identifier name—$counter in the above example—any name you like. The second expression sets conditions under which the loop should continue to execute, or to look at it another way, sets the terminating condition; the loop continues to execute as long as the value of the second expression is `true`. The third expression controls how the counter is incremented or decremented. The counter is often incremented or decremented in steps of 1, but you can use other values as appropriate. It is up to you to make sure that these three related expressions are consistent and will actually cause the loop to terminate. For example, the loop

```
for ($i=1; $i=12; i+=2)
```

will never terminate because $i will never equal 12. Perhaps you meant to write the second expression as $i<=12;. If so, then the loop will execute for $i=1, 3, 5, 7, 9, and 11.

Now, consider Document 5.4, which displays the integers 0–10, in order. The counter $k is initialized to 1. It is incremented in steps of 1, and the loop executes as long as $k is less than 10. Use of the shortcut incrementing or decrementing operators, as in $k++, is very common in `for` loops.

Document 5.4 (`counter.php`)

```php
<?php
echo "Here's a simple counter:<br />";
for ($k=0; $k<=10; $k++) {
   echo $k. "<br />";
}
?>
```

Here's a simple counter:
0
1
2
3
4
5
6
7
8
9
10

Document 5.5 shows a version of Document 5.4 which counts backward from 10.

Document 5.5 (`countdown.php`)

```php
<?php
echo "Countdown...<br />";
for ($k=10; $k>=0; $k--) {
   echo $k. "<br />";
}
echo "FIRE!!<br />";
?>
```

5.5.2 Conditional Loops

It is often the case that conditions under which repetitive calculations will or will not be executed cannot be determined in advance. Instead, conditions controlling the execution or termination of a loop structure will be determined by values calculated inside the loop, while the script is running. Such circumstances require conditional loops.

There are two kinds of conditional loops: pre-test and post-test loops. The statements in pre-test loops may or may not be executed at all, depending on the original values of loop-related variables. Post-test loops are always executed at least once, and the values of loop-related variables are tested at the end of the loop. The syntax is different:
pre-test loop:

```
while ({logical expression}) {
   {statements that result in changing the value of the pre-test logical
   expression}
}
```

post-test loop:

```
do {
   {statements that result in changing the value of the post-test logical
   expression}
} while ({logical expression});
```

Conditional loops can always be written either as post- or pre-test loops. The choice is based on how a problem is stated. Consider this problem:

A small elevator has a maximum capacity of 500 pounds. People waiting in line to enter the elevator are weighed. If they can get on the elevator without exceeding the load limit, they are allowed to enter. If not, the elevator leaves without trying to find someone who weighs less than the person currently first in line. If the elevator is overloaded, it crashes. It is possible that there might be a large gorilla in line, weighing more than 500 pounds. This gorilla shouldn't be allowed on the elevator under any circumstances. Write a document that will supply random weights for people (or gorillas) waiting in line, control access to the elevator, and stop allowing people (or gorillas) to enter if the weight limit would be exceeded.

One solution to this problem is shown in Document 5.6.

Document 5.6 (elevator.php)

```php
<?php
   echo "The elevator problem...<br />";
   $limit=500;
   echo "maximum weight = ".$limit." pounds<br />";
      $totalWeight=0; $maxWeight=550;
   do {
      $newWeight=rand(0,$maxWeight);
      if (($totalWeight + $newWeight) <= $limit) {
         $totalWeight += $newWeight;
         echo "New weight = ".$newWeight.",
            Total weight = ".$totalWeight."<br />";
         $newWeight=0;
      }
      else echo "You weigh ".$newWeight." pounds.
         I'm sorry, but you can't get on.<br />";
   } while (($totalWeight+$newWeight) <= $limit);
?>
```

This code uses PHP's `rand()` function (more about PHP math functions later) to generate random weights between 0 and 550 pounds. The calculations are done inside a post-test

> The elevator problem...
> maximum weight = 500 pounds
> New weight = 179, Total weight = 179
> New weight = 104, Total weight = 283
> New weight = 84, Total weight = 367
> New weight = 72, Total weight = 439
> You weigh 190 pounds. I'm sorry, but you can't get on.

loop. The code is arranged so that the effect of adding a new person to the elevator is tested before the person is allowed on the elevator.

In principle, count-controlled loops can also be written as conditional loops. However, it is better programming style to reserve conditional loop structures for problems that actually need them. Clearly, Document 5.6 is such a problem because there is no way for the script to determine ahead of time what weights the `rand()` function will generate.

5.6   More Examples

5.6.1   The Quadratic Equation Revisited

Previously, and with good reason, this book has emphasized the advantages of separating input to a computational problem from doing the required calculations and generating output. An HTML document provides the input interface and a separate PHP application does the rest.

But, as discussed for the compound interest problem in Section 4.3.2, it may be useful to combine these two documents into a single HTML/PHP document. Consider again the problem of solving a quadratic equation with code that allows user input of the coefficients a, b, and c.

Solve a quadratic equation of form $ax^2 + bx + c = 0$, for which the roots are obtained from

$$\frac{-b \pm \sqrt{b^2 - 4ac}}{2a}$$

If the discriminant, $b^2 - 4ac$, is greater than 0, there are 2 real roots. If it is 0, there is 1 real root. If it is negative, there are no real roots.

Document 5.7 (`quadrat1.php`)

```
<html>
<head>
<title>Solving the Quadratic Equation</title>
</head>
<body>
<form method="post"
     action="<?php $_SERVER ['PHP_SELF'] ; ?>">
<h3> Solving the quadratic equation</h3>
Enter coefficients for ax<sup>2</sup> + bx + c = 0:
<br />
a = <input type="text" value="1" name="a" />
  (must not be 0) <br />
b = <input type="text" value="2" name="b" /><br />
c = <input type="text" value="-8" name="c" /><br />
<br /><input type="submit"
   value="click to get roots..." />
</form>
</body>
</html>
<?php
$a = $_POST ["a"] ; $b = $_POST ["b"] ; $c = $_POST ["c"] ;
$d = $b* $b - 4* $a* $c;
if ($d == 0) {
  $r1 = $b/ (2* $a) ; $r2 = "undefined";
}
else if ($d < 0) {
  $r1 = "undefined"; $r2 = "undefined";
}
else {
$r1 = (-$b + sqrt ($b* $b - 4* $a* $c) ) /2/ $a; ;
$r2 = (-$b - sqrt ($b* $b - 4* $a* $c) ) /2/ $a; ;
}
echo "r1 = " . $r1 . ", r2 = " . $r2;
?>
```

Combining HTML documents and PHP scripts involves literally combining an HTML document (everything inside the `html` element) with a PHP script inside the `<$php ... ?>` tags. The only change to the HTML document occurs in the `form` element:

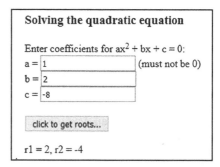

```
<form method="post"
      action="<?php $_SERVER[ 'PHP_SELF'] ; ?>">
```

Instead of referencing a separate PHP application, the action attribute references itself—that is, the PHP code inside the same document—through the `action` attribute of the `form` element.

5.6.2   Newton's Square Root Algorithm

Another example of a problem that demands a conditional loop calculation is Newton's algorithm for finding the square root of a number.

> Given a number n:
>
> 1. Make a guess (g) for the square root of n. n/2 is a reasonable guess.
> 2. Replace g with (g + n/g)/2.
> 3. Repeat step 2 until the absolute difference between g^2 and n is smaller than some specified value.

This algorithm is easy to write as a conditional loop. Consider Document 5.8.

Document 5.8 (`newton.php`)

```php
<html>
<head>
<title></title>
</head>
<body>
<form method="post"
      action="<?php $_SERVER ['PHP_SELF'] ; ?>">
<h3>Newton's square root algorithm</h3>
Enter a positive number:
<input type="text" value="9" size="4" name="n" />
<br /><input type="submit"
      value="click to calculate square root" />
</form>
</body>
</html>
<?php
$n = $_POST ["n"] ;
$g=$n/2;
do {
    $g = ($g + $n/$g) /2.;
} while (abs($g*$g-$n) > 1e-5);
echo "square root = ".$g. "<br />";
?>
```

This algorithm is implemented as a post-test loop because a reasonable assumption is that the calculation inside the loop will always need to be done at least once. In fact, considering that the initial guess for the square root of n is n/2, this assumption is true

> **Newton's square root algorithm**
>
> Enter a positive number: 9
>
> click to calculate square root
>
> square root = 3.0000000000393

for all values of n except 4. The statement `$g=($g+n/$g)/2;` is an excellent example of how an assignment operator differs from the same symbol when it is used in an algebraic context. This kind of "replacement assignment" is often seen in conditional loops but, of course, it makes no algebraic sense whatsoever.

The terminating condition `while (abs($g*$g-$n)>1e-5);` is important. It is not obvious whether g^2 will be larger or smaller than n. So, you must test the absolute value of (g^2 – n) to ensure that the value being compared to 10^{-5} is always positive (because any negative number is less than $+10^{-5}$).

This algorithm will work for any positive number. But, except for 4 (not even for 1) it will not give the *exact* square root even for perfect squares, as shown in the example for n = 9. (The result is exact for 4 only because initializing the "guess" at n/2 gives the actual square root of 4.) These results, which also appear in other real number calculations, are a result of how real numbers are stored and how numerical calculations are performed on them. PHP does not "know" (or care!) that 9 is a perfect square! Newton's square root algorithm is a numerical approximation, so in general, it will only *approach* the actual answer within the specified accuracy. Except for annoying strings of zeros and digits for the square root of perfect squares, as in the output shown here for n = 9, these discrepancies are usually of no practical concern. If desired, the extraneous digits can be removed by rounding the result to an appropriate number of significant figures. Especially in problems dealing with physical measurements and their units, "extra" digits can be extraneous and misleading when they cannot be justified on the basis of measurement accuracy. For example, there is no justification for expressing a dew point temperature as 15.2340987 °C regardless of how that number comes to exist as the result of a calculation! (See Document 7.1.)

Arrays

6

This chapter provides an introduction to array syntax and use. The PHP array model provides several ways of accessing and manipulating data.

6.1 Array Definition and Properties

The concept of arrays is extremely important in programming, as it provides a way to organize, access, and manipulate related quantities. It is important to form a mental model of how arrays are implemented, as shown in the sketch below. It may be helpful to think of a post office analogy. The post office has a name, equivalent to the name of an array. Inside the post office are numbered mail boxes. The numbers on the boxes correspond to array "addresses," called indices. The contents of the boxes correspond to array elements.

In many programming languages, including PHP, the default numbering of array indices begins at 0 rather than 1. This is because the array index is considered as an "offset" from the beginning of the location in memory where the array is stored; that is, the first element is located at an offset of 0 bytes.

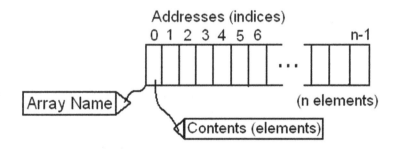

In this model, the largest index of an array with n elements is $n - 1$, not n. PHP's implementation of arrays includes but is not limited to this model, which is all that is needed for many kinds of scientific and engineering problems.

© Springer International Publishing AG 2017
D.R. Brooks, *Programming in HTML and PHP*, Undergraduate Topics in Computer Science, DOI 10.1007/978-3-319-56973-4_6

In PHP, arrays are created with the `array()` constructor:

$ArrayName = `array` (*[(mixed data types)...]*)

where *$ArrayName* is a generic representation of a user-supplied array name. Starting with version 5.4, PHP arrays also can be defined like this:

$ArrayName = *[(mixed data types)...]*

Arrays can contain a mixture of data types. The elements can be specified either when the array is defined, or later. Document 6.1 shows some basic array operations.

Document 6.1 (`basicArray.php`)

```php
<?php
$A=array(17.7,3,'z',"PHP");
for ($i=0; $i<sizeof($A); $i++) {
    echo $A[$i] . "<br />";
}
echo "<br />";
$B=array();
for ($i=0; $i<10; $i++) {
    $B[$i] =rand(0,100);
    echo $B[$i] . "<br />";
}
?>
```

```
17.7
3
z
PHP

25
6
34
21
96
82
43
93
45
6
```

For arrays based on the simple model where indices start at 0, `for...` loops are often used to access elements, as shown in Document 6.1. For array `$B`, which doesn't have pre-defined elements, it is not necessary to use the array constructor and the code will work the same without it. However, it is always good practice to declare a variable name as an array if that is how you will use that name.

Note the use of "square bracket" notation for identifying array elements, which can always be accessed through their indices.

PHP has many functions for dealing with arrays, including the `sizeof()` function used to set the terminating condition for the `for...` loop. (A summary of array-related functions is given in Chap. 8.) Remember that, by default, array indices start at 0, not 1. This means that the loop counter must stop not at the size of the array (4 in the case of `$A`, but 3—the number of elements (`sizeof()`) minus 1.

As a further clarification, for the `for...` loop using the `$B` array, the size of which has not yet been defined, it would be OK as a matter of syntax to write (for example):

```
for ($i=1; $i<=10; $i++)
```

but this would mean that the size of $B would be 11, not 10, and the first element $B[0] would be undefined.

For the $A array in Document 6.1, writing

```
for ($i=0; $i<=sizeof($A); $i++)
```

will generate an "undefined offset" error because the element 4 doesn't exist.

For long arrays with defined elements, the elements can be continued on more than one line. Thus, $A could be defined like this:

| 17.7 |
| 3 |
| z |
| PHP |
| 18 |
| 38 |
| 55 |
| 90 |
| 15 |
| 74 |
| 65 |
| 70 |
| 18 |
| 69 |

```
$A=array(17.7,    or    $A=[17.7,
    3,                      3,
    'z',                    'z',
    "PHP"                   "PHP"
);                      ];
```

In an extension of the basic array model, each element of a PHP array can have its own user-defined index (key) value:

```
$a = array($key1 => $value1, $key2 => $value2,
      $key3 => $value3,…);
```

The => operator associates a key with its value. The keys can be numbers, characters, or strings, and you can name them however you like. Numerical keys can start with any value, not just 0 (which would correspond to the simple array model), and they don't even have to be sequential (although they usually are). Document 6.2 shows an example of an array with named keys.

Document 6.2 (keyedArray.php)

```php
<?php
// Create an array with user-specified keys...
echo '<br />A keyed array:<br />';
$stuff = array('mine' => 'BMW', 'yours' => 'Lexus',
   'ours' => 'house');
foreach ($stuff as $key => $val) {
  echo '$stuff[' . $key . '] = '. $val . '<br />';
}
?>
```

A for... loop will not work for an array with string names or non-sequential numerical values for keys. Instead, a foreach... loop is used, with syntax as shown in the shaded statement. It is the syntax following the as keyword that makes the

A keyed array:
$stuff[mine] = BMW
$stuff[yours] = Lexus
$stuff[ours] = house

association between a key name and its array element. Note that a foreach... loop does not require or even allow that you specify the length of the array.

This code won't work for a keyed array because the indices have arbitrary names rather than sequential values:

```
/* This won't work!
for ($i=0; $i<sizeof($stuff); $i++)
   echo $stuff[$i] . '<br />';
*/
```

If the keys specified are the default integer keys starting at 0, then it is straightforward to use a for... loop, as in the previous code examples. It is also possible to use a for... loop if a keyed array is created with a starting index other than 0, or if it has consecutive character keys; these possibilities are also illustrated in Document 6.3.

Document 6.3 (consecutiveKeyArray.php)

```
<?php
$a = array('david', 'apple', 'Xena', 'Sue');
echo "Using for... loop<br />";
for ($i=0; $i<sizeof($a); $i++)
   echo $a[$i] . '<br />';
echo "Using implied keys with foreach... loop<br />";
foreach ($a as $i => $x)
   echo 'a[' . $i . '] = ' . $x . '<br />';
echo "An array with keys starting at an integer other than
0<br />";
$negKey = array(-1 => 'BMW', 'Lexus', 'house');
for ($i=-1; $i<2; $i++)
   echo $negKey[$i] . '<br />';
echo 'A keyed array with consecutive character keys...<br />';
$stuff = array('a' => 'BMW', 'b' => 'Lexus', 'c' => 'house');
for ($i='a'; $i<='c'; $i++)
   echo $stuff[$i] . '<br />';
?>
```

```
Using for... loop
david
apple
Xena
Sue
Using implied keys with foreach... loop
a[0] = david
a[1] = apple
a[2] = Xena
a[3] = Sue
An array with keys starting at an integer other than 0
[-1] = BMW
[0] = Lexus
[1] = house
A keyed array with consecutive character keys...
[a] = BMW
[b] = Lexus
[c] = house
```

Document 6.3 demonstrates that even if specific key definitions are omitted, they still exist and are given default integer values starting at 0. It also shows that it is possible to define just the first key, and the other keys will be assigned consecutively. When `foreach...` is used with assigned keys even if just the first key is assigned, all keys are automatically displayed along with their values. Note that it isn't allowed to assign a key to a non-existent element. That is,

```
$a = array(1 =>);
```

makes no sense, although you might like to use this syntax as a way to define a keyed array without assigning its elements as part of its declaration.

The ability to specify just the starting key provides an easy way to start array indices at 1 rather than 0, as might be convenient for labeling columns and rows in a table or the 12 months in a year:

```
$a = array(1 => 63.7, 77.5, 17, -3);
$m = array(1 => January,February,March,April,May,June,
       July,August,September,October,November,December);
```

The first index has a value of 1 and the remaining unspecified indices are incremented by 1. Either a `foreach...` or a `for...` loop can be used to access the values, as shown in Document 6.4.

Document 6.4 (base_1Array.php)

```php
<?php
echo '<br />A keyed array with indices starting at 1...<br
/>';
$a = array(1 => 63.7, 77.5, 17, -3);
foreach ($a as $key => $val) {
   echo 'a[' . $key . '] = '. $val . '<br />';
}
for ($i=1; $i<=sizeof($a); $i++)
   echo $a[$i] . '<br />';
?>
```

```
A keyed array with indices starting at 1...
a[1] = 63.7
a[2] = 77.5
a[3] = 17
a[4] = -3
63.7
77.5
17
-3
```

Two-dimensional arrays—you can think of them as row-and-column tables—can be formed from an array of arrays, as shown in Document 6.5.

Document 6.5 (two-D.php)

```php
<?php
echo '<br />A 2-D array<br />';
$a = array(
  0 => array(1,2,3,4),
  1 => array(5,6,7,8),
  2 => array(9,10,11,12),
  3 => array(13,14,15,16),
  4 => array(17,18,19,20)
);
$n_r=count($a); echo '# rows = ' . $n_r . '<br />';
$n_c=count($a[0]); echo '# columns = ' . $n_c . '<br />';
for ($r=0; $r<$n_r; $r++) {
   for ($c=0; $c<$n_c; $c++)
      echo $a[$r][$c] . ' ';
   echo '<br />';
}
?>
```

Document 6.5 uses the `count()` function to determine the number of rows and columns in the array; this function is completely equivalent to and interchangeable with `sizeof()`. The number of elements in $a, the "rows," is returned by `count($a)`. Each element in $a is another array containing the "columns," and `count($a[0])` (or any other index) returns the number of elements in this array. The `count()` function counts only defined array

| A 2-D array |
| # rows = 5 |
| # columns = 4 |
| 1 2 3 4 |
| 5 6 7 8 |
| 9 10 11 12 |
| 13 14 15 16 |
| 17 18 19 20 |

elements, so in order for it to work as expected, every element in an array must have a value. In Document 6.5, defining the first row as

```
0 => array(1,2,3)
```

will result in the number of columns being identified as 3 rather than 4 if you use `count($a[0])`.

Higher-dimension arrays can be defined by extending the above procedure

6.2   Array Sorting

Sorting data stored in an array is a common computing task and PHP supports several functions for this task. Consider Document 6.6, which uses PHP's `sort()` function.

Document 6.6 (`sort1.php`)

```php
<?php
// Create and sort an array...
$a = array('david', 'apple', 'sue', 'xena');
echo 'Original array:<br />';
for ($i=0; $i<sizeof($a); $i++)
    echo $a[$i] . '<br />';
sort($a);
echo 'Sorted array:<br />';
for ($i=0; $i<sizeof($a); $i++)
    echo $a[$i] . '<br />';
?>
```

This code produces the expected results with the array as defined, but it won't do what you might expect for this change to the array, in which two names are capitalized:

```
$a = array('david', 'apple', 'Xena', 'Sue');
```

The problem has to do with how a string is evaluated as "less" or"greater"than another string. "Sue" is less than "sue" because the uppercase alphabet comes earlier in the ASCII character sequence than the lowercase alphabet because S is less than s. (See Appendix 3.)

```
david
apple
sue
xena
Sorted
array:
apple
david
sue
xena
```

```
Original array:
david
apple
Xena
Sue
Sorted array:
Sue
Xena
apple
david
```

PHP's sort() function works as expected with numbers.

Document 6.7 (sort2.php)

```
<?php
    $a=array(3.3,-13,-0.7,14.4);
    sort($a);
    for ($i=0; $i<sizeof($a); $i++)
       echo $a[$i] . '<br />';
?>
```

```
-13
-0.7
3.3
14.4
```

PHP offers several ways to sort arrays of strings and other combinations of elements, but it is also possible to define your own way of deciding whether one array element is less than, equal to, or greater than another: use the usort() function and provide your own code for comparing one array element against another. A user-supplied comparison function must return an integer value less than 0 if the first argument is to be considered less than the second, 0 if they are equal, and greater than 0 if the first argument is greater than the second. For an array with strings containing upper- and lowercase letters, the very simple function shown in Document 6.8 uses `strcasecmp()` to perform a case-insensitive comparison of two strings, producing the elements in the order you probably want to see: apple, david, Sue, Xena.

Document 6.8 (`sort3.php`)

```php
<?php
function compare($x,$y) {
  return strcasecmp($x,$y);
}
// Create and sort an array...
$a = array('Xena', 'Sue', 'david', 'apple');
echo 'Original array:<br />';
for ($i=0; $i<sizeof($a); $i++)
  echo $a[$i] . '<br />';
echo 'Sorted array with user-defined comparisons of
elements:<br />';
usort($a, "compare");
for ($i=0; $i<sizeof($a); $i++)
  echo $a[$i] . '<br />';
?>
```

6.3   Stacks, Queues, and Line Crashers

Stacks and queues are abstract data types familiar to computer science students. They are used to store and retrieve data in a particular way. A stack uses a last-in first-out

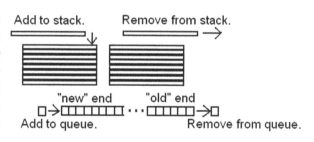

(LIFO) data storage model. You can think of it as a stack of dinner plates. You put new dinner plates on the top of the stack, and when you retrieve a dinner plate, it always comes from the top of the stack. So, the last value added on a stack is the first value retrieved.

A queue uses a first-in first-out (FIFO) data storage model. It operates like a queue (a line, in American English) of people waiting. A new person joins the line at the end, and people leave the line according to who has been in line the longest. So, a value removed from the queue is always the "oldest" value.

PHP provides a very friendly environment for implementing stacks and queues because arrays can be resized dynamically, while a script is running. Because PHP's array model supports keyed arrays, the possibilities for adding elements to and removing them from stacks or queues are extensive and complicated. This discussion will deal only with the basics, assuming arrays with integer indices that start at 0. This limited approach is sufficient for many science and engineering problems.

The basic PHP functions are `array_pop()`, `array_push()`, `array_shift()`, and `array_unshift()`. Document 6.9 demonstrates the use of each of these functions.

Document 6.9 (`stacksAndQueues.php`)

```php
<html>
<head>
<title>Stacks and Queues</title>
</head>
<body>
<?php
  $a = array (-17, "David", 33.3, "Laura");
// Treat $a like a stack (last in, first out)...
  echo "The original array (element [0] is the \"oldest\"
element):<br />";
  print_r($a);
// Add two elements to $a...
  array_push($a, "Susan", 0.5);
  echo "<br />Push two elements on top of stack:<br />";
  print_r($a);
// Remove three elements from $a...
  array_pop($a);   array_pop($a);   array_pop($a);
  echo "<br />Remove three elements from top of stack:<br
/>";
  print_r($a);
// Treat $a like a queue (first in, first out)...
  $a = array (-17, "David", 33.3, "Laura");
  echo "<br />Back to original array:<br />";
  print_r($a);
  echo "<br />Remove two elements from front of queue:<br
/>";
  array_shift($a);
  array_shift($a);
  print_r($a);
  echo "<br />Add three elements to end of queue:<br />";
  array_push($a, "Susan", 0.5, "new_guy");
  print_r($a);
```

```
  echo "<br />Add a \"line crasher\" to the beginning of the
queue:<br />";
  array_unshift($a, "queue_crasher_guy");
  print_r($a);
?>
</body>
</html>
```

```
The original array (element [0] is the "oldest"
element):
Array ( [0] => -17 [1] => David [2] => 33.3
[3] => Laura )
Push two elements on top of stack:
Array ( [0] => -17 [1] => David [2] => 33.3
[3] => Laura [4] => Susan [5] => 0.5 )
Remove three elements from top of stack:
Array ( [0] => -17 [1] => David [2] => 33.3 )
Back to original array:
Array ( [0] => -17 [1] => David [2] => 33.3
[3] => Laura )
Remove two elements from front of queue:
Array ( [0] => 33.3 [1] => Laura )
Add three elements to end of queue:
Array ( [0] => 33.3 [1] => Laura [2] => Susan
[3] => 0.5 [4] => new_guy )
Add a "line crasher" to the beginning of the queue:
Array ( [0] => queue_crasher_guy [1] => 33.3
[2] => Laura [3] => Susan
[4] => 0.5 [5] => new_guy )
```

Document 6.9 deserves close study if you need to do this kind of data manipulation in an array.

6.4 More Examples

6.4.1 The Quadratic Equation Revisited

In Document 4.5 (quadrat.htm and quadrat.php), three coefficients of a quadratic equation were passed from an HTML document and retrieved by name:

```
$a = $_POST["a"];
$b = $_POST["b"];
$c = $_POST["c"];
```

   This code requires the PHP application to "know" what names the form
fields were given in the corresponding HTML document ("a", "b", and
"c"). In PHP terminology, you can think of the form fields being passed as
a keyed array, with the key names corresponding to the form field names.
For this and similar kinds of problems, it might be desirable to make the
code less dependent on names given in the HTML document. Document
6.10 shows one way to do this.

Document 6.10a (quadrat2.htm)

```html
<html>
<head>
<title>Solving the Quadratic Equation</title>
</head>
<body>
<form method="post" action="quadrat_2.php">
Enter coefficients for ax<sup>2</sup> + bx + c = 0:
<br />
a = <input type="text" value="1" name="coeff[0]" />
  (must not be 0)<br />
b = <input type="text" value="2" name="coeff[1]" /><br />
c = <input type="text" value="-8" name="coeff[2]" /><br />
<br /><input type="submit" value="click to get roots..." />
</form>
</body>
</html>
```

Document 6.10b (quadrat2.php)

```php
<?php
var_dump($_POST["coeff"]);
echo "<br />";
$coefficientArray=array_keys($_POST["coeff"]);
$a = $_POST["coeff"][$coefficientArray[0]];
$b = $_POST["coeff"][$coefficientArray[1]];
$c = $_POST["coeff"][$coefficientArray[2]];
$d = $b*$b - 4.*$a*$c;
if ($d == 0) {
  $r1 = $b/(2.*$a);
  $r2 = "undefined";
}
else if ($d < 0) {
  $r1 = "undefined";
  $r2 = "undefined";
}
else {
$r1 = (-$b + sqrt($b*$b - 4.*$a*$c))/2./$a;;
$r2 = (-$b - sqrt($b*$b - 4.*$a*$c))/2./$a;;
}
echo "r1 = " . $r1 . ", r2 = " . $r2;
?>
```

array(3) { [0]=> string(1) "1" [1]=> string(1) "2" [2]=> string(2) "-8" }
r1 = 2, r2 = -4

Document 6.10a is similar to Document 4.5a, but there is an important difference, marked with shaded code. Instead of each coefficient having a unique name, each one is assigned to an element of an array named `coeff`.

The calculations of the real roots in Document 6.10b are identical to those in Document 4.5b, but this code assumes that the PHP script does not automatically "know" the names of the quadratic coefficients, and that an array containing those coefficients may use keys other than consecutive integers starting at 0. The `array_keys()` function is used to extract the key names through the `coeff[]` array, available in `$_POST[]`; the contents of `$_POST[]` are displayed by using the `var_dump()` function. First, the values are placed in `$coefficientArray`, which uses default integer keys starting at 0. These values are then used as indices to the `coeff` array passed to the `$_POST[]` array.

Because integer array keys starting at 0 are used, the code for retrieving the coefficients can be simplified a little, as shown in the shaded lines of Documents 6.11a and 6.11b, which are otherwise identical to Documents 6.10a and 6.10b.

Document 6.11a (`quadrat3.htm`)

```html
<html>
<head>
<title>Solving the Quadratic Equation</title>
</head>
<body>
<form method="post" action="quadrat3.php">
Enter coefficients for ax<sup>2</sup> + bx + c = 0:
<br />
a = <input type="text" value="1" name="coeff[]" />
  (must not be 0)<br />
b = <input type="text" value="2" name="coeff[]" /><br />
c = <input type="text" value="-8" name="coeff[]" /><br />
<br /><input type="submit" value="click to get roots..." />
</form>
</body>
</html>
```

Document 6.11b (quadrat3.php)

```php
<?php
var_dump($_POST["coeff"]);
echo "<br />";
$coefficientArray=$_POST["coeff"];
$a = $coefficientArray[0];
$b = $coefficientArray[1];
$c = $coefficientArray[2];
$d = $b*$b - 4.*$a*$c;
if ($d == 0) {
  $r1 = $b/(2.*$a);
  $r2 = "undefined";
}
else if ($d < 0) {
  $r1 = "undefined";
  $r2 = "undefined";
}
else {
$r1 = (-$b + sqrt($b*$b - 4.*$a*$c))/2./$a;;
$r2 = (-$b - sqrt($b*$b - 4.*$a*$c))/2./$a;;
}
echo "r1 = " . $r1 . ", r2 = " . $r2;
?>
```

Note that because no index values are specified for the coeff[] array in Document 6.11a, PHP assumes that they are integers starting at 0. You could also specify the keys, for example, as integers starting at 1, but you must then tell the PHP application what the keys are, either by using array_keys() or by "hard coding" the key values:

(in the HTML document)
```
a = <input type="text" value="1" name="coeff[1]" />
    (must not be 0)<br />
b = <input type="text" value="2" name="coeff[2]" /><br />
c = <input type="text" value="-8" name="coeff[3]" /><br />
```

(in the PHP script)
```php
$coefficientArray=$_POST["coeff"];
$a = $coefficientArray[1];
$b = $coefficientArray[2];
$c = $coefficientArray[3];
```

This code is easier to write with consecutive integer keys than with arbitrarily named keys, but that approach would essentially defeats the purpose of simplifying access to form fields, which the example in Document 6.11 was originally intended to demonstrate.

You might conclude that the code presented in these examples is not much of a simplification and is not worth the extra effort, because the PHP application still needs to "know" the name of the coefficient array entered into the HTML document's form fields. However, if only one name is needed—the name of that array—this approach might provide some code-writing economy for a longer list of inputs.

6.4.2 Reading HTML `checkbox` Values

The HTML `<input type= "checkbox" … />` form field is used to associate several possible values with a single form field name. Unlike a `type="radio"` field, which allows only one selection from a list, checkboxes allow multiple values to be selected. How can PHP deal with these choices? Consider this problem, referring back to Document 3.10:

> Report cloud observations by checking boxes for cloud types divided into four categories: high, mid, low, and precipitating. Each category has more than one possible cloud type, and multiple cloud types in one or all categories may be observed:
>
> High: cirrus, cirrocumulus, cirrostratus
> Mid: altostratus, altocumulus
> Low: stratus, stratocumulus, cumulus
> Precipitating: nimbostratus, cumulonimbus

Write an HTML document to enter cloud observations and a PHP script that will report all the cloud types reported.

Document 6.12a (`cloudObs.htm`)

```
<html>
<head>
<title>Cloud Observations</title>
</head>
<body bgcolor="#aaddff">
</h1>Cloud Observations</h1>
<strong> Cloud Observations </strong>(Select as many cloud
types as observed.)
```

```html
<br />
<form method="post" action="CloudObs.php" />
<table>
  <tr>
   <td><strong>High</strong> </td>
    <td>
     <input type="checkbox" name="high[]"
       value="Cirrus" /> Cirrus</td>
    <td>
     <input type="checkbox" name="high[]"
       value="Cirrocumulus" /> Cirrocumulus </td>
    <td>
       <input type="checkbox" name="high[]"
         value="Cirrostratus" /> Cirrostratus </td></tr>
  <tr>
    <td colspan="4"><hr noshade color="black" />
     </td></tr>
  <tr>
    <td> <strong>Middle</strong> </td>
    <td>
       <input type="checkbox" name="mid[]"
         value="Altostratus" /> Altostratus </td>
    <td>
       <input type="checkbox" name="mid[]"
         value="Altocumulus" /> Altocumulus</td></tr>
  <tr>
    <td colspan="4"><hr noshade color="black" />
     </td></tr>
  <tr>
    <td> <strong>Low</strong></td>
    <td>
       <input type="checkbox" name="low[]" value="Stratus" />
         Stratus</td>
    <td>
       <input type="checkbox" name="low[]"
         value="Stratocumulus" /> Stratocumulus</td>
    <td>
      <input type="checkbox" name="low[]" value="Cumulus" />
         Cumulus </td></tr>
   <tr>
    <td colspan="4"><hr noshade color="black" />
       /td></tr>
   <tr>
    <td> <strong>Rain-Producing </strong> </td>
    <td>
       <input type="checkbox" name="rain[]"
```

```
          value="Nimbostratus" /> Nimbostratus</td>
     <td>
     <input type="checkbox" name="rain[]"
          value="Cumulonimbus" /> Cumulonimbus </td></tr>
</table>
<input type="submit" value="Click to process..." />
</form>
</body>
</html>
```

Cloud Observations

Cloud Observations (Select as many cloud types as observed.)

High	☐ Cirrus	☑ Cirrocumulus	☑ Cirrostratus
Middle	☐ Altostratus	☐ Altocumulus	
Low	☐ Stratus	☐ Stratocumulus	☐ Cumulus
Rain-Producing	☐ Nimbostratus	☑ Cumulonimbus	

Click to process...

It is very easy to process these data with PHP if the HTML document is written correctly, as shown in Document 6.13a. Each cloud category—high, mid, low, or precipitating—must be specified as an array, $high[] rather than just $high, for example. You do not need to specify the index values. The $_POST [...] operation performed in PHP will return an array including just those cloud types that have been checked. That is, PHP *automatically* does the work that you would otherwise have to do yourself to separate checked boxes from unchecked ones. But...

If you don't check any boxes for a cloud category, then no array is created for that category and your code must provide a way to see if this has happened. Not surprisingly, there is a helpful PHP function for this task. For example: if (isset($_POST["high"])) returns a value of true if a variable (in this case, an array) exists or false if it doesn't. The PHP code for this problem is in Document 6.12b.

Document 6.12b (`cloudObs.php`)

```php
<?php
// high clouds
  if (isset($_POST["high"])) {
    $high = $_POST["high"];
    $n = count($high);
     echo "For high clouds, you observed <br />";
    for ($i=0;$i<$n;$i++)
       echo $high[$i] . "<br>";
  }
  else echo "You didn't observe any high clouds.<br />";
// mid clouds
    if (isset($_POST["mid"])) {
    $mid = $_POST["mid"];
    $n=count($mid);
     echo "For mid clouds, you observed<br />";
    for ($i=0; $i<$n; $i++)
       echo $mid[$i] . "<br />";
    }
    else echo "You didn't observe any mid clouds.<br />";
// low clouds
    if (isset($_POST["low"])) {
    $low = $_POST["low"];
    $n=count($low);
     echo "For low clouds, you observed<br />";
     for ($i=0; $i<$n; $i++)
        echo $low[$i] . "<br />";
    }
    else echo "You didn't observe any low clouds.<br />";
// rain clouds
    if (isset($_POST["rain"])) {
    $rain = $_POST["rain"];
    $n=count($rain);
     echo "For rain clouds, you observed<br />";
     for ($i=0; $i<$n; $i++)
        echo $rain[$i] . "<br />";
    }
    else echo "You didn't observe any rain clouds.<br />";
?>
```

The number of boxes checked for each category is contained in the value of $n. (Depending on your needs, you could create a different variable name for each category.) For mid and low clouds, no boxes are checked, so their corresponding arrays are empty and their for... loops are not executed.

> For high clouds, you observed
> Cirrocumulus
> You didn't observe any mid clouds.
> You didn't observe any low clouds.
> For rain clouds, you observed
> Cumulonimbus

6.4.3   Building a Histogram Array

> Write a PHP application that reads scores between 0 and 100 (possibly
> including both 0 and 100) and creates a histogram array whose ele-
> ments contain the number of scores between 0 and 9, 10 and 19, etc.
> The last "box" in the histogram should include scores between 90 and
> 100. Use a function to generate the histogram. You will have to create
> your own data file for this problem.

The solution shown in Document 6.13 is a minimalist approach to this problem. In general, you would want to provide a data file containing the values
used for generating a histogram array, but this code just uses a random number
generator to create some data for testing—integers between –100 and +100.
Once this code is working, it is easy to add code to read data from a file.

Document 6.13 (histo.php)

```php
<?php
// Generate data array for testing.
  $a=[ ] ; $n=10; $n_boxes=10;
  $low=-100; $high=100; $range=$high-$low;
  for ($i=0; $i<$n; $i++) $a[$i] =rand($low,$high);
  //for ($i=0; $i<$n; $i++) $a[$i]=rand($low,$high);
  // Test some data values to make sure they're
  // boxed properly.
  $a[0] =110;
// Create histogram array.
  $h=[ ] ; $h[0] =$n; // use $h[0] to hold # of data points.
  for ($i=1; $i<=$n_boxes; $i++) $h[$i] =0;
  $dn=$range/$n_boxes;
  $out=0; // # of boxes outside of histogram range
// Fill histogram boxes.
  for ($i=0; $i<sizeof($a) ; $i++) {
    if ( ($a[$i] >$high) || $a[$i] <$low) {
    $out++;
    }
    else {
     if ($a[$i] ==$high) $box_num=$n_boxes;
     else $box_num=floor( ($a[$i] -$low) /$dn) +1;
     $h[$box_num] ++;
     echo $a[$i] . " ".$box_num. "<br />";
    }
  }
echo "Total # of data points: ".$h[0] ."<br />";
echo "Total # of points outside of range: ".$out. "<br />";
echo "Histogram counts:<br />";
```

```
for ($i=1; $i<=$n_boxes; $i++) echo $i." ".$h[$i]."<br />;
?>
```

The `rand()` function generates only integers, but you can convert those integers to real numbers by dividing them by some real number; dividing integers from –100 to +100 by `10.` results in real numbers between –10.0 and +10.0. (Don't forget the decimal point for the divisor, to insure that real arithmetic is being done!)

This code in Document 6.1.34 assumes that the specified number of histogram bins evenly divides the data range. (Specifying bins of different sizes would require a *lot* more code!) With the values and bins specified, a value of –80 goes in bin number 2. Values outside the allowed range are not put in any histogram box.

This code is a good example of the need to plan carefully when you define counter

```
23 7
35 7
-21 4
-58 3
23 7
70 9
36 7
-13 5
66 9
Total # of data points: 10
Total # of points outside of range: 1
Histogram counts:
1 0
2 0
3 1
4 1
5 1
6 0
7 4
8 0
9 2
10 0
```

variable ranges `for...` loops. The data and histogram arrays are initialized without specifying their size. A choice was made to number the histogram boxes from 1 to n. If the default way of indexing arrays, starting at 0, is used, then for this code the histogram array will have a size of 11. With the histogram box numbering starting at 1, element `$h[0]` won't be given any values based on looking at the data. Instead, it is used to hold the total number of data values considered. It would also make sense to use this element to hold just the number of data values falling inside the specified data range.

A value equal to the maximum allowed value will try to put itself into a "next higher" box. That is, for the code as shown, a value of 100 would try to put itself into histogram array element 11, which isn't defined for this problem. The statement `if ($a[$i] ==$high) $box_num=$n_boxes;` prevents this. You could also replace

```
if ($a[$i] ==$high) $box_num=$n_boxes;
else $box_num=floor(($a[$i] -$low)/$dn)+1;
```

with

```
$box_num=min(floor(($a[$i] -$low)/$dn)+1, $n_boxes);
```

although this solution would not be obvious until you have learned about PHP's built-in math functions in Chap. 7.

Functions

7

This chapter introduces the concept of user-defined functions in programming and shows how to use functions in PHP scripts. A summary of PHP built-in math constants and functions is provided.

7.1 The Purpose of Functions

Functions are self-contained code modules that accept input, perform operations on that input, and return one or more results. They are an important concept in any programming language. Here are three reasons to use functions:

1. *Organizing solutions to computational problems*

   A problem to be solved on a computer often consists of several related parts, in which output from one part is used as input to the next part. Functions provide a mechanism for creating a code structure that reflects the nature of this kind of problem. By organizing code into a series of self-contained modules, and by controlling the flow of information among these modules, the problem can be solved in a logical fashion, one part at a time. Basically, this is a matter of separating large problems into smaller and more manageable parts.

2. *Creating reusable code*

   Often, identical calculations must be done several times within a program, but with different values. Functions allow you to write code to perform the calculations just once, using variable names as "placeholders" that will represent actual values when the function is used. Once a function has been written and tested, it can be used in other programs, too, allowing you to create a shareable library of useful calculations.

© Springer International Publishing AG 2017
D.R. Brooks, *Programming in HTML and PHP*, Undergraduate Topics in Computer Science, DOI 10.1007/978-3-319-56973-4_7

3. *Sharing authorship of large programming projects*
     Large programming projects often involve more than one person.
When a project is broken down into several smaller tasks, individual programmers can work independently and then collaborate to assemble the
finished product. Without the separation of tasks made possible by functions, this kind of collaborative approach would be much more difficult.

     The sketch below shows schematically how this task-based approach
works. A problem is stated and the inputs required to solve the problem are
defined and a conceptual solution is outlined. Inputs are sent to tasks and the
output for each task serves as input to another task. The process continues
until the solution is reached. Some problems might not have such a "linear"
solution structure—there may be several branches for required tasks. In any
case, a function-based approach makes it easier to organize a solution to a
large problem; the more complicated the problem the more useful a
task-oriented approach will be.

     Functions are "called" (or "invoked") from a main program or from
another function. Each function performs some operations and then returns a
result.

     In addition to providing a mechanism for modularizing the solution to a
problem, functions play an important role in program design. The syntax of
function implementation forces a programmer (or, for large projects, groups
of programmers) to think carefully about a problem and its solution: "Can I
state the problem and propose a step-by-step solution? What information
must be provided to complete this task? What information is provided when
the task is completed? What steps are required to solve the problem? Can the
problem be divided into smaller independent but related parts? How does
each part relate to the others? Are the specified inputs and outputs for each
part consistent with the relationships among the parts?" Once these questions are answered, the structure of a program should be clear. Often,
working out an appropriate function structure is the hardest part of solving a
large computational problem.

7.2   User-Defined Functions

User-defined functions are an essential part of PHP and other programming languages. It is important to understand how information is provided to and extracted from a function. The model shown in the sketch is applicable to PHP and many other languages. A function resides in an isolated subset of computer memory. Communications with the contents of this

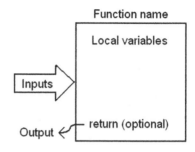

space are strictly controlled and limited to specific pathways. The box represents the computer memory set aside for the function. This space and the operations carried out within it are not visible to the rest of a script, including to other functions within that script, except along two specific paths.[1] The large arrow represents the path into to the function, through its parameter list. The small arrow represents a single output from the function, generated as a result of a `return` statement.

Here is the syntax for a generic function.

```
function doSomething($input1,$input2,$input3,...) {
    $local1,$local2,$local3,... $outputName;
    {Statements using any desired combination of input parameters
        and locally defined variables.}
    return $outputName;
}
```

The `function` keyword is required at the beginning of every function. Every function must have a user-provided name, `doSomething` in this generic example. Function names are case-insensitive. Spaces between parts of a function name are not allowed, but underlines are. So, for example, you could name the function `do_something`, but not `do something` (because `do something` is interpreted as two tokens rather than one). As in all aspects of programming, it will be helpful in your own work to settle upon a function-naming convention and use it consistently.

---

[1]Note that BASIC, which was for many years the introductory programming language of choice, and which is still used today, does not support this "walled-off" memory model for functions.

The parameter list contains the names of one or more input parameters, separated by commas and enclosed in parentheses. These names are placeholders for input values (the "calling arguments") passed to the function when it is called. Occasionally, a function will have no values in its parameter list. However, parentheses are still required.

All the code in a function constitutes a statement block, enclosed in right and left curly brackets. The opening bracket can appear either at the end of the `function {name}()` line or on the next line. Your code will be more easily readable if you adopt a consistent style of indenting the body of the code, as shown in the generic example shown above.

Within a function, one or more local variables can be defined. Local variables may not be required for some calculations, but code may be clearer if the results of intermediate calculations are stored in separate variables. In any event, the required task for the function is carried out using appropriate combinations of the input parameters and local variables. The general programming rule that a variable should never be used until it has first been assigned a value applies equally to local variables in functions. To put it another way, a local variable should never appear on the right hand side of an assignment operator until it has first appeared on the left. The function assumes that variables passed as parameters have already been given appropriate values. The value of parameter variables can be changed within the function, if needed, but those changes do not affect the values in the calling program or function.

It is important to understand that the local variables defined within a function and calculations performed in a function are invisible to the rest of your script, including to other functions. This means that you can select local variable names, assign values, and change those values without regard to what happens in other functions and elsewhere in a script, even when the same variable name is used elsewhere.

The result of calculations performed in a function is returned to the place from which the function was called by using the `return` keyword in a statement. Only one `return` statement can be executed in a function. A function can have more than one `return` statement, perhaps in various branches of an `if...` construct, but only one of these can actually be executed. The value to be returned can be declared as a local variable, too, as shown in the shaded items in the code above, but it is also possible to return the result of a calculation without first assigning that result to a variable name.

In summary, here are two critical points about functions:

> The parameter list is a one-way path for input only. Information can be passed *in* to the function along this path, but no information passes *out* along this path.

> The `return` statement is a one-way path for a single value flowing *out* of the function.

Successful programming requires accurate mental pictures of how programming paradigms work. The function model shown here, including the restricted input/output paths and the protected nature of variables locally declared inside a function, is one of the most important paradigms in all of programming. It makes it possible to separate large and complex computational problems into a series of smaller (and hopefully simpler) problems, linked through a series of function interfaces. This modularization makes even small scripts easier to write, and it also makes it practical for large programming projects to be written, tested, and maintained by more than one person. It is true that use-defined functions are rarely actually *required*, but it is often very good programming practice to use them.

As a simple example, consider this problem:

Dew point temperature is the temperature at which moisture in the atmosphere condenses to water. For air temperature T ($0°C \leq 60°C$) and relative humidity RH $(0.01 - 1.00)^2$:

$a = 17.27$ $b = 237.7[°C]$ $\beta(T, RH) = (a \cdot T)/(b + T) + ln(RH)$
$T_d = (b \cdot \beta)/(a - \beta)$

Write a script that calculates dew point temperature for user-supplied values of air temperature and relative humidity

Document 7.1 (`dewpoint.php`)

```
<html>
<body>
<h3>Calculate dew point temperature</h3>
<form method="post" action="<?php $_SERVER ['PHP_SELF'] ; ?>">
    Air temperature, &deg;C (0<= T <= 60) :
    <input type="text" size="4" name="T" value="25" /><br />
```

---

[2]See, for example, http://www.paroscientific.com/dewpoint.htm.

```
Relative humidity, %:
<input type="text" size="4" name="RH" value="60" /><br />
<input type="submit" value="Calculate dew point
temperature" />
</form>
</body>
</html>
<?php
   $T=$_POST["T"];
   $RH=$_POST["RH"]/100.; // convert from % to fraction
   $Td=getDewpoint($T,$RH);
   echo "dew point temperature (deg C): ".$Td."<br />";
   function getDewpoint($T,$RH) {
      $a=17.27; $b=237.7;
      $beta=$a*$T/($b+$T)+ log($RH); // log() is base-e log
      $Td=$b*$beta/($a-$beta);
      return round($Td,1);
   }
?>
```

Calculate dew point temperature

Air temperature, °C (0<= T <= 60): 25

Relative humidity, %: 60

Calculate dew point temperature

dew point temperature (deg C): 16.7

Clearly, this problem could easily be done without the use of a function. But, this code illustrates how to use functions, and it might be useful to have available a function for calculating dew point temperature without having to look up the equations every time you needed that calculation.

The fact that only a single value can be returned from a function might impose some limitations. Fortunately, there is an easy solution: the single "value" returned from a function can be an array. A simple example is shown in Document 7.2, which uses a function to calculate the area and circumference of a circle. Again, this is a very simple problem which can be done without a function. Its only purpose is to show how to return multiple values from a function. The only issue is that you need to keep track of which values are stored in which array elements.

Document 7.2 (`circle.php`)

```
<html>
<head>
<title></title>
</head>
<body>
<h3>Calculate the area and circumference of a circle.</h3>
<form method="post" action="<?php $_SERVER['PHP_SELF']; ?>">
   radius: <input type="text" size="4" name="r" value="25"
/><br />
   <input type="submit" value="Calculate area and
circumference" />
```

```
</form>
</body>
</html>
<?php
   $r=$_POST["r"];
   $a=[]; // [0] is circumference, [1] is area
   $a=circleStuff($r);
   echo "circumference: ".$a[0]." area: ".$a[1]."<br />";
   function circleStuff($r) {
      $a=[];
      $a[0] =round(2.*pi()*$r,2); // circumference in[0]
      $a[1] =round(pi()*$r*$r,2); // area in [ 1]
      return $a;
   }
?>
```

7.3 Recursive Functions

There is an important class of calculations that can be implemented with recursive algorithms. A standard example is the factorial function n!, defined for non-negative integers as:

$n! = 1$ for $n = 1$ or $n = 0$
$n! = n \cdot (n - 1)!$ for $n > 1$

For example, $5!=5 \cdot 4 \cdot 3 \cdot 2 \cdot 1=120$. This is a recursive definition, in which each value of n! for n greater than 1 is defined in terms of $(n-1)!$.

Like other modern programming languages, PHP supports recursive functions—functions that call themselves. Document 7.3 implements the recursive algorithm for n!.

Document 7.3 (factorial.php)

```
<html><head><title>calculate n!</title>
</head><body>
<h3>Calculate n!</h3>
<form action="<?php $_SERVER['PHP_SELF']; ?>" method="post">
Enter n (integer >=0):
<input type="text" name="n" value="8" size="3" /><br />
<input type="submit" name="submit" value="Calculate n!" />
</form>
<?php
$n=$_POST["n"];
echo "max integer: ".PHP_INT_MAX."<br />";
echo "Calculate n! for n=".$n."<br />";
```

```
$nfact=nFactorial($n);
echo $nfact. "<br />";
function nFactorial($n) {
    if ($n<=1) return 1;
    else return $n* nFactorial($n-1);
}
?>
</body></html>
```

The shaded line contains the critical code, in which the function calls itself. For certain mathematical functions, such as n!, the structure

max integer: 2147483647
Calculate n! for n=8
40320

of the recursive function is easy to see from the mathematical definition of the function. Recursive algorithms always require at least two branches. One branch generates a recursive call and the other terminates the function. In Document 7.3, the relationship between the recursive definition for n! and the code required to evaluate n! should be obvious. Note that this code does not check to make sure that only non-negative integer values of n have been entered as input. (You might want to add that code yourself.) Also, there can be problems with large values of n because of the limited range of integers; n! grows rapidly with increasing n. The maximum allowed integer is system-dependent. Document 7.3 displays the value of PHP_INT_MAX which, as its name implies, tells you what the maximum integer value is for your system. However, for larger values, the result will be converted to a floating point number. For the PHP installation used to execute Document 7.3, the code gives 18! = 6.402373705728E+15 (the right value), but 19! = 1.2164510040883E +17, for which the correct (integer) value is 121645100408832000.

The success of recursive functions depends on the function model discussed at the beginning of this chapter, in which information flows into a function through the parameter list. When the function is called with the current value of $n-1$, this value is associated with the parameter n in the new call. Because of how the algorithm is written, the local value of $n-1$ will eventually equal 1 (for any value of n originally greater than 1) and the recursive calls will be terminated. The intermediate values of the factorial function are stored within the programming environment. Table 7.1 shows the sequence of events for calculating 4!.

You can think of each function call as adding a plate to a stack of plates. The initial call plus the three recursive calls add a total of four plates to the stack. At the third recursive call, n = 1 and a value of 1 is returned. Executing a return statement is equivalent to removing one of the plates. Subsequently, the three remaining plates are removed as the deferred multiplications are carried out and a value is returned. When the function returns control of the script back to the point from which it was initially called, all the "plates" have been removed from the stack.

Table 7.1 Calculating 4! using a recursive algorithm

Local value of n	Action	Value returned
n = 4	Initial call	Deferred
n = 3	1st recursive call	Deferred
n = 2	2nd recursive call	Deferred
n = 1	3rd recursive call	1
n = 2	Complete multiplication $2 \cdot 1$	2
n = 3	Complete multiplication $3 \cdot 2$	6
n = 4	Complete multiplication $4 \cdot 6$	24

For more complicated recursive algorithms, it can be difficult to follow the course of the calculations. Fortunately, it isn't necessary to do this. As long as the algorithm is properly designed, with a condition that will appropriately terminate the recursive calls, the programming environment takes care of keeping track of all the intermediate values generated during the execution of the algorithm.

Here's another example of a well-known function that is defined recursively. The Fibonacci numbers F_n that form the sequence 1, 1, 2, 3, 5, 8, 13, 21,... are defined for positive integer values of n as

$$F_n = 1 \text{ if } n = 1 \text{ or } n = 2 \quad F_n = F_{n-1} + F_{n-2} \text{ if } n > 2$$

Document 7.4 shows how simple it is to evaluate this function using a recursive algorithm.

Document 7.4 (fibonacci.php)

```php
<?php
$n=8;
echo "Calculate the first ".$n." Fibonacci numbers.<br />";
for ($i=1; $i<=$n; $i++) {
    echo $i." ".Fib($i)."<br />";
}
function Fib($n) {
    if ($n<=2) return 1;
    else return Fib($n-1)+Fib($n-2);
}
?>
```

It is not easy to follow the sequence of events as this recursive algorithm does its job. However, you don't have to worry about that!

Recursive algorithms can also be formulated using count-controlled or conditional loop structures. However, a recursive formulation is often much shorter and more direct to implement

Calculate the first 8 Fibonacci numbers.
1 1
2 1
3 2
4 3
5 5
6 8
7 13
8 21

in code. The famous "Towers of Hanoi" problem is an excellent example of a problem that is difficult to solve "directly" but is trivial to solve recursively.

Consider three poles, on one of which are stacked 64 golden rings. The bottom ring is the largest and the others decrease in size. The object is to move the 64 rings from one pole to another, using the remaining pole as a temporary storage place for rings. There are two rules for moving rings:

1. Only one ring can be moved at a time.
2. A ring can never be placed on top of a smaller ring.

Describe how to move the entire stack of rings from one pole to another.

It can be shown that it will take $2^n - 1$ moves to move n rings. For n = 64, if you could move one ring per second without ever making a mistake, it would take roughly 100 times the estimated age of the universe! However, it is not difficult to develop a recursive algorithm that will work in principle for any number of rings and apply it to a value of n that is small enough to be practical. For n = 4, 15 moves are required.

In a conceptual sense, the solution is simple (but perhaps not obvious). Suppose the poles are labeled A, B, and C. Initially, all the rings, numbered 1 through n, smallest

Towers of Hanoi moves for 4 rings.
Move ring 1 from A to B
Move ring 2 from A to C
Move ring 1 from B to C
Move ring 3 from A to B
Move ring 1 from C to A
Move ring 2 from C to B
Move ring 1 from A to B
Move ring 4 from A to C
Move ring 1 from B to C
Move ring 2 from B to A
Move ring 1 from C to A
Move ring 3 from B to C
Move ring 1 from A to B
Move ring 2 from A to C
Move ring 1 from B to C

to largest, are on A and the goal is to move them all to C. The steps are:

1. Move n – 1 rings from A to B.
2. Move the nth ring from A to C.
3. Move n – 1 rings from B to C.

This solution is "conceptual" in the sense that it doesn't specify precisely how to do steps 1 and 3; only step 2 defines a specific action that can be taken. However, the power of recursive functions allows us to solve this problem without giving additional specific steps, as shown in Document 7.5.

Document 7.5 (towers.htm)

```php
<?php
$n=4;
echo "Towers of Hanoi moves for ".$n." rings.<br />";
move($n, 'A', 'C',' B' );
function move($n,$start,$end,$intermediate) {
  if ($n > 0) {
     move($n-1,$start,$intermediate,$end);
    echo "Move ring ".$n." from ".$start." to ".$end."<br />";
     move($n-1,$intermediate,$end,$start);
  }
}
?>
```

Although this seems almost too simple to be true, in fact this simple "conceptual" code is all that is required to solve this problem in the sense that all the steps are explicitly written out; try it yourself using a real set of rings or blocks. You can also try writing an equivalent non-recursive solution. (Good luck!)

The success of this algorithm depends, once again, on how parameter lists work—passing information into a function along a "one-way street." This algorithm will generate *many* intermediate values and, as n increases it will eventually run out of memory space; it still works for n = 10, which requires 1023 moves.

7.4 Built-In Math Constants and Functions

PHP's math functions return integer or floating-point results, with a system-dependent precision that is often about 14 significant digits for floating-point numbers. This is sufficient for all but the most specialized calculations. There are also several pre-defined mathematical constants, all of which are floating-point numbers. These constants and functions are built into PHP, with no need for external software libraries. Trigonometric functions always assume input parameters in radians or produce angle outputs in radians.

Constants and built-in math functions are listed in Table 7.2. Data types are shown in parentheses, for example, `(float)`. Optional arguments are enclosed in square brackets. "x" (and other arguments, in some cases) always represents a variable of the appropriate type, even though they are shown without the $ symbol (Table 7.3).

Table 7.2 Math constants

Named constants	Description
`M_1_PI`	$1/\pi$
`M_2_PI`	$2/\pi$
`M_2_SQRTPI`	$2/(\pi^{1/2})$
`M_E`	Base of the natural logarithm, $e = 2.71828\ldots$
`M_EULER`	Euler's constant* $= 0.577215665\ldots$
`M_LN2`	Natural logarithm of $2 = 0.693147\ldots$
`M_LN10`	Natural logarithm of $10 = 2.302585\ldots$
`M_LNPI`	Natural logarithm of $\pi = 1.1447299\ldots$
`M_LOG2E`	Log to the base 2 of $e = 1.442695\ldots$
`M_LOG10E`	Log to the base 10 of $e = 0.434294\ldots$
`M_PI`	$\pi = 3.1415927\ldots$
`M_PI_2`	$\pi/2 = 1.5707963\ldots$
`M_PI_4`	$\pi/4 = 0.7853981\ldots$
`M_SQRT1_2`	$1/(2^{1/2}) = 0.7071067\ldots$
`M_SQRT2`	$2^{1/2} = 1.4142136\ldots$
`M_SQRT3`	$3^{1/2} = 1.7320508\ldots$
`M_SQRTPI`	$\pi^{1/2} = 1.7724539\ldots$

*Euler's constant e is the limit as $n \to \infty$ of $(1 + 1/2 + 1/3 + \cdots + 1/n)$

Table 7.3 Math functions

Functions	Returns
`(number)abs((number)x)`	Absolute value of x, a floating-point or integer number, depending on x
`(float)acos((float)x)`	Inverse cosine of x, $\pm\pi$, for $-1 \le x \le 1$
`(float)acosh((float)x)`	Inverse hyperbolic cosine of x
`(float)asin((float)x)`	Inverse sine of x, $\pm\pi/2$, for $-1 \le x \le 1$
`(float)asinh((float)x)`	Inverse hyperbolic sine of x
`(float)atan((float)x)`	Inverse tangent of x, $\pm\pi/2$, for $-\infty < x < \infty$ (compare with `atan2(y,x)`)
`(float)atan2((float)y,` `(float)x)`	Inverse tangent of angle between x-axis and the point (x,y), $0 \rightarrow 2\pi$, measured counterclockwise
`(float)atanh((float)x)`	Inverse hyperbolic tangent of $x^{(2)}$
`(float)ceil((number)x)`	Smallest whole number (still type `float`) greater than or equal to x
`(float)cos((float)x)`	Cosine of x, ± 1
`(float)cosh((float)x)`	Hyperbolic cosine of x
`(float)deg2rad((float)x)`	Convert x in degrees to radians
`(float)exp((float)x)`	e to the x power (e^x)
`(float)floor((float)x)`	Greatest whole number (still type `float`) less than or equal to x
`(float)fmod((float)x,` `(float)y)`	Floating-point remainder of x/y
`(float)log((float)x[,` `(float)b])`	Logarithm of x to base e unless optional base argument b is included, x > 0
`(float)getrandmax` `((void))`	Max value returned by call to `rand()`
`(float)log10((float)x)`	Base-10 logarithm of x

`(mixed)max((mixed)x,`
`(mixed)y,…)`
`(mixed)max((array)x)`
	Largest of two or more values, or maximum value in an array

`(mixed)min((mixed)x,`
`(mixed)y,…)`
`(mixed)min((array)x)`
	Smallest of two or more values, or minimum value in an array

`(float)pi()`	Returns value of π, identical to `M_PI`
`(number)pow((number)x,` `(number)y)`	x to the y power (x^y), returns a whole number when appropriate
`(float)rad2deg((float)x)`	Convert radian value x to degrees

`(int)rand()`
`(int)rand([(int)min,`
`(int)max])`
	Random integer in the range 0–RAND_MAX, optionally between `min` and `max`

`(float)round((float)x[,` `(float)p])`	x rounded to specified precision (p digits after decimal point), or to whole number without argument p
`(float)sin((float)x)`	Sine of x
`(float)sinh((float)x)`	Hyperbolic sine of x
`(float)sqrt((float)x)`	Square root of (positive) x

(continued)

Table 7.3 (continued)

Functions	Returns
*(float)*srand([*(int)*seed])	Seeds random number generator, optionally with specified integer seed
*(float)*tan(*(float)*x)	Tangent of x, $\pm\infty$
*(float)*tanh(*(float)*x)	Hyperbolic tangent of x

7.5 More Examples

7.5.1 Loan Repayment Schedule

Given the principal amount P of a loan, an annual interest rate R in percent, and a repayment period of n months, the monthly payment M is given by:

$$r = R/(100 \cdot 12), \; M = (P \cdot r)/[1 - 1/(1 + r)^n]$$

Create a document that asks the user to enter P, R, and n and then calculates and displays the monthly payment.

This is a straightforward problem. Computing payments on a loan is a standard calculation that is a good candidate for writing as a function that can be reused in other code; there is no need to have to remember the formula the next time you need it.

Document 7.6 (loanPayment.php)

```
<html><head>
<title>Loan Calculator</title>
<body>
<h3>Loan Calculator</h3>
<form method="post" action="<?php $_SERVER['PHP_SELF'] ; ?>">
Principal Amount: $:
<input type="text" name="amount" size="9"
   maxlength="9" value="10000" /><br />
Annual rate: %<input type="text" name="rate" size="6"
   maxlength="6" value="4.5" />
<br />
Number of Months: <input type="text" name="n" size="3"
   maxlength="3" value="24" /><br />
<input type="submit" value="Click here to get monthly
      payment." />
</form></body></html>
<?php
    $P=$_POST["amount"] ; $r=$_POST["rate"] ; $n=$_POST[ "n"] ;
```

```php
$monthlyPayment=getPayment($P,$r,$n);
echo "Your monthly payment is $"
    .round($monthlyPayment,2)."<br />";
echo "The total cost of your loan is $"
    .round($monthlyPayment*$n,2)."<br />";
function getPayment($P,$r,$n) {
    $r=$r/100/12; $M=$P*$r/(1-1/pow(1+$r,$n)); return $M; }
?>
```

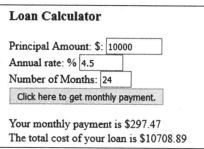

Loan Calculator

Principal Amount: $: 10000
Annual rate: % 4.5
Number of Months: 24

Click here to get monthly payment.

Your monthly payment is $297.47
The total cost of your loan is $10708.89

7.5.2   Legendre Polynomials

A set of functions called Legendre polynomials are sometimes used in science and engineering applications.[3] Here is a table of the first 8 Legendre polynomials.

n	$P_n(x)$
0	1
1	x
2	$(3x^2 - 1)/2$
3	$(5x^3 - 3x)/2$
4	$(35x^4 - 30x^2 + 3)/8$
5	$(63x^5 - 70x^3 + 15x)/8$
6	$(231x^6 - 315x^4 + 105x^2 - 5)16$
7	$(429x^7 - 693x^5 + 315x^3 - 35x)/16$

By making use of the fact that $P_0(x) = 1$ and $P_1(x) = x$, Legendre polynomials of order n $\geq$ 2 can be generated through a recursion relation:

$$P_n(x) = [(2n-1)/n]xP_{n-1}(x)-[(n-1)/n]P_{n-2}(x)$$

Write an application that will generate the value of the first n Legendre polynomials for any value of x and n $\geq$ 0.

---

[3]Legendre polynomials are solutions to Legendre's differential equation.

Document 7.7 (`legendre.htm`)

```php
<?php
  $n=8; $x=1.5;
  echo "Legendre polynomials for x = ".$x."<br />";
  for ($i=0; $i<=$n; $i++) {
     $L=getLegendre($i,$x);
     echo $i." ".$L."<br />";
  }
  function getLegendre($n,$x) {
     if ($n==0) return 1;
     elseif ($n==1) return $x;
     else return (2.*$n-1)/$n* getLegendre($n-1,$x) -
       ($n-1)/$n* getLegendre($n-2,$x);
  }
?>
```

This is another example of a calculation that is very easy to implement as a recursive algorithm, because that is how the function is defined. The solution requires nothing more than a straightforward translation of the definition into code. Note the multiple `return` statements in the function; only one of those statements is executed, depending on the current value of `$n`.

Legendre polynomials for x = 1.5
0 1
1 1.5
2 1.75
3 1.9166666666667
4 2.0416666666667
5 2.1416666666667
6 2.225
7 2.2964285714286
8 2.3589285714286

7.5.3   Kepler's Equation

The period of an Earth-orbiting object τ is $\tau = 2\pi a\sqrt{a/\mu}$, where $\mu = 398601.2$ km^3/s^2 is Earth's gravitational constant; $a = (r_p + r_a)/2$ is the semimajor axis; r_p and r_a are the perigee (closest) and apogee (farthest) distances from Earth's center:

$$r_p = a(1 - e)$$
$$r_a = a(1 + e)$$

where e is the eccentricity, 0 for a circular orbit and less than one for a closed (periodic) orbit. For typical near-Earth orbits at an altitude of a few hundred kilometers, the period is roughly 100 minutes.

The angular position M of an object in a circular orbit with radius a at time t, the mean anomaly, is $M = 2\pi\, t/\tau$ radians, measured from an arbitrarily specified perigee. For an object in a closed non-circular orbit, $0<e<1$, with a as defined above, the angular distance from perigee, the true anomaly f, is obtained from Kepler's equation:

$$M = E - e\sin(E)$$

$$f = \cos^{-1}\left(\frac{\cos(E) - e}{1 - e\cos(E)}\right)$$

where E is the so-called eccentric anomaly. Both M and f are measured from perigee.

The transcendental equation which relates E to M can be solved iteratively. Select $E = M$ as a first guess. Then "solve" for a new value of E: $E_{new} = M + e\sin(E)$. Replace E with E_{new} and repeat until the absolute value of $E - E_{new}$ is less than some specified small number.

Write a script to calculate the true anomaly of an orbiting object as a function of time from perigee for a specified semimajor axis and eccentricity. Earth's radius is about 6378 km, so for an object in a circular orbit at 300 km, for example, $a = 6678$ km.[4]

Document 7.8 (KeplerEquation.php)

```
<html>
<head>
<title>Calculate true anomaly of orbiting object</title>
<body>
<h3>Calculate true anomaly of orbiting object</h3>
<form method="post"
      action="<?php $_SERVER['PHP_SELF'] ; ?>">
Semimajor axis (km) :
<input type="text" name="a" size="5" value="7000" /><br
/>

Eccentricity (0 to &lt;1) :
<input type="text" name="e" size="5" value="0.7" />
<br />
Time steps along orbit path (how many, even #) :
<input type="text" name="n" size="3" value="10" /><br />
```

---

[4]Earth is not a perfect sphere, but that fact can be overlooked for this calculation.

```
<input type="submit"
value="Click here to generate true anomalies." />
</form>
</body>
</html>
<?php
    $a=$_POST["a"] ; $e=$_POST["e"] ; $n=$_POST["n"] ;
    $tau=2.*pi()*$a*sqrt($a/398601.2);
    $dt=($tau/60)/$n;
    echo "Period, minutes: ".round($tau/60,3)."<br />";
    echo "time, mean anomaly, true anomaly (deg)<br />";
    for ($t=0; $t<($tau/60); $t+=$dt) {
        $M=2*pi()*$t*60/$tau;
        echo round($t,4)." ".round(180/pi()*$M,3);
        if ($e == 0) $f=$M; // for circular orbit
        else {
            $E=getE($e,$M,$M); // E = M as initial value
            $f=acos((cos($E)-$e)/(1-$e*cos($E)));
        }
        $f=180/pi()*$f;
        if ($t/($tau/60) > 0.5) $f=360-$f;
        echo " ".round($f,3)."<br />";
    }
    echo round($tau/60,3)." ".round(360,3).
        " ".round(360,3)."<br />";
    function getE($e,$M,$E) {
        $newE=$M + $e*sin($E);
        if (abs($newE-$E) < 1e-5) return $newE;
        else return getE($e,$M,$newE); // recursive
    }
?>
```

This code is a good example of how to use PHP's trigonometric functions. Angles must always be expressed in radians. Writing `sin(30)` won't cause any problems for PHP, which is perfectly happy to calculate the sine of 30 radians. But, if what you really want is the sine of 30° you must convert the angle to radians: `sin(30*pi()/180)`. Or use the `deg2rad()` function. Likewise, the `asin()` function returns an angle in radians. Because confusing degrees with radians doesn't cause a syntax error, it is very easy to write code that looks OK but which will, at best or at worst, depending on your point of view, give incorrect answers and, at worst or best, may eventually cause your script to crash. You can convert radians back to degrees with the `rad2deg()` function or by multiplying radians by 180/π.

The equation defining E as a function of M lends itself to a recursive implementation, although it is also possible to use a conditional loop.

At time t = τ/2, an orbiting object will be at a true anomaly of 180° regardless of its eccentricity; the time intervals for use in the `for...` loop are defined to include this value. The results for $e = 0$ and $e = 0.7$ show that objects in non-circular orbits move faster near perigee and slower near apogee.

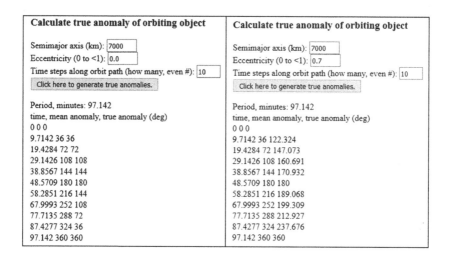

Calculate true anomaly of orbiting object	Calculate true anomaly of orbiting object
Semimajor axis (km): 7000 Eccentricity (0 to <1): 0.0 Time steps along orbit path (how many, even #): 10 Click here to generate true anomalies.	Semimajor axis (km): 7000 Eccentricity (0 to <1): 0.7 Time steps along orbit path (how many, even #): 10 Click here to generate true anomalies.
Period, minutes: 97.142 time, mean anomaly, true anomaly (deg) 0 0 0 9.7142 36 36 19.4284 72 72 29.1426 108 108 38.8567 144 144 48.5709 180 180 58.2851 216 144 67.9993 252 108 77.7135 288 72 87.4277 324 36 97.142 360 360	Period, minutes: 97.142 time, mean anomaly, true anomaly (deg) 0 0 0 9.7142 36 122.324 19.4284 72 147.073 29.1426 108 160.691 38.8567 144 170.932 48.5709 180 180 58.2851 216 189.068 67.9993 252 199.309 77.7135 288 212.927 87.4277 324 237.676 97.142 360 360

Input/Output and Functions to Files, Strings, and Arrays

8

This chapter deals with handing input and output. It presents a summary of PHP functions for reading and writing files, viewing the content of variables, and manipulating strings. It also includes summaries of some array-related and miscellaneous functions.

8.1 File Handling and Input/Output Functions

As noted previously in Chap. 4, file access is one of the primary justifications for using a language such as PHP. As a general rule, PHP can read files from anywhere on a local computer, but you may need to set appropriate access permissions to write or modify files. You may need to need to ask your system administrator about write access on a host computer. Problems with assigning write permissions manifest themselves when PHP refuses to open a file in write ('w') or append ('a') mode.

A previous example involved reading data from an external file, an essential requirement for many computing tasks. (See Document 4.4.) The PHP language has an extensive set of functions for reading and writing files. This section summarizes a subset of those functions. In these descriptions, the data type of an input parameter or return value is given in italicized parentheses, e.g., *(string)*. Programmer-supplied text is printed in *{italicized Times Roman font}* inside curly brackets. Often, generic variable names are given in *italicized Courier font*, e.g., *$fileHandle*. Optional parameters are enclosed in square brackets.

8.1.1 Opening, Closing, and Moving Files

Files are typically opened for either reading *or* writing, but not both at the same time. Files are always assumed to be sequential access only, which means their contents cannot be accessed in any order except from the beginning or, in "append" mode, moving forward from the end. Table 8.1 summarizes the three common access modes.

© Springer International Publishing AG 2017
D.R. Brooks, *Programming in HTML and PHP*, Undergraduate Topics in Computer Science, DOI 10.1007/978-3-319-56973-4_8

Table 8.1 Text file access modes for fopen()

Mode	Description
'r' or "r"	Open for reading only, starting at beginning of file
'w' or "w"	Open for writing only. If the file exists, its contents will be overwritten. If not, it will be created
'a' or "a"	Open for writing only, starting at the end of an existing file. If the file does not it exist, it will be created

The fopen() function is used to open files regardless of their access mode. As previously noted in Chap. 4, fopen() returns a file handle," to be associated with a physical file identified by the name under which it is stored either locally or remotely, along with its directory as needed.

When a file is opened in "read" mode, its file handle points to the location of the first byte of the file in memory. Reading from a sequential access file implies that you always must read the contents of the file starting at the beginning, even if you discard some of the information. You cannot jump ahead or backwards to a random location within the file.

In "write" mode, data are written to the file sequentially, starting at the beginning of a blank file if the named file does not already exist. If the file handle represents a physical file that already exists, then the old file is replaced by the new data. (Be careful!)

In "append" mode, the pointer to the file is positioned initially at the end of the file, just before the end-of-file character. New data are added to the end of the file without changing whatever was previously in the file.

When you are done with a file, whether in read, write, or append mode, it should be closed with fclose(). If a PHP script terminates properly, it will automatically close all open files, but it is good programming practice to include code to close files, especially if more than one file is needed at different places in your script.

$fileHandle = fopen(*(string) $fileName*, *(string) {mode}*)
   $fileHandle is a pointer to the beginning of a file in 'r' or 'w' mode or at the end of a file, just before the end-of-file mark, in 'a' mode. *$fileName* can be a variable name assigned an appropriate value or a string literal.

(bool) fclose(*$fileHandle*)
   Closes a previously opened file pointed to by a file handle.

In this code fragment, $in, $out, and $out_add are file resource handles.

```
$inFile = "dataFile.dat";
$in = fopen($inFile,'r');
$out = fopen("outputFile.csv",'w');
$out_add=fopen("appendFile.txt",'a');
```

When working with files, it is sometimes desirable for your script to be able to determine whether a specified file already exists before trying to open it. There is a PHP function for doing that.

> *(bool)* file_exists(*(string) $filename*)
>   Returns a boolean value of true if the specified file or directory exists, and false otherwise.

There are functions for copying, renaming, and deleting files within a script. You should be careful about using these functions, to make sure you really intend for the requested operations to be carried out.

> *(bool)* copy(*(string) $sourceFile,*)
>   *(string) $destinationFile*)
> *(bool)* rename(*(string) $sourceFile,*)
>   *(string) $destinationFile*)
> *(bool)* unlink(*(string) $fileName*)
>   copy() copies the entire contents of *$sourceFile* to *$destinationFile*. rename() renames a file. unlink() deletes a file. These functions return a boolean value of true if successful and false if not.

8.1.2   Format Specifiers

Some of the PHP input/output (I/O) functions described below for reading input or displaying output require format specifiers that control how input is interpreted and how output is displayed. Each format conversion specifier starts with a percent sign (%) followed by, in order, one or more of these elements, all of which except the data type specifier are optional.

Table 8.2 lists three data types and the type specifiers used with them. Table 8.3 gives details for each of these specifiers.

Table 8.2 PHP data types

Data Type	Format Specifiers
Strings	s
Integers	d, u, c, o, x, X, b
Floats	g, G, e, E, f, F

Table 8.3 Data type specifiers for input and formatted output

Specifier	Description
%b	Treats argument as integer and displays binary equivalent
%c	Treats argument as an integer, displays an integer as the character having that base-10 ASCII value (assuming the character is printable)
%d	Displays numerical value as a signed base-10 integer
%e or %E	Displays numerical value in scientific notation, for example, 7.444e-3
%f or %F	Reads or displays a value as a floating-point number
%g or %G	Display is shorter of %e, %E, %f or %F
%o	Treats argument as integer and displays octal equivalent
%s	Reads or displays a value as a string
%u	Reads or displays a numerical value as a base-10 integer
%x or %X	Treats argument as integer and displays hexadecimal equivalent
(alignment) —	Right-aligns output "%-s"
(sign display)	Forces + or − sign to be displayed. By default, only negative numbers are displayed with their sign "%+d",17 → +17
(padding, width) '{char}{num}	Left-pads an output with *{char}* (default is a space) in a total field of *{width}* characters "%' 5d",17.7 → _17.7 (_ = space) "%'*10s","hi" → ********hi
(precision) .{num}	Specifies number of decimal digits to right of decimal point or maximum string length. Rounds numbers appropriately if needed "%.2f",17.7 → 17.70 "%.3f",17.7346 → 17.735

In some cases, the format specifiers act like data type converters. The %c specifier converts an integer into its corresponding ASCII character, assuming it exists. (See Appendix 3.) The %s specifier will display a number as a string. Sometimes the conversions will not make much sense.

A numerical width specifier defines the minimum number of spaces allocated for display of a number or string. If the width specifier is too small, it will be overridden to allow display of the entire number or string.

A numerical precision specifier, preceded by a decimal point, defines how many digits to the right of the decimal point should be displayed for floating-point numbers. It is often used along with the width specifier, for example, 8.3. When significant digits are lost, the result is rounded rather than truncated. For example, an *n*.3 specifier applied to 17.4567 will display the number as 17.457. Numbers are right-padded with 0's as needed For example, an *n*.3 format specifier applied to 17.5 will display 17.500. When applied to a string, this value defines the maximum number of characters displayed.

Table 8.4 shows some escape sequences for inserting special characters such as a tab or characters that would otherwise be confused with other characters that have special meanings in PHP. Escape sequences are preceded by a backslash (the "escape character") or a percent sign within format strings.

Table 8.4 Escape characters

Escape character	Description
%%	Display percent sign
\n	Insert linefeed, ASCII base-10 value10
\r	Insert carriage return, ASCII base-10 value 13
\t	Insert tab, ASCII base-10 value 9
\$	Display dollar sign
\'	Display single quote
\"	Display double quote
\\	Display backslash character

Document 8.1 shows how to use some of these format specifiers and escape characters when writing files. Some of the specifiers, \r and \n in particular, will not work when printing to your screen because white space characters are ignored. Also, <br /> just looks like characters, not a line break, when printing to a file.

Document 8.1 (`formatTest.php`)

```php
<?php
  $out=fopen ("formatTest.txt", 'w');
  $a=67;
  $b=.000717;
  $c=-67;
  $d=83.17;
  fprintf ($out,
  "right justified, with sign and precision specifier\r\n");
  fprintf ($out, "%+12.6f\r\n",$a);
  fprintf ($out, "%+12.6f\r\n",$b);
  fprintf ($out, "%+12.6f\r\n",$c);
  fprintf ($out, "%+12.6f\r\n",$d);
  fprintf ($out, "display integer %d as character\r\n",$a);
  fprintf ($out, "%c\r\n",$a);
  fprintf ($out, "display number as string\r\n");
  fprintf ($out, "%s\r\n",$b);
  $line1="1/14/2013 17:3:1";
  $formatString="%'02d/%'02d/%4d %'02d:%'02d:%'02d";
  sscanf ($line1, "%i/%i/%i %d:%d:%d",
     $mon, $day, $yr, $hr, $min, $sec);
  fprintf ($out, "Display %s padded with 0's: ",$line1);
  fprintf ($out, $formatString, $mon, $day, $yr, $hr, $min, $sec);
  echo "Created output file.";
  fclose ($out);
?>
```

```
right justified, with sign and precision specifier
  +67.000000
   +0.000717
  -67.000000
  +83.170000
display integer 67 as character
C
display number as string
0.000717
Display 1/14/2013 17:3:1 padded with 0's: 01/14/2013 17:03:01
```

8.1.3 Reading Files

A text file opened in 'r' mode can be read one character at a time, one value at a time according to a specified format, a specified number of characters at a time, an entire line at a time, or in its entirety. Of these functions, you will use most often use `fgets ()` to read an entire line as a string and `fscanf ()` to read values according to a format.

(string) fgetc(*(resource) $fileHandle*)
   Returns a single character from the file pointed to by *$fileHandle*.

(string) fgets(*(resource) $fileHandle[, (int) $length]*)
   Returns a string of up to *$length* − 1 bytes from the file pointed to by *$fileHandle*, or to an end-of line or end-of-file mark. If the optional length parameter is not provided, fgets() will read to the end of the line or the end of the file, whichever comes first.

(array) = file(*(string) $filename*)
   Reads an entire file into array *$a*. Each line in the file becomes an array element.

(string) file_get_contents(*(string) $fileName*)
   Returns the entire contents of *$fileName* as a string.

(string) fread(*(resource) $fileHandle, (int) $length*)
   Reads up to *$length* bytes from *$fileHandle*, or to the end-of-file mark, and returns the result in a string.

(mixed) fscanf(*(resource) $fileHandle,*
              $formatString[, (mixed) $var...])
   Reads a line of text from a file and parses input according to a specified format string. Without optional *$var* parameters, the function creates create an array, the elements of which are determined by the format string. If *$var* parameters are included, fscanf() returns the number of parameters parsed. fscanf() will not read past the end-of-line mark if more format specifiers are provided than there are values in the line. Any white-space character in the format string matches any whitespace in the input stream. For example, a tab escape character (\t) in the format string can match a space character in the input stream.

   When reading a file of unknown length, it is often useful (in conditional loops, for example) to know when you have come to the end of a file.

(bool) feof(*(resource) $fileHandle*)
   Tests for the end-of-file marker on *$fileHandle*. Returns a value of true if the end-of-file marker is found and false otherwise.

It is sometimes useful to read an entire line with `fgets()` and then use `sscanf()` to read the string to extract values according to a format specifier string. In this case, the *(resource)* is not a file handle, but a string.

> *(mixed)* sscanf(*(string)* $line,
> $formatString[, *(mixed)* $var...])
> Reads $line and parses its contents according to the format specifier string. Without optional $var parameters, the output is used to create an array, the elements of which are determined by the format string. If $var parameters are included, sscanf() returns the number of parameters parsed. sscanf() will not read past the end of $line if more format specifiers are provided than there are values in the line.

Text files created on one system may cause problems when used on a different system. Table 8.5 shows three small text files viewed in an editor that displays file contents byte-by-byte.[1] The first file was created with Notepad on a Windows computer. The first byte in the Windows file contains hex value 48, the ASCII code value for "H". The third character from the end, 2E, is the hex code value for ".". Pressing the Enter key in Notepad terminates a line with a carriage return character (ASCII hex 0D) and a new line character (0A). These "non-printable" characters are represented by a period in this editor.

The second file was created with a text editor on a UNIX computer. Pressing the Enter key on a UNIX computer terminates a line with just a new line character. The third file is the Windows file saved without pressing the Enter key at the end of the line. For the first two files, the end-of-line characters are displayed as a period because they are non-printable characters. All three files contain an invisible "end-of-file" character.

```
fscanf($inFile,"%u,%f",$i,$x);
```

implies that a line in the input file contains an integer and a floating-point number, with a comma directly after the integer. The number of spaces between a comma and the following number does not matter. For example, it does not matter whether two values in a file are stored as

```
17,33.3
```

or (with a "tab" or multiple spaces)

```
17,          33.3
```

---

[1] I have used the freeware HxD editor (https://mh-nexus.de/en/hxd/).

Table 8.5 End-of-line characters in text files

```
Offset(h)  00 01 02 03 04 05 06 07 08 09 0A 0B 0C 0D 0E 0F
00000000   48 65 72 65 20 69 73 20 61 20 73 61 6D 70 6C 65   Here is a sample
00000010   20 74 65 78 74 20 66 69 6C 65 2E 0D 0A            text file...
```

"carriage return" character   "new line" character

Text file created on a Windows computer.

```
Offset(h)  00 01 02 03 04 05 06 07 08 09 0A 0B 0C 0D 0E 0F
00000000   48 65 72 65 20 69 73 20 61 20 55 4E 49 58 20 74   Here is a UNIX t
00000010   65 78 74 20 66 69 6C 65 2E 0A                     ext file..
```

"new line" character

Text file created on a UNIX computer.

```
Offset(h)  00 01 02 03 04 05 06 07 08 09 0A 0B 0C 0D 0E 0F
00000000   48 65 72 65 20 69 73 20 61 20 73 61 6D 70 6C 65   Here is a sample
00000010   20 74 65 78 74 20 66 69 6C 65 2E                  text file.
```

Windows text file saved without pressing Enter key at end of line.

The same format specifier used for output would display one integer and one floating-point number in default format, separated by a comma. With screen output, multiple spaces embedded in a format string are collapsed into a single space when they are displayed in a browser, but those spaces are retained if the output is sent to a file.

8.1.4   Creating and Writing Files

There are several functions for creating or adding to files opened in 'w' or 'a' mode. The format specifiers used to interpret the contents of files opened in 'r' mode are then used to specify how output values should be written to a file.

```
(int) fprintf( (resource) $fileHandle,
    (string) [format string]
    [ ,[one or more values to be displayed, comma-separated]] )
```

Writes a text string and optionally (but usually) one or more values according to the format conversion specifier string, to the file pointed to by *$fileHandle*. The format type specifiers should match the data type of the values.

fprintf() returns an integer value equal to the number of characters written to *$fileHandle*. Typically, the return value is not needed. The format string is usually specified as a string literal, but it may be assigned to a variable prior to calling fprintf(). This capability allows for script-controlled formatting.

(int) fwrite(*(resource) $fileHandle,*
(string) $s[, (int) $length])

Writes the contents of *$s* to the specified file or, optionally, the first *$length* characters of *$s*. (For the inverse operation, see file_get_contents().)

Including commas in the output format string makes it is easy to create comma-delimited files that can be opened directly in a spreadsheet. Typically, these files have a .csv extension. Lines written to a text file usually need to be terminated with \r\n, but a .csv file to be opened in a spreadsheet can be terminated with just \n.

Document 8.2 shows how to read a text file with a "header" line and some data consisting of three values separated by spaces or tabs, and create a second file where the data values are separated by commas, saved with a .csv extension for opening in a spreadsheet. There are a few subtleties in this code.

The header line is read with fgets() and echoed to your monitor. For the .csv file, the "Site Longitude Latitude" string should be written as "Site,Longitude,Latitude" so the data titles will go in their own columns. To reach this goal, the explode() function is used. (See Sect. 8.2, below, for more about array string-related functions.) In this case, by specifying a blank space as a separator between words, an array is created that contains Site, Longitude, and Latitude as its three elements. Then these three values can be written to a file, separated by commas.

In general, code for reading a file should not assume how many lines of data are in the file. The while()... loop takes care of this by looking for the end-of-file mark. However, suppose the last line of data in the file has an end-of-line mark, which would usually be the case. Then the code will still read the next "line" containing only an end-of-file mark. Because there is nothing there, the values for $site, $lon, $lat will not be changed and they would be echoed and written to the file as a duplicate set of data values. This can be avoided by using `fgets()` to read the line. Then the `strlen()` function is used to check the length of the line just read. It is possible that the data file might contain a blank line with only an end-of-line mark, and the assumption in this code is that such lines should be ignored. Hence, values are extracted from a line with `sscanf()` only if it is longer than three characters.

The top box shows the contents of `siteFile.txt` and the lower box shows `siteFile.csv` opened in a spreadsheet. As is typically the case for examples in this book, the input file is stored in the `\wamp\www` folder and the output file is written to the same folder.

Document 8.2 (`siteFile.php`)

```php
<?php
$in=fopen("siteFile.txt",'r');
$out=fopen("siteFile.csv",'w');
$header=fgets($in);
$h=array();
$h=explode(' ',$header);
echo $header."<br />";
fprintf($out,"%s,%s,%s",$h[0],$h[1],$h[2]);
while (!feof($in)) {
    $line=fgets($in);
    if (strlen($line)>3) {
        sscanf($line,"%s %f %f",$site,$lon,$lat);
        echo $site.",".$lon.",".$lat."<br />";
        fprintf($out,"%s,%f,%f\n",$site,$lon,$lat);
    }
}
fclose($in); fclose($out);
?>
```

```
Site Longitude Latitude
site1 -80.02 43.77
site2 133.55 -18.3
site3 0 90
```

	A	B	C
1	Site	Longitude	Latitude
2	site1	-80.02	43.77
3	site2	133.55	-18.3
4	site3	0	90

8.1.5   Examining Variables and Displaying Output

The basic function for displaying output on your screen is `printf()`. It is often used to display output that mirrors the format of data being read from a file. There are other functions for displaying the contents of variables that are especially useful during code development

(int) printf(*(string) $formatString*
                [, *(mixed) $var...*])

Displays a text string according to the format conversion specifier, to the open window. The returned value, the number of characters written, is usually not needed. *$formatString* is usually given as a string literal, but it may be assigned to a variable prior to calling printf(), a capability that allows for script-controlled output formatting.

(mixed) print_r(*(mixed) $expression*[, *(bool) $return*])
Displays information about *$expression*, often an array, in a readable format. Setting *$return* to true copies the output into a variable rather than displaying it.

(string) sprintf(*(string) $formatString*
              [, *(mixed) $var...*])
Returns a string built according to the format specifier string and optional arguments. *$formatString* is usually given as a string literal, but may be assigned to a variable prior to calling printf(), a capability that allows for script-controlled formatting.

(void) var_dump(*(mixed)* $expression[, *(mixed)* ...])
Displays information about one or more mixed expressions, including data types and values. Like print_r(), often used to display the contents of arrays.

(int) vprintf(*(string) $formatString, (array) $a*)
Displays a string built from the arguments of array *$a*, formatted according to the format string specifier.

Format specifiers for output have been given above in Table 8.3 Document 8.3 Shows some examples of examining variables and modifying how outputs are displayed.

Document 8.3 (displayVariables.php)

```php
<?php
$a=array("Monday","Tuesday");
$s="I'm supposed to be in class on %s and %s.<br />";
echo "Using printf() and sprint()<br />";
printf($s,$a[0],$a[1]);
echo sprintf($s,$a[0],$a[1]);
```

```
echo "Using print_f()<br />";
print_r($a);
echo "<br />Using var_dump()<br />";
var_dump($a);
echo "Using vprintf()<br />";
$b=array('A',17.7,TRUE);
vprintf("Building a string from an array: %s, %s, %u",$b);
?>
```

> Using printf() and sprint()
> I'm supposed to be in class on Monday and Tuesday.
> I'm supposed to be in class on Monday and Tuesday.
> Using print_f()
> Array ([0] => Monday [1] => Tuesday)
> Using var_dump()
>
> C:\wamp\www\displayVariables.php:10:
> array (size=2)
>   0 => string 'Monday' (length=6)
>   1 => string 'Tuesday' (length=7)
>
> Using vprintf()
> Building a string from an array: A, 17.7, 1

8.2   String Handling Functions

A great deal of programming involves working with strings of characters rather than numerical values. PHP includes a large number of functions for accessing, comparing, and manipulating strings.

> *(string)* chr(*(int)* $ASCII)
> *(int)* ord(*(string)* $s)
>   chr() and ord() are complementary functions. chr() returns the single-character string corresponding to the $ASCII value. ord() returns the base-10 ASCII value of the first character of $s. Appendix 3 contains a list of the 256 standard ASCII codes (base 10, 0-255) and their character representations for Windows computers. The lowercase alphabet starts at ASCII (base-10) 97 and the uppercase alphabet starts at ASCII 65. Nearly all ASCII characters can be displayed and printed by using their ASCII codes.

> *(mixed)* count_chars(*(string)* $s[, *(int)* $mode])
>   Counts the number of occurrences of every byte (with ASCII value 0...255) in $s and returns it according to $mode:

0 – the default value, returns an array with the byte value as its keys and the number of occurrences of every byte as its values.
1 – same as 0, but only byte values that actually occur in the string are listed.
2 – same as 0, but only byte values that do not occur are listed.
3 – a string containing all unique characters is returned.
4 – a string containing all characters not appearing in s is returned.

(string) ltrim (*(string)* $s[, (string)* $charlist])
(string) rtrim (*(string)* $s[, (string)* $charlist])
(string) trim (*(string)* $s[, (string)* $charlist])

Without the optional list of characters, strips whitespace characters from the left, right, or both left and right ends of a character string. A list of other characters to be trimmed can be specified with the optional $charlist$ parameter. These functions are useful for removing blank characters and return/linefeed characters from strings.

Document 8.4 gives examples using the trim and explode() functions.

Document 8.4 (splitString.php)

```php
<?php
$str="x x Mississippi x x";
echo ltrim($str, "x ") . "<br />";
echo rtrim($str, "x ") . "<br />";
echo trim($str, "x ") . "<br />";
$A=array();
$A=explode(' ',$str);
var_dump($A);
?>
```

```
Mississippi x x
x x Mississippi
Mississippi

C:\wamp\www\splitString.php:8:
array (size=5)
  0 => string 'x' (length=1)
  1 => string 'x' (length=1)
  2 => string 'Mississippi' (length=11)
  3 => string 'x' (length=1)
  4 => string 'x' (length=1)
```

(int) strcasecmp(*(string)* $s1, (string)* $s2)

Performs a case-insensitive comparison of $s1$ and $s2$. strcasecmp() returns 0 if $s1$ and $s2$ are identical, an integer less than 0 if $s1$ is less than $s2$ (in the lexical sense), and an integer value greater than 0 if $s1$ is greater than $s2$.

(int) strcmp(*(string) $s1, (string) $s2*)

   Performs a case-sensitive comparison of *$s1* and *$s2*. strcmp() returns 0 if *$s1* and *$s2* are identical, an integer value less than 0 if *$s1* is less than *$s2* (in the lexical sense), and an integer value greater than 0 if *$s1* is greater than *$s2*.

(string) stristr ((string) *$s*, (mixed) *$lookFor*)

   Returns all of *$s* from the first occurrence of *$lookFor* to the end of *$s*. If *$lookFor* is not found, returns false. The search is case-*in*sensitive. If *$lookFor* is not a string, it is converted to an integer and interpreted as the ordinal value of a character.

(int) strlen(*(string) $s*)*;*

   Returns the length (number of characters) in *$s*.

(int) strncasecmp(*(string) $s1, (string) $s2,*
                   (int) $n_char)

   Performs a case-insensitive comparison on the first *$n_char* characters of *$s1* and *$s2*. strncasecmp() returns 0 if *$s1* and *$s2* are identical, an integer value less than 0 if *$s1* is less than *$s2* (in the lexical sense), and an integer value greater than 0 if *$s1* is greater than *$s2*.

(int) strncmp(*(string) $s1, (string) $s2, (int) $n_char*)

   Performs a case-sensitive comparison on the first *$n_char* characters of *$s1* and *$s2*. strncmp() returns 0 if *$s1* and *$s2* are identical, an integer value less than 0 if *$s1* is less than *$s2* (in the lexical sense), and an integer value greater than 0 if *$s1* is greater than *$s2*.

(int) strpos(*(string) $s, (mixed) $lookFor*
                   [, *(int) $offset*])

   Returns the numeric position of the first occurrence of *$lookFor* in *$s*. If the optional $offset parameter is provided (default is 0), the search starts at the specified offset position rather than at the beginning of $s.

(string) strtolower(*(string) $s*)
(string) strtoupper(*(string) $s*)

   strtolower() converts the alphabetic characters in *$s* to lowercase. strtoupper() converts the alphabetic characters in *$s* to uppercase.

(string) substr(*(string) $s, (int) $start*
         [, *(int) $length*])

Returns *$length* characters of *$s*, starting at *$start*. The first character in a string is at position 0. If the length of *$s* is less than or equal to *$start* characters long, a warning message will be displayed. If *$length* is not specified, all the characters from position *$start* will be returned.

(int) substr_compare(*(string) $s1,*
   (string) $s2, (int) $offset [, *(int) $length*
  [, *(bool) $case_insensitivity*]]

Returns 0 if *$s1* is equal to *$s2*, <0 if *$1* is less than *$s2*, and >0 if *$s1* is greater than *$s2*. If the optional *$length* parameter is supplied (default is 0), the comparison uses *$length* characters of *$s1*. If *$length* is greater than or equal to the length of *$s1*, a warning message will be displayed. If the optional *$offset* parameter is specified (default is 0), the comparision starts at the specified offset from the beginning of *$s1*. If *$offset* is negative, the comparison starts counting from the end of the string. If the optional *$case_insensitivity* parameter is given a value of true (default is false), the comparison is case-insensitive.

(int) substr_count(*(string) $s, (string) $what*
  [, *(int) $offset* [, *$length*]])

Returns the number of times the string *$what* occurs in *$s*, optionally starting at *$offset* (default is 0) and including the next *$length* characters.

Document 8.5 shows output from some of the string functions.

Document 8.5 (stringCompare.php)

```php
<?php
echo strcasecmp("Dave","David")."<br />";        // returns -4
echo strcasecmp("DAVID","david")."<br />";        // returns 0
echo strcmp("david","DAVID")."<br />";            // returns 1
echo strcmp("Dave","David")."<br />";             // returns -1
echo strcmp("DAVID","david")."<br />";            // returns -1
echo strcmp("david","DAVID")."<br />";            // returns 1
$len = min(strlen("Dave"),strlen("David"));
echo strncasecmp("Dave","David",$len)."<br />"; // returns -4
echo strncmp("Dave","David", 3)."<br />";         // returns 0
```

```php
echo stristr ("David", 'v') . "<br />";        // returns vid
echo strpos ("David", 'i') . "<br />";         // returns 3
echo strtolower ("David") . "<br />";          // returns david
echo strtoupper ("David") . "<br />";          // returns DAVID
echo substr ("David", 3) . "<br />";           // returns id
echo substr_compare ("Mississippi", "Missouri", 0, 5) . "<br />";
                                               // returns -1
echo substr_count ("Mississippi", "ss");       // returns 2
?>
```

8.3 Array-Related Functions

Except for array_keys (), these functions apply to the kinds of arrays that are most relevant to the topics discussed in this book. (Look online for more information about functions to work with user-keyed arrays.)

(array) array_keys ((array) $a)
    Returns an array containing the keys of the $a array.

(mixed) array_pop ((array) $a)
    Treats $a as a stack and removes and returns the last (newest) element of $a, automatically shortening $a by one element. A value of NULL will be returned if the array is already empty. This functions resets the array pointer to the beginning of the array after the element is removed.
    Example:

```php
<?php
$stack = array ("orange", "banana", "apple", "lemon");
$fruit=array_pop ($stack);
print_r ($stack);
?>
```

Array ([0] => orange [1] => banana [2] => apple)

The variable $fruit will be assigned a value of *lemon*.

(int) array_push ((array) $a, (mixed) $var[, (mixed) ...])
    Treats $a as a stack, and pushes the passed variable(s) onto the end of $a. The length of $a increases by the number of variables pushed. Returns the number of elements in the array after the push.

Example:
```php
<?php
$stack = array("red", "grn");
$n = array_push($stack, "blu", "wh");
print_r($stack);
$stack[] = "blk";
printf("<br />%u<br />",$n);
print_r($stack);
printf("<br />%u<br />",sizeof($stack));
?>

Array ([0] => red[1] => grn[2] => blu[3] => wh)
4
Array ([0] => red[1] => grn[2] => bl
        [3] => wh[4] => blk)
5
```

The example shows how a new variable can be "pushed" onto the end of an array simply by assigning a new element to the array. Because this avoids whatever overhead might be associated with a function call, and it is shorter to write, it might make sense to use array_push() when you wish to add multiple new values at the same time.

(mixed) array_shift(*(array) $a*)

Removes the first element of *$a* (the "oldest" element) and returns it, then shortens *$a* by one element and moves everything down one position. Numerical keys will be reset to start at 0. Literal keys are unchanged. array_shift() is used to remove the oldest element from an array treated as a queue. It resets the array pointer to element 0 after it is used. Returns value removed or null if array is already empty.

Example:
```php
<?php
$queue = array("orange", "banana", "raspberry", "mango");
print_r($queue);
$rottenFruit = array_shift($queue);
echo '<br />' . $rottenFruit;
echo '<br />' . count($queue);
?>

Array ([0] => orange[1] => banana[2] => raspberry
[3] => mango)
orange
3
```

(number) array_sum(*(array)* $a)

Returns the sum of numerical values in an array, float or int.

(int) array_unshift(*(array)* $a),
                        (mixed) $var[, *(mixed)* ...])

Adds one or more elements to the "front" of the array (the "old" end). The entire list is inserted in order, so the first item in the list to be added is the first element in the modified array. Numerical keys are reset to start at 0. Literal keys are unchanged. Returns number of new elements added.

Example:

```php
<?php
$a = array("orange", "banana", "raspberry", "mango");
print_r($a);
array_unshift($a, "papaya", "mangosteen");
echo '<br />' . count($a) . '<br />';
print_r($a);
?>
```

```
Array ([0] => orange [1] => banana [2] => raspberry
   [3] => mango)
6
Array ([0] => papaya [1] => mangosteen [2] => orange
   [3] => banana [4] => raspberry [5] => mango)
```

(int) count(*(mixed)* $a[, $mode])
(int) sizeof(*(mixed)* $a[, $mode])

count() and sizeof() are equivalent. They return the number of elements in the array $a. If the value of $mode if it is not specified, its default value is 0. Setting $mode to 1 or to COUNT_RECURSIVE will count elements recursively in a multidimensional array.

The "recursive count" might not do what you expect. In a two-dimensional array with 5 "rows" and 4 "columns" (see Document 9.4, two-D.php), the recursive count option counts 5×4 rows, and then 5 rows again, and returns a value of 25. But, the number of elements in this two-dimensional array is not 25, but $25 - 5 = 20$.

(bool) sort(*(mixed)* $a[, $sort_flag])
(bool) usort(*(mixed)* $a, *(string)* compare_function_name)

sort() sorts an array in ascending order. The $sort_flag is optional:

SORT_REGULAR (default value) compares items without changing types

SORT_NUMERIC compares items as though they are numbers

SORT_STRING compares items as though they are strings

usort() sorts an array by calling a user-supplied function that compares two elements in an array. This can be used to sort an array in descending rather than the default ascending order.

sort () and usort() will work with keyed arrays, but the key information is lost.

8.4 Some Miscellaneous Functions and Constructs

break[*(int) $n*]

Exits the current conditional or count-controlled loop structure. An optional argument following break (not in parentheses) specifies the number of nested structures to be exited.

(bool) ctype_alpha(*(string) $s*)

Returns true if all the characters in *$s* (which could be just one character) are letters, a-z or A-Z, false otherwise. This function will not detect some letters in non-English languages that lie outside the a-z or A-Z range in the ASCII collating sequence.

die([*(string) $status*])   die([*(int) $status*])
exit([*(string) $status*])   exit([*(int) $status*])
Equivalent functions to exit a script. If the argument is a string, it will be printed on exit. An integer argument, in the range 0–254, is available for use as an exit error code in other applications, but it is not printed.

(array) explode(*(string) $delimiter, (string) $s,*
    [*(int) $n]*)
(string) implode(*(string) $delimiter, (array) $a*)

explode() returns an array of strings consisting of substrings of the string $s, in which the substrings are separated by the *$delimiter*. When *$n* is present, explode() will build array elements from the first $n values, with the last element containing the remainder of the string. The delimiter must match the file contents exactly. For example, a " " (single space) delimiter implies that the values are separated by one and only one space. In a file with numerical values, the elements of the returned array can be treated as numbers in subsequent code.

implode() returns all elements of *$a* as a concatenated string, with the elements separated by *$delimiter*.

(void) list(*(mixed) {arguments}*) = *$array*
Assigns contents of an array to several variables.

(string) number_format((float) $n[, (int) *$decimals*,]
[*(string) $character, (string) $separator*)])
Formats $n, as specified by one, two, or four parameters (not three parameters). With one parameter, a comma is placed between each group of thousands, with no decimal point or fractional digits. With two parameters, $n will include $decimals digits to the right of a decimal point, and with a comma between each group of thousands. With four parameters, $character will be used before the significant digits and $separator designates the character used to separate groups of thousands.
Example:

$n=17343789.936;
**echo number_format($n)."
";**
**echo number_format($n,2)."
";**
**echo number_format($n,2,',',' ')."
";**

17,343,790
17,343,789.94
17 343 789,94

(int) strtotime(*(string) $time*)
Converts a date and time description, in any common format, into the number of seconds from January 1, 1970, 00:00:00 GMT. For dates specified in xx/xx/xx or xx/xx/xxxx format, strtotime() assumes the U.S. custom of supplying dates as mm/dd/yy or mm/dd/yyyy. (The custom in many other countries is to specify dates as dd/mm/yy or dd/mm/yyyy.) strtotime() can be used to determine whether a date comes before or after another date.
Example:

echo strtotime("12/04/2007"); yields the result 1196744400

(int) strval(*(mixed) $var*)
Converts any scalar variable (not an array) into a string.

More examples:

Using this data file, `LatLon.dat`:

```
Site Lat Lon
brooks 40.01 -75.99
europe 50.5 5.3
south -30 88
farsouth -79 -167
```

Document 8.6 (`ExplodeArray.php`)

```php
<?php
  $a=file("LatLon.dat");
  var_dump($a);
  echo "<br />";
  for ($i=1; $i<sizeof($a); $i++) {
    list($s,$la,$lo)=explode(" ",$a[ $i] );
    echo $s.", ".$la.", ".$lo."<br />";
  }
  foreach ($a as $s) {
    list($site,$Lat,$Lon)=explode(" ",$s);
    echo $site.", ".$Lat.", ".$Lon."<br />";
  }
?>
```

```
array(5) { [0]=> string(14) "Site Lat Lon " [1]=> string(21) "brooks
40.01 -75.99 " [2]=> string(17) "europe 50.5 5.3 " [3]=> string(14)
"south -30 88 " [4]=> string(17) "farsouth -79 -167" }
brooks, 40.01, -75.99
europe, 50.5, 5.3
south, -30, 88
farsouth, -79, -167
Site, Lat, Lon
brooks, 40.01, -75.99
europe, 50.5, 5.3
south, -30, 88
farsouth, -79, -167
```

Document 8.7 (varDump.php)

```php
<?php
$a = array('david', 'apple', 'Xena', 'Sue');
$b = array();
list($b[0], $b[1], $b[2], $b[3]) = $a;
var_dump($b);
?>
```

```
array(4) {
[3] => string(3) "Sue" [2] => string(4) "Xena" [1] => string(5)
"apple"
[0] => string(5) "david" }
```

Document 8.8 (arrayList.php)

```php
<?php
$stuff = array('I', 'love', 'PHP.');
list($who, $do_what, $to_what) = $stuff;
echo "$who $do_what $to_what" . "<br />";
list($who, , $to_what) = $stuff;
echo "$who $to_what<br />";
$a = array('david', 'apple', 'Xena', 'Sue');
$b = array();
list($b[0], $b[1], $b[2], $b[3]) = $a;
var_dump($b);
echo "<br />Access with for... loop.<br />";
for ($i=0; $i<count($b); $i++) echo $b[$i] . "<br />";
echo "Access with foreach... loop.<br />";
foreach ($b as $key => $x) echo "a[" . $key . "] = " . $x . "<br /
>";
?>
```

> I love PHP.
> I PHP.
> array(4) { [3]=> string(3) "Sue" [2]=> string(4) "Xena"
> [1]=> string(5) "apple" [0]=> string(5) "david" }
> Access with for... loop.

```
I love PHP.
I PHP.
array(4) { [3]=> string(3) "Sue" [2]=> string(4) "Xena"
[1]=> string(5) "apple" [0]=> string(5) "david" }
Access with for... loop.
david
apple
Xena
Sue
Access with foreach... loop.
a[3] = Sue
a[2] = Xena
a[1] = apple
a[0] = david
```

Note that with scalar, named variables, as in

```
$stuff = array('I', 'love', 'PHP.');
list($who, $do_what, $to_what) = $stuff;
```

the result is what you expect. However, if the target of the list operation is an array, as in

```
$a = array('david', 'apple', 'Xena', 'Sue');
$b = array();
list($b[0], $b[1], $b[2], $b[3]) = $a;
```

then the output shows that the order of the keys is reversed. That is, the first key for the $b array is 3 and not 0. If you use a for... loop with the numerical indices, you can still get elements printed in the same left-to-right order in which they are defined in $a, but if you use a foreach... loop to display the contents of $b, the order will be reversed.

8.5 More Examples

8.5.1 Processing Wind Speed Data

A text file contains wind speed data:

```
1 1991 31
 3.2, 0.4, 3.8, 4.5, 3.3, 1.9, 1.6, 3.7, 0.8, 2.3, 2.8,
2.4, 2.5, 3.2, 4.1, 3.9, 5.0, 4.4, 4.4, 5.5, 3.0, 3.7,
2.2, 2.0
```

```
 2.6, 2.8, 2.3, 2.3, 1.2, 2.4, 3.1, 4.0, 3.6, 2.9, 6.0,
 4.4, 0.8, 3.8, 3.5, 4.5, 2.7, 3.4, 6.6, 5.2, 1.6, 1.2,
 2.3, 2.4
...
 2 1991 28
   4.6, 5.9, 3.1, 3.2, 4.5, 4.4, 3.9, 4.4, 7.5, 8.4,10.2,
 9.2, 8.1, 6.3, 3.1, 3.5, 2.2, 1.4, 0.4, 4.2, 5.4, 4.0,
 2.9, 1.7
 2.5,  2.3,  2.1,  1.5,  2.3,  4.1,  5.3,  6.0,  6.0,
 9.7,11.3,12.7,13.0,13.0,11.6, 9.9, 9.6, 8.7, 5.4, 5.1,
 5.3, 5.6, 4.4, 4.2
...
```

The three numbers in the first line of the file are the month, year, and number of days in the month. Then, for each day in the month, 24 hourly wind speeds are given (in units of miles per hour), separated by commas. Each set of 24 hourly values is on the same line of text in the file, even though each of those lines occupies three lines as displayed here (to fit the page). This pattern is repeated for all 12 months. Missing data are represented by a value of −1.

Write a PHP script that will read this file and count the number of missing values for each month. The script should display as output the number of each month (1–12) the year, and the number of missing values for that month. Write the results into a file and save it.

The calculations required for this problem are not difficult, but reading the data file correctly requires some care. Document 8.9 shows the code for this problem.

Document 8.9 (windspd.php)

```php
<?php
$inFile="windspd.dat";
$outFile="windspd.out";
$in = fopen($inFile, "r") or die("Can't open file.");
$out=fopen($outFile, "w");
while (!feof($in)) {
// Read one month, year, # of days.
  fscanf($in, "%u %u %u", $m, $y, $nDays);
  if (feof($in)) exit;
  echo $m . ', ' . $y . ', ' . $nDays . '<br />';
  $nMissing=0;
  for ($i=1; $i<=$nDays; $i++) {
```

```
  $hrly_string=fgets($in);
  $hrly=explode(',',$hrly_string);
   for ($hr=0; $hr<24; $hr++) {
    if ($hrly[$hr] == -1) $nMissing++;
   }
 }
  echo 'Number of missing hours this month is ' .
     $nMissing.'.<br />';
  fprintf($out,"%u, %u, %u\r\n",$m,$y,$nMissing);
}
echo "All done.<br />";
// fclose($in);
// fclose($out);
?>
```

1, 1991, 31 Number of missing hours this month is 22. 2, 1991, 28 Number of missing hours this month is 0. All done
…Screen display
1, 1991, 23 2, 1991, 0
…Output file, windspd.out

As in previous examples, the input file required by Document 8.9, windspd.dat, is stored in the PHP document folder, and the output file is written to the same directory. You could create separate directories just for output files created by PHP scripts, or for a particular project. The output shown here is for a short version of this file, with data for only two months.

It is possible to write a format string with 24 %f format specifiers to read all 24 hourly values directly into an array, using fscanf(). But, it is easier to read the entire line into a string and use explode() to put the comma-separated hourly values in an array.

It is often the case that code to read data from a data file should not assume ahead of time how many values are in the file. Thus, a conditional loop is most often the appropriate approach. The feof() function is used to test for an end-of-file mark that, when found, uses exit to close all open files and terminate the program. If additional processing is required after reaching the end of the file, the alternative is to use break rather than exit; and then fclose().

```
while (!feof($in)) {
// Read one month, year, # of days.
    fscanf($in,"%u %u %u",$m,$y,$nDays);
    if (feof($in)) break;
    …
}
echo "All done.<br />";
fclose($in);
fclose($out);
// possibly more code here…
```

8.5.2   Calculating the Mass of Solid Objects

Write an HTML document that allows a user to select a solid object shape and enter its dimensions and the material from which it is made. The choices could be a cube, a rectangular block, a cylinder, or a sphere. You could choose a number of possible materials—air, gold, water, etc. Then call a PHP application that will find the mass of the object by calculating its volume based on the specified shape and the density of the material as retrieved from a data file.

In a common type of computing problem, data relevant to certain calculations are stored in a file and accessed as needed. In this application, there will be two data files. One contains densities for several materials. The other will contain *code* that can be accessed as needed to calculate the volume. Document 8.10a shows the HTML interface for this problem. The possible shapes and materials are placed in < select> lists.

Document 8.10a (getMass.htm)

```
<html>
<head>
<title>Calculate mass</title>
</head>
<body>
<form method="post" action="getMass.php">
Enter length: <input type="text" name="L" value="3" /><br />
Enter width: <input type="text" name="W" value="2" /><br />
Enter height: <input type="text" name="H" value="10" /><br/>
Enter radius: <input type="text" name="R" value="3" /><br />
   <select name="shapes" size="10">
      <option value="cube">cube</option>
      <option value="cylinder">cylinder</option>
      <option value="block">rectangular block</option>
      <option value="sphere">sphere</option>
   </select>
   <select name="material" size="10">
      <option value="air">air</option>
      <option value="aluminum">aluminum</option>
      <option value="gold">gold</option>
      <option value="oxygen">oxygen</option>
      <option value="silver">silver</option>
      <option value="water">water</option>
   </select><br />
 <input type="submit" value="Click to get density.">
```

```
</form>
</body>
</html>
```

Note that the `value` attribute of the `<option>` tag can be, but does not have to be, the same as the text for the option. For the "rectangular block" shape, `value` is assigned as a single word (`block`), which will look like a single string literal value when it is used later in the PHP application.

For all but the simplest problems, it is never a good idea to try to write an entire application all at once. In this case, the HTML document helps to organize the problem by organizing all the required inputs. Once you are happy with Document 8.10a, then write a single-line PHP application that uses `print_r()` to display what is posted to the `$_POST` array:

Enter length:	3
Enter width:	2
Enter height:	10
Enter radius:	3

cube		air	
cylinder		aluminum	
rectangular block		gold	
sphere		oxygen	
		silver	
		water	

Click to get mass.

```
<?php
  print_r($_POST);
?>
```

This code will display something like this:

Array ([L] => 3 [W] => 2 [H] => 10 [R] => 3 [shapes] => cylinder [material] => silver)

and the results show that, really without any programming effort on your part, all the input data have been passed to the PHP application.

Once you are convinced that the inputs are successfully passed to PHP, then the calculations can be done. The first step is to create a data file containing materials and their densities:

```
(density.dat)
material density (kg/m^3)
water 1000
aluminum 2739
gold 19320
silver 10429
oxygen 1.429
air 1.205
```

The header line is optional, but it is always a good idea to describe the contents of a data file, including, in this case, the physical units in which the densities should be supplied.

The next step is less obvious. Although it is certainly possible to "hard code" volume calculations for each allowed shape, a more interesting solution is to create a second data file that contains PHP code for calculating the volume of each shape:

```
(volume.dat)
shape volume
cube $L*$L*$L
sphere 4./3.*M_PI*$R*$R*$R
cylinder M_PI*$R*$R*$L
block $L*$W*$H
```

The code string for each allowed shape assumes specific variable names for the dimensions—L, $W, $H, and $R—which must correspond to the names defined in 8.10a.

Continue building the PHP application like this:

```php
<?php
print_r($_POST);
$material=$_POST["material"];
$shape=$_POST["shapes"];
$L=$_POST["L"];
$W=$_POST["W"];
$H=$_POST["H"];
$R=$_POST["R"];
echo "<br />" . $material . ", " . $shape . "<br />";
?>
```

This code will display:

Array ([L] => 1 [W] => 1 [H] => 1 [R] => 3 [shapes] => cube [material] => oxygen)
oxygen, cube

Now it is clear that the PHP application is properly receiving the inputs passed from Document 8.10a and has stored them in local variables. (You could also echo the values of $L, $W, $H, and $R if you like.) In Document 8.10a, the fields were given the names L, W, H, and R, but this would not need to be the case. All that is important for the PHP application is to give the variables the same names used in the volume.dat file.

Document 8.10b gives the entire PHP code for this problem. This code should be written in three sections: first, the definition of the variables as shown above, then the code to search for the material in its data file, and finally the code to do the mass calculation.

Document 8.10b (getMass.php)

```php
<?php
print_r($_POST);
//exit;
$material=$_POST["material"];
$shape=$_POST["shapes"];
//exit;
$L=$_POST["L"];
$W=$_POST["W"];
$H=$_POST["H"];
$R=$_POST["R"];
echo "<br />" . $material . ", " . $shape . "<br />";
$materialFile=fopen("density.dat","r");
$shapeFile=fopen("volume.dat","r");
// Read materials file.
$found=false;
$line=fgets($materialFile);
while ((!feof($materialFile)) && (!$found)) {
  $values=fscanf($materialFile,"%s %f",$m,$d);
  if (strcasecmp($material,$m) == 0) {
    echo "density = ".$d." kg/m^3<br />";
    $found=true;
  }
}
// Read volume file.
$found=false;
$line=fgets($shapeFile);
while ((!feof($shapeFile)) && (!$found)) {
  $values=fscanf($shapeFile,"%s %s",$s,$v);
  if (strcasecmp($shape,$s) == 0) {
    echo $shape . ", " . $v . "<br />";
    $found=true;
  }
}
fclose($materialFile);
fclose($shapeFile);
$vv=$v . "*$d";
echo $vv . "<br />";
echo "Mass = " .eval("return round($vv,3);") . " kg<br />";
?>
```

In the interests of demonstrating just the essential code needed to solve this problem, Document 8.10b does not include code to determine whether the supplied material is included in the file of materials or whether there is a match with the shape supplied, but this would not be difficult to do.

The not-so-obvious and rather clever part of this application is included in the two shaded lines of code in Document 8.10b:

```
$vv=$v . "*$d";
echo "Mass = " . eval("return round($vv,3);") . "<br />";
```

The first of these lines appends `"*$d"` to the volume calculation string—mass equals volume times density. This string now looks like "legal" PHP code, for example:

```
M_PI* $R* $R* $L* $d
```

(You could `echo` the value of `$vv` if you want to see what it contains.) The next line of code "executes" this statement, using the `eval()` construct (it looks like a function, but is not). The `return` keyword is required to get back the numerical result, and the `round()` function is applied to the calculation to remove extraneous digits from the output.

The obvious advantage of this approach is that you can add new materials and shapes without altering the PHP code, assuming that, at most, four variables—length, width, height, and radius—will be sufficient to describe all dimensions needed for the volume calculations. For more complicated shapes, it might be necessary to add new variables or apply different interpretations to existing variables.

8.5.3 Processing .bmp Image Files

Image files come in a variety of formats—jpeg, gif, bmp, etc. You would normally consider these to be "binary" files rather than the text files dealt with in the rest of this chapter. However, although the code can be complicated, all files are "text" files in the sense that they can be dealt with one byte at a time. Although PHP isn't intended as an image-processing language, it is nonetheless possible to use it in this way.

Of the popular image files, bitmap files are conceptually the simplest. A bitmap file (with a `.bmp` extension) consists of two sections—an information section that contains information about the structure of the file, and the image section itself. For 24-bit color images, the image is represented as a series of three bytes per pixel, with each byte containing values for the red, green, and blue color "guns" (always in that RGB order) that are used to produce the pixel. This arrangement allows for $256 \times 256 \times 256 = 16,777,216$ possible colors.

Because each pixel in a 24-bit color image requires three color bytes to define, bitmap images can be very large. In principle, .bmp files can be compressed, but for this programming exercise there is no point in doing that because a compressed bitmap file would need to be uncompressed back to its original state before it can be analyzed.

The structure of .bmp files makes them very easy to analyze with PHP by considering each byte in the file as a "character." Here are the details about the contents of each section in a .bmp file:

Header record

The header consists of 14 8-bit bytes:

Table 8.6 Contents of header record

Byte Position (offset index + 1)	Contents
1-2	Image type field (BM)
3-6	File size, bytes
7-10	Not used
11-14	Offset to image data, bytes

Image information record

The image information record consists of 40 bytes.

Table 8.7 Contents of file information record

Byte Position (offset index + 1)	Contents
1-4	Header size, in bytes
5-8	Width of image, bytes
9-12	Height of image, bytes
13-14	Number of color planes
15-16	Bits per pixel
17-20	Compression type (0 for uncompressed 24-bit color images)
21-24	Image size, bytes
25-28	X-resolution
29-32	Y-resolution
33-36	Number of colors
37-40	Important colors

Image data

The image pixels are stored "upside down." That is, the first pixel in the image section represents the lower left-hand corner of the image as it is viewed. The pixels proceed from left to right, and row-by-row to the top of the i[mage. If required, each row in the image is padded on the right end with extra bytes so that each row contains a multiple of 4 bytes. The value of these bytes is not specified, but they are not necessarily filled with zeros.

As an example of extracting from these records the values needed to work with a .bmp image, consider this 24-bit color image of a male wild turkey, in a .bmp file format. (It is printed here in black and white, of course.) Document 8.11 reads the header and image information records and interprets the values according to

Tables 8.6 and 8.7. If you want to try this code, you will of course need to use your own .bmp image. Any photo processing utility should let you save an image in .bmp format, or you can create your own bitmap image with a drawing utility such as Windows' Paint program.

Document 8.11 (bmp_info.php)

```php
<?php
$inFile="turkey.bmp";
// Get the size of this file.
echo "File size: " . filesize($inFile) . "<br />";
$in=fopen($inFile, 'r');
$c=array(); // Read header.
for ($i=0; $i<14; $i++) {
    $c[$i]=ord(fgetc($in));
    echo $c[$i] . " ";
}
echo "<br />";
// Calculate file size.
$size=$c[5]*16777216+$c[4]*65536+$c[3]*256+$c[2];
echo "File size = ".$size." bytes.<br />";
// Find offset to start of image.
$offset=$c[10];
echo "Offset to start of image = ".$offset."<br />";
// Read image information record.
for ($i=0; $i<40; $i++) {
    $c[$i]=ord(fgetc($in));
    echo $c[$i] . " ";
}
```

```
echo "<br />";
// Get # of rows and columns.
$cols=$c[7] * 16777216+$c[6] * 65536+$c[5] * 256+$c[4] ;
$rows=$c[11] * 16777216+$c[10] * 65536+$c[9] * 256+$c[8] ;
echo "This image has ".$rows." rows and ".$cols."
  columns.<br />";
$nPlanes=$c[ 13] * 256+$c[ 12] ; // Get some other information.
echo "# of color planes = ".$nPlanes."<br />";
$bitsPerPixel=$c[ 15] * 256+$c[ 14] ;
echo "Bits per pixel = ".$bitsPerPixel."<br />";
$compressionType=$c[ 19] * 16777216+$c[ 18] * 65536+$c[ 17] * 256+
  $c[16] ;
echo "Compression type = ".$compressionType."<br />";
$imageSize=$c[23] * 16777216+$c[22] * 65536+$c[21] * 256+$c[20] ;
echo "Image size = ".$imageSize."<br />";
$Xresolution=$c[27] * 16777216+$c[26] * 65536+$c[25] * 256+$c[24] ;
echo "X-resolution = ".$Xresolution."<br />";
$Yresolution=$c[31] * 16777216+$c[30] * 65536+$c[29] * 256+$c[28] ;
echo "Y-resolution = ".$Yresolution."<br />";
$nColors=$c[35] * 16777216+$c[34] * 65536+$c[33] * 256+$c
[32] ;
echo "number of colors = ".$nColors."<br />";
$importantColors=$c[39] * 16777216+$c[38] * 65536+$c[37] * 256+$c
[36] ;
echo "important colors = ".
$importantColors."<br />";
// Close the file.
fclose($in) ;
?>
```

The shaded line of code in Document 8.11 shows how to use `fgetc()` to read a single character and then to use `ord()` to convert that character into its base-10 integer value.

As indicated in Table 8.6, the first two bytes, $c[0] and $c[1], contain ASCII values 66 and 77, corresponding to the uppercase letters B and M, which identify this as a bitmap file. Bytes $c[2] through $c[5] contain the file

```
File size: 36882
66 77 18 144 0 0 0 0 0 54 0 0
File size (from header) = 36882 bytes.
Offset to start of image = 54
40 0 0 0 131 0 0 0 93 0 0 0 1 0 24 0 0 0 0 0
220 143 0 0 19 11 0 0 19 11 0 0 0 0 0 0 0 0
0 0
This image has 93 rows and 131 columns.
# of color planes = 1
Bits per pixel = 24
Compression type = 0
Image size = 36828
X-resolution = 2835
Y-resolution = 2835
number of colors = 0
important colors = 0
```

size, represented as a 32-bit integer. This integer is stored in four bytes, in low-to-high (reversed) order, and the base-10 integer is extracted like this:

```
file size = $c[ 2] +256* $c[3] +65536*
$c[4] +16777216* $c[5]
```

(= 18 + 144•256 + 0 + 0 = 36882)

This value is the same as the value obtained from `filesize($inFile)`.

The next four bytes can be ignored. The last four bytes give the offset to the start of the image data, also stored in four reverse-order bytes even though for 24-bit images only the first (lowest order) byte will have a value other than 0:

Offset to image =

`$c[10] +256* $c[11] +65536* $c[12] +16777216* $c[13]` = 54

This value is as expected because 14 + 40, the number of bytes in the header and image information records, equals 54.

The image information record shows that this image is 93 pixels high and 131 pixels wide. The only compression type of interest in this discussion is 0, for an uncompressed image.

There are three bytes (24 bits) per color: 3•131=393 color bytes per row. If required, image rows are padded so the number of bytes in each row is evenly divisible by 4. So with 3 padding bytes there are 396 bytes per row. Hence the image size is 396•93=36,828, equal to the file size minus 54 bytes for the header and image information records. The X- and Y-resolutions are given in the somewhat puzzling units of pixels per meter, which might be useful for deciding how to display this image on a computer monitor. For 24-bit color images, the number of colors is not specified here, and all colors are "important," so the number of important colors can be ignored.

With this information, it is now possible to read and interpret the image section of a `.bmp` file. As a test of whether images are being interpreted properly, a reasonable goal is to read the image, convert the pixels to their grayscale equivalent, and create a new `.bmp` file containing this grayscale image. This conversion is done by averaging the red, green, and blue values for each pixel and replacing each of those values with that average value. With this approach, the format of the grayscale image file will be exactly the same as the 24-bit color image.

Document 8.12 shows how to read a `.bmp` file.

Document 8.12 (`bmp_read.php`)

```php
<?php
$inFile="turkey.bmp";
echo filesize($inFile) . "<br />";
$in=fopen($inFile, 'r');
// Read header.
```

```php
$ch=array();
for ($i=0; $i<14; $i++) {
    $ch[$i]=ord(fgetc($in));
    echo $ch[$i]." ";
}
echo "<br />";
//$offset=$ch[10];
for ($i=0; $i<40; $i++) {
    $ch[$i]=ord(fgetc($in));
    echo $ch[$i]." ";
}
echo "<br />";
$cols=$ch[5]*256+$ch[4]; $bytes=3*$cols;
// Each row is padded to contain a multiple of 4 bytes.
$nPad=4-$bytes%4;
echo "# of pad bytes = ".$nPad."<br />";
$rows=$ch[9]*256+$ch[8];
echo "rows and columns: ".$rows." ".$cols."<br />";
// Read image.
for ($r=1; $r<=$rows; $r++) {
    for ($c=1; $c<=$cols; $c++) {
        for ($i=0; $i<=2; $i++) {
            $ch[$i]=fgetc($in); echo ord($ch[$i]);
        }
        echo " ";
    }
    // Read pad bytes at end of line.
    for ($p=1; $p<=$nPad; $p++) {
        $pad=fgetc($in); echo "pad";
    }
    echo "<br />";
}
fclose($in);
?>
```

36882

66 77 18 144 0 0 0 0 0 0 54 0 0 0

40 0 0 0 131 0 0 0 93 0 0 0 1 0 24 0 0 0 0 0 220 143 0 0 19 11 0 0 19 11 0 0 0 0 0 0 0 0 0
0

# of pad bytes = 3

rows and columns: 93 131

488478 488478 488478 659993 75109103 639791 85119113 599387 609488 78110105
92124119 80112107 83113108 649489 88118113 83113108 86116111 97129124
669893 75103103 679393 729597 668789 8199106 607885 8096103 95111117 769298
99118121 80100101 82104102 749896 436864 729793 729793 729995 709591
98125121 92117113 618884 739894 649187 85110106 77104100 689389 588680
659086 7510397 84109105 81109103 508172 599382 6710190 7611099 77111100
629685 619584 80116104 6810492 478573 569482 84122110 81119107 6610694
6110189 6710593 6710593 6710593 6610191 85119109 77108101 7610399 114138138
138159161 126145150 115133140 110125134 146161170 124139148 137154163
101120128 112134140 130152158 80108109 92128122 73113102 115155144
74114103 79119108 76116105 6010089 101141130 78118107 122162151 121160152
90130119 88127119 97137126 101140132 101140132 80122111 74118105 107152136
122167151 88131116 100141126 115156141 86124112 101139127 106143133
111148138 81121110 539584 82123115 84127118 84129120 106146141 142171176
126149157 92118124 87116120 104135136 87122118 6710397 74114103 569684
87127115 7011196 347560 529176 79118103 padpadpad
1392685 1392685 1392685 1392685 1392685 1392685 1392685 1392685 1392685
1392685 1392685 1392685 1392685 1392685 1392685 1392685 1392685 1392685
1392685 1392685 1392685 1392685 1392685 1392685 1392685 1392685 1392685
1392685 1392685 1392685 1392685 1392685 1392685 1392685 1392685 1392685
1392685 1392685 1392685 1392685 1392685 1392685 1392685 1392685 1392685
1392685 1392685 1392685 1392685 1392685 1392685 1392685 1392685 1392685
1392685 1392685 1392685 1392685 1392685 1392685 1392685 1392685 1392685
1392685 1392685 1392685 1392685 1392685 1392685 1392685 1392685 1392685
1392685 1392685 1392685 1392685 1392685 1392685 1392685 1392685 1392685
1392685 1392685 1392685 1392685 1392685 1392685 1392685 1392685 1392685
1392685 1392685 1392685 1392685 1392685 1392685 1392685 1392685 1392685
1392685 1392685 1392685 1392685 1392685 1392685 1392685 1392685 1392685
1392685 1392685 1392685 1392685 1392685 1392685 1392685 1392685 1392685
1392685 1392685 1392685 1392685 1392685 padpadpad

Document 8.13 is a version of Document 8.12 that reads the original file and modifies the color values to create a grayscale version of the image.

Document 8.13 (bmp_grayscale.php)

```php
<?php
$inFile="turkey.bmp";
$outFile="turkey_grayscale.bmp";
echo filesize($inFile)."<br />";
$in=fopen($inFile,'r');
$out=fopen($outFile,'w');
// Read header.
$ch=array();
for ($i=0; $i<14; $i++) {
  //$ch[$i]=ord(fgetc($in));
  //echo $ch[$i]." ";
  //fwrite($out,chr($ch[$i]),1);
  fwrite($out,fgetc($in));
}
echo "<br />";
//$offset=$ch[10];
for ($i=0; $i<40; $i++) {
  $ch[$i]=ord(fgetc($in));
  echo $ch[$i]." ";
  fwrite($out,chr($ch[$i]),1);
}
echo "<br />";
$bytes=3*$cols;
$nPad=4-$bytes%4; // Each row padded to contain a multiple of
4 bytes.
echo "# of pad bytes = ".$nPad."<br />";
$rows=$ch[ 9]*256+$ch[8];
echo "rows and columns: ".$rows." ".$cols."<br />";
// Read image.
for ($r=1; $r<=$rows; $r++) {
  for ($c=1; $c<=$cols; $c++) {
    for ($i=0; $i<=2; $i++) {
      $ch[$i]=fgetc($in);
    }
    $avg=(ord($ch[0])+ord($ch[1])+ord($ch[2]))/3;
    fwrite($out,chr($avg),1); fwrite($out,chr($avg),1);
    fwrite($out,chr($avg),1);
  }
```

```
   // Read pad bytes at end of line.
   for ($p=1; $p<=$nPad; $p++) {
     $pad=fgetc($in);
     fwrite($out,$pad);
   }
}
fclose($in);
fclose($out);
echo "A grayscale file has been created.<br />";
?>
```

All that is required to create a new .bmp file is to write every character that is read from the original file into a new file. If no changes are made in these characters, then the new file is a copy of the original file. In this case, the color values will be changed. The resulting grayscale image created by Document 8.13 is not shown here because it looks just like the original image of the turkey shown above, which was converted to grayscale for printing.

The second block of shaded in Document 8.13 shows that it is not necessary to convert the character to its decimal value, using the ord() function, unless these values are actually needed for something. In this case, the character is read from the original file and written to the new file in a single statement, using the fwrite() function.

The third block of highlighted text shows the code used to replace the color settings with their average grayscale settings before writing them to the new file. In this case, it is necessary to convert the characters to base-10 values in order to compute their average.

This simple example of how to manipulate the contents of a .bmp file opens the door to many possibilities for processing images. The contrast in images can be stretched or compressed, linearly or nonlinearly. Starting with a grayscale image, it is easy to generate false-color images based on the grayscale values. All these possibilities are applicable to medical and other kinds of X-ray imaging, for example.

A less obvious application is to use .bmp files to transmit text messages. In fact, although it seems like a silly use of the .bmp file format, there is no reason why a .bmp file can't contain *just* text in the bytes that assign RGB color settings, rather than "real" color values. "Image processing" then becomes simply a matter of appropriately interpreting the file contents as text.

Because of the structure of .bmp files, it is easy to embed hidden" text within an image. Even in a relatively small bitmap image, there are places to hide text where it will be virtually undetectable in the image itself. Individual color values can be replaced with ASCII character codes that still look like legitimate color settings. Even better, the padding bytes that may be added to the end of each row of an image (depending on its width, to make each row a multiple of four bytes) are completely invisible within the image. Those bytes are not needed for anything and they can be used to store text. Sizing an image so each row will require three padding bytes provides the most "invisible" space in the image.

Within the 14-byte image header record, there are four unused bytes that can be used to hold the location—perhaps the row and column—of the start of the text message. This information could also be included in the padding bytes for the first (bottom) row of the image, for example. While not actually encrypted, a small text message embedded within a large .bmp file will be very hard to find unless you know what you are looking for and where to look for it.

Document 8.14 writes the message "Please don't eat me!" into the padding bytes, starting at row 9; this value is written into the unused seventh byte of the header record.

Document 8.14 (bmp_hidetext.php)

```php
<?php
$inFile="turkey.bmp";
$outFile="turkey_text.bmp";
echo filesize($inFile)."<br />";
$in=fopen($inFile,'r');
$out=fopen($outFile,'w');
$hiddenText="Please don' t eat me!";
$startRow=9;
// Read header.
$ch=array();
for ($i=0; $i<14; $i++) {
  $ch[$i]=ord(fgetc($in));
  echo $ch[$i]." ";
  // Write starting row for text here, in unused byte.
  if ($i==6) fwrite($out,chr($startRow),1);
  else fwrite($out,chr($ch[$i]),1);
}
```

```
echo "<br />";
for ($i=0; $i<40; $i++) {
  $ch[$i] =ord(fgetc($in));
  echo $ch[$i] ." ";
  fwrite($out,chr($ch[$i]),1);
}
echo "<br />";
$cols=$ch[7] * 16777216+$ch[6] * 65536+$ch[5] * 256+$ch[4];
$bytes=3*$cols;
$nPad=4-$bytes%4; // Each row padded to contain a multiple
of 4 bytes.
echo "# of pad bytes = ".$nPad."<br />";
$rows=$ch[11] * 16777216+$ch[10] * 65536+$ch[9] * 256+$ch[8];
echo "rows and columns: ".$rows." ".$cols."<br />";
// Read image.
$K=strlen($hiddenText);
$knt=0;
for ($r=1; $r<=$rows; $r++) {
  for ($c=1; $c<=$cols; $c++) {
    for ($i=0; $i<=2; $i++) {
      $ch[$i] =fgetc($in);
    }
    $avg=(ord($ch[0] )+ord($ch[1] )+ord($ch[2] ))/3;
    fwrite($out,chr($avg),1);
    fwrite($out,chr($avg),1);
    fwrite($out,chr($avg),1);
  }
  // Read pad bytes at end of line.
  for ($p=1; $p<=$nPad; $p++) {
   $pad=fgetc($in);
   if (($r>=$startRow) && ($knt<$K)) {
    // Write text into pad bytes.
    fwrite($out,substr($hiddenText,$knt,1),1);
    $knt++;
   }
   else fwrite($out,$pad,1);
  }
}
fclose($in);
fclose($out);
echo "A grayscale file has been created.<br />";
?>
```

Using turkey_text.bmp as the input file, the output from Document 8.11, for row 9, looks like this:

```
949494 949494 949494 939393 808080 757575 898989 787878 848484 929292 939393
108108108 929292 104104104 898989 999999 949494 939393 939393 898989 868686
100100100 777777 686868 797979 848484 616161 797979 828282 636363 606060
515151 737373 666666 666666 505050 707070 555555 383838 585858 575757 505050
303030 353535 292929 111111 222 222 444 111 666 222222 232323 161616 161616
141414 888 111111 777 777 555 181818 111 111 111 111 111 111 222 666 151515
161616 343434 828282 100100100 696969 333 444 666 000 171717 343434 838383
133133133 102102102 105105105 145145145 102102102 123123123 110110110
117117117 132132132 120120120 153153153 115115115 137137137 120120120
138138138 129129129 129129129 122122122 878787 969696 989898 989898
115115115 112112112 929292 989898 979797 979797 123123123 114114114
120120120 106106106 124124124 120120120 909090 808080 959595 109109109
979797 888888 888888 797979 858585 979797 747474 119119119 939393 113113113
Ple
```

The first three characters in the text message ("Ple") are found in the three padding bytes at the end of row 9. Remember that this text doesn't affect the image in *any* way. This code doesn't retrieve the location of the first row containing the text message from the header record, to tell you where to start looking for the text message, but it could easily do that.

8.5.4 Converting Strings Containing Dates and Times to Numerical Values

It is occasionally useful to be able to convert strings containing date and time information into numerical values. For example, it might be desired to know the elapsed time between two calendar dates and times. These sorts of calculations are done by converting dates and times back and forth between a large list of possible date/time formats and the UNIX timestamp, which is the (integer) number of seconds since January 1, 1970 00:00:00 UTC—an arbitrarily chosen but universally used "time zero" value. This approach, which might seem cumbersome, is useful because it is based on very efficient integer arithmetic and it allows programmers to bypass the complexities inherent in the calendar system.

Document 8.15 shows some examples of these conversions, using the date_create(), date_format(), and strtotime() functions. You can find a more complete description of the many recognized input formats for strtotime() online.

Document 8.15 (DateTimeConversions.php)

```php
<?php
echo "seconds from 1/1/1970 to now: ";
# converts time from 1/1/1970 (UNIX time stamp) to current
echo strtotime("now")."<br />";
$date=date_create();
echo date_format($date, "U = Y-m-d H:i:s")." UTC <br />";
$Dec10=strtotime("10 December 2016");
echo "December 10, 2016".$Dec10."<br />";
$Dec11=strtotime("11 December 2016");
echo "December 11, 2016".$Dec11."<br />";
echo "difference = ".($Dec11-$Dec10)." seconds<br />";
echo "one day from today: ".strtotime("+1 day")."<br />";
echo "one week, 2 days, 12 hours, 52 seconds from today: ".
strtotime("+1 week 2 days 4 hours 2 seconds")."<br />";
echo "next Monday: ".strtotime("next Thursday")."<br />";;
echo "last Saturday: ".strtotime("last Monday")."<br />";
?>
```

```
seconds from 1/1/1970 to now: 1481222240
1481222240 = 2016-12-08 18:37:20 UTC
December 10, 20161481328000
December 11, 20161481414400
difference = 86400 seconds
one day from today: 1481308640
one week, 2 days, 12 hours, 52 seconds from today: 1482014242
next Monday: 1481760000
last Saturday: 1480896000
```

PHP Graphics

9

This chapter introduces the PHP GD graphics library. Applications are developed for creating pie charts, bar graphs, and line graphs suitable for displaying scientific and engineering data.

9.1 Introduction

GD is a library of graphics functions usable directly from PHP scripts (and several other programming languages). This library is included as part of current PHP downloads and is activated by default when PHP is installed. Like PHP itself, GD graphics is supported by an active online user community. It is widely used in web applications for dynamically creating images and it is a natural choice for creating science and engineering graphing applications to augment PHP's computational and data processing capabilities.

GD includes functions for drawing text, lines, and shapes. These functions work at the pixel level. To draw a line, for example, you must supply the starting and ending coordinates and line width, in pixel units. It requires careful planning and sometimes a lot of code to use these functions to build graphics applications for displaying data.

GD will create images in several popular graphics formats, including GIF, JPG, and PNG. (The applications in this chapter will use GIF graphics.) A typical scientific and engineering application for using GD with PHP is to access data on a server and create graphic output "on the fly" that can then be displayed by your browser. It is also easy to save that output image as a separate file and, in fact, you can do both from within the same application. Saved files can be accessed with any photo display or processing application.

This chapter presents complete HTML/PHP applications for pie charts, bar graphs, and line graphs. In each case, tradeoffs have been made between simplicity and the ability to customize aspects of the final result.

© Springer International Publishing AG 2017
D.R. Brooks, *Programming in HTML and PHP*, Undergraduate Topics
in Computer Science, DOI 10.1007/978-3-319-56973-4_9

9.2 Creating a Space for Graphics Applications

The first step in any graphics application is to create a "canvas"—a framework within which an image space can be defined. Document 9.1 shows how to build this basic framework.

Document 9.1 (graphingSpace.php)

```php
<?php
Header ("Content-type: image/gif");
// define title
$TitleString = "Chart Title";
// dimensions of plotting space
$x_max = 300; $y_max = 200;
// starting point for title
$x_title = 10; $y_title = 30.;
// (0,0) for axes
$x0=40; $y0= 170;
// axis lengths
$x_length=180; $y_length=120;
// create image space
$im = ImageCreate($x_max,$y_max) or die
   ("Cannot Initialize new GD image stream");
// define colors -- first call fills background
$background_color = ImageColorAllocate($im, 200, 200, 200);
// define text color
$black = ImageColorAllocate($im,0,0,0);
// display text
ImageString($im,5,0,0,"(0,0)",$black);
ImageString($im,5,$x_title,$y_title,$TitleString,$black);
ImageString($im,5,$x_max-80,$y_max-16,"(300,200)",$black);
// draw x-y axis
ImageSetThickness($im,2);
ImageLine($im,$x0,$y0,$x0+$x_length,$y0,$black);
ImageLine($im,$x0,$y0,$x0,$y0-$y_length,$black);
// display image
ImageGIF($im);
// release resources
ImageDestroy($im);
?>
```

Consider the code a few lines at a time:

```php
Header ("Content-type: image/gif");
```

This line is required for every graphics application. It indicates that for this script, a gif image will be created; other possibilities include JPEG and PNG images.

```
// define title
$TitleString = "Chart Title";
// dimensions of plotting space
$x_max = 300; $y_max = 200;
// starting point for title
$x_title = 10; $y_title = 30.;
// (0,0) for axes
$x0=40; $y0= 170;
// axis lengths
$x_length=180; $y_length=120;
```

These lines define a chart title and provide values which define the width and height of the image space in pixels, the starting coordinates for the title, the starting point (0,0) for the axes of an x-y graph, and the length of the x and y axes.

An important point about the image space is that the (0,0) coordinates are in the upper left-hand corner and the pixels (300,200) are in the lower right-hand corner; that is, the x-axis plots from left to right, as you would expect, but the y-axis plots from top to bottom, "upside down" relative to how you would normally think of graphing in (x,y) space. In Document 9.1, the starting coordinates for an x-y graph axis are 40 pixels from the left-hand side of the image space and 30 pixels "up" (y_max-y0=300-270) from the bottom of the image space.

```
// create image space
$im = ImageCreate($x_max,$y_max)
   or die ("Cannot Initialize new GD image space");
// define colors -- first call fills background
$background_color = ImageColorAllocate($im, 200, 200, 200);
// define text color
$black = ImageColorAllocate($im,0,0,0);
```

These lines initialize the image space and give it a resource handle. The "or die" part of the statement is optional; as a practical matter, there should never be a reason why the new image can't be created. The $background_color = statement actually creates the space, in this case colored grey according to the RGB components (200,200,200). Black (0,0,0) will be used for drawing lines and text.

```
// display text
ImageString($im,5,0,0,"(0,0)",$black);
ImageString($im,5,$x_title,$y_title,$TitleString,$black);
ImageString($im,5,$x_max-80,$y_max-16,"(300,200)",$black);
```

The `ImageString()` function draws text. The basic and not particularly attractive monospaced GD font comes in five sizes, from 1 to 5, smallest to largest.[1] The (x,y) coordinates refer to the upper left-hand corner of the first character of the text string, which explains the offsets for the string printed in the lower right-hand corner of the graphing space. The size 5 font appears to be 16 pixels tall by 9 pixels wide. It is possible to use more attractive TrueType fonts, but this might be considered as just an afterthought for the applications in this chapter. Text placement is more complicated because most TrueType fonts are proportionally space (that is, the individual characters are not all the same width) and the (x,y) offset coordinates for locating the start of a text string are different from what they are for the default GD fonts—see `ImageTTFText()` in Sect. 9.7.3.

```
// draw x-y axis
ImageSetThickness($im,2);
ImageLine($im,$x0,$y0,$x0+$x_length,$y0,$black);
ImageLine($im,$x0,$y0,$x0,$y0-$y_length,$black);
```

These lines set the thickness for drawing lines, in pixels, and then draw the bottom and left-hand lines for an X-Y graph. If you don't include `ImageSetThickness()` the default line width is 1 pixel. You can change the line thickness at any time in a script.

```
// display image
ImageGIF($im);
// release resources
ImageDestroy($im);
```

Finally, these two functions actually create and display the graph and then free the resources used to create the graph. There are many other GD library functions which will be used in the following sections and summarized at the end of the chapter.

Developing code for graphics applications can be a challenge. The favored strategy for creating text-based applications is to write the code no more than a few steps at a time, using the `echo` command or a function such as `print_r()` to display temporary output and check the results for each new section of code. Once the code has been thoroughly tested, then the temporary outputs can be removed.

The same strategy is not available for GD graphics applications. Once an image space has been defined, it is no longer possible to mix text commands such as `echo` with graphics commands. The nearest GD

---

[1]The default GD font bears a striking resemblance to fonts from the very early days of dot-matrix printers.

equivalent of `echo` is `ImageString()`. But, because the purpose of this function is only to output a user-supplied string, not including variables, and because this function must include coordinates to position the text at a particular location within the image space, it is not nearly as convenient to implement as an `echo` command.

When graphics code contains an error, the image space simply won't be created. This will happen whenever you provide inappropriate input to a GD graphics routine even when the error doesn't create a syntax error message you can see on your screen. But, error messages *will* be recorded in a log file—on Windows computers, `php_error.log` in the `\wamp\logs` directory. (This file can become quite large, so you can simply erase it at any time and it will be recreated as needed.)

In any event, when you write graphics code, you should start with something very simple, such as defining an image space with a non-white background color (so you can see how big the space is on your monitor) and displaying some text or drawing axes. After that, *every* step in developing your code should be tested before proceeding. If you try to write an entire graphics application all at once without lots of intermediate testing, you will be sorry!

One strategy for developing a graphing application that requires calculations to convert values to coordinate positions in an image space is first to write code to do the calculations in a text-based function. For a pie chart, for example, it is necessary to convert the data values into angles that will define the starting and ending points of the pie slices. For other applications, data values need to be converted to pixel locations within a defined X-Y graphing space. It may be helpful to display the results of these calculations before actually trying to draw the chart. When the results have been checked, then the `echo` commands can be commented out or removed and the graphics functions can be added.

Typically, graphics applications will require input from other sources such as external data files. However, for each type of graph, it may be helpful to include a default set of data in a PHP script so the application can display some representative output without needing any external output. This speeds up the process of developing the application because you can concentrate on writing code for developing the graphics output and you don't have to call the function from an HTML document every time you make a change to the PHP code.

In this chapter, there will be two separate scripts for the pie and horizontal bar chart applications—one with "hard-coded" input data for testing and another which will receive input passed from an HTML document or read from an external data file. For example, the user-supplied input required for testing a pie chart application consists of an array of up to 12 values to generate the pie slices, and another array containing an equal number of legends to be associated with those values. For all the applications shown here in their completed versions, rest assured that each of them was developed using a step-by-step approach with code testing after each step even when those intermediate steps aren't shown!

9.3 Pie Charts

A pie chart application is considered first because it is the simplest to implement, using GD library functions that make it easy to draw a colored segment of a circle. Document 9.2a creates a pie chart using hard-coded data for 12 pie "slices." In principle, there is no upper limit on the number of slices, but 12 seems like a reasonable practical limit that will allow displaying a year's worth of monthly data; change it if you like.

Document 9.2a (pie2.php)

```php
<?php
Header ("Content-type: image/gif");
$TitleString = "Pie Chart";
$A=array(60,50,40,100,50,50,75,5,10,15,20,35);
$legends = array("Item1","Item2","Item3","Item4","Item5",
"Item6","Item7","Item8","Item9","Item10","Item11","Item12");
// dimensions of plotting space
$x_max = 800; $y_max=500;
// center point for pie chart
$x0 = 200; $y0 = 250;
// diameter of pie
$dia = 360;
// starting point for title
$x_title = 40; $y_title = 40.;
// upper left-hand corner of legend space
$x0_legend = 400; $y0_legend = 75;
// size of legend color boxes
$legend_size = 25;
// vertical space between legend color boxes;
$dy_legend = $legend_size+5;
// create image space
$im = ImageCreate($x_max,$y_max) or die ("Cannot Initialize
new GD image stream");
// define colors
$background_color = ImageColorAllocate($im, 234, 234, 234);
// first call fills background
$black=ImageColorAllocate($im,0,0,0);
```

```php
// pie section colors for up to $n_max sections
$ColorCode =

array ("255,0,0","51,0,255","51,255,51","255,153,0","0,204,
   153","204,255,102","255,102,102","102,204,255","204,153,
   255","255,51,153","204,0,255","255,255,51");
$n_max = count ($ColorCode);
$PieColor = array ();
for ($i=0; $i<$n_max; $i++) {
  $ColorCodeSplit = explode (',',$ColorCode[ $i] );
  $PieColor[ $i] = ImageColorAllocate ($im,
  $ColorCodeSplit[ 0] ,$ColorCodeSplit[ 1] ,$ColorCodeSplit[ 2] );
}
// Convert data array into angles, total of 360 deg.
$sum = array_sum ($A);
$n = count ($A);
$start = array ();
$end = array ();
$start[ 0] = 0;
for ($i=0; $i<$n; $i++) {
  $slice = $A[ $i] /$sum* 360;
  if ($i>0) $start[ $i] = $end[ $i-1] ;
  $end[ $i] = $start[ $i] + $slice;
}
// Display title
ImageString ($im, 5,$x_title,$y_title,$TitleString,$black);
// draw filled arcs
for ($i=0; $i<$n; $i++) {
   ImageFilledArc ($im,$x0,$y0,$dia,$dia,$start[ $i] ,$end[ $i] ,
     $PieColor[ $i] , IMG_ARC_PIE);
}
// Display legend
for ($i=0; $i<$n; $i++) {
   ImageFilledRectangle ($im,$x0_legend,
     $y0_legend+$dy_legend* $i,$x0_legend+$legend_size,
     $y0_legend+$dy_legend* $i+$legend_size,$PieColor[ $i] );
   ImageString ($im, 5,$x0_legend+$legend_size+5,
     $y0_legend+$dy_legend* $i+5,$legends[ $i] ,$black);
}
// Display and release allocated resources.
ImageGIF ($im);
ImageDestroy ($im);
?>
```

The sizing of the pie slices is done in the shaded code, making use of the `array_sum()` function to sum the values of all elements in the data array. With the starting angle set to 0°, the starting point for the pie slices drawn with `ImageFilledArc()` is the "three o'clock position—the position of the positive x-axis in a conventional x-y

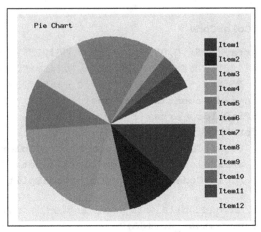

coordinate space, with angles increasing clockwise from there.

The final steps for this application are to convert the code from Document 9.2a to a function, write HTML code with input values, and write PHP code to pass input to the graphing function. Documents 9.2b and 9.2c give the code:

Document 9.2b (pieChart.htm)

```
<html>
<head>
<title></title>
</head>
<body>
<form method="post" action="pieChart.php" />
<h3> Pie Chart Test</h3>
   Pie chart data (chart title, values & legends) from:
<input type="text" value="pieChart.dat" name="fileName" />
<br />
   Data file format:<br />
   <font face="Courier">
   Title<br />
   Value    Legend<br />
   Value Legend<br />
   ...
   <br /></font>
   Size of graphing space (pixels): X <input type="text"
value="800" name="$x_max" size="4" />
   Y <input type="text" name="$y_max" value="500" size="4" />
<br />
   Center of pie chart (pixels): X <input type="text"
name="x0" value="200" size="4" />
   Y <input type="text" name="y0" value="250" size="4" />
<br />
   Diameter of pie chart (pixels): <input type="text"
```

```
    name="dia" value="360" size="4" /><br />
  Size of legend boxes (pixels): <input type="text"
    name="legend_size" size="3" value="25" /><br />
  <input type="submit"
    value=
  "Click here to generate pie chart from specified file." />
</form>
</body>
</html>
```

The `pieChart.dat` file for this chart looks like this:

```
Quarterly Sales
17.7 January-March
15 April-June
19.2 July-September
30 October-December
```

This file is very easy to read because the text for the legends contains no spaces between words. You will have to work harder if there *are* spaces in these legends! (In that case, it might be easiest to put each legend on its own line, separate from the data value, so you can read the entire line as a single string.)

The final version of the PHP pie chart application is given in Document 9.2c. Much of the code is copied directly from Document 9.2a, with some hard-coded values replaced with input values received from the corresponding HTML document.

Document 9.2c (`pieChart.php`)

```php
<?php
function
generatePie($Title,$A,$legends,$x_max,$y_max,$x0,$y0,
  $legend_size,$dia,$x0_legend,$y0_legend) {
Header ("Content-type: image/gif");
// vertical space between legend color boxes;
$dy_legend=$legend_size+5;
$x_title=10; $y_title=20; // locates plot title
// create image space
$im = ImageCreate($x_max,$y_max) or
  die ("Cannot Initialize new GD image stream");
// define some colors
// $background_color creates background
$background_color = ImageColorAllocate($im, 200, 200, 200);
$black=ImageColorAllocate($im,0,0,0); // for drawing
// colors for up to 12 sections
$ColorCode =
array("255,0,0", "51,0,255", "51,255,51", "255,153,0",
```

```php
    "0,204,153", "204,255,102", "255,102,102", "102,204,255",
    "204,153,255", "255,51,153", "204,0,255", "255,255,51");
$PieColor=array();
for ($i=0; $i<12; $i++) {
  $ColorCodeSplit = explode(',',$ColorCode[$i]);
  $PieColor[$i] = ImageColorAllocate($im,
  $ColorCodeSplit[0],$ColorCodeSplit[1],$ColorCodeSplit[2]);
}
// Convert data array into angles, total of 360 deg.
$sum=array_sum($A); $n=count($A);
$start=array(); $end=array();
$start[0]=0;
for ($i=0; $i<$n; $i++) {
  $slice=$A[$i]/$sum*360;
  if ($i>0) $start[$i]=$end[$i-1];
  $end[$i]=$start[$i]+$slice;
}
// Display title
ImageString($im,5,$x_title,$y_title,$Title,$black);
// draw filled arcs
for ($i=0; $i<$n; $i++) {
  ImageFilledArc($im,$x0,$y0,$dia,$dia,$start[$i],$end[$i],
    $PieColor[$i],IMG_ARC_PIE);
}
// Display legend
for ($i=0; $i<$n; $i++) {
  ImageFilledRectangle($im,$x0_legend,
      $y0_legend+$dy_legend*$i,$x0_legend+$legend_size,
      $y0_legend+$dy_legend*$i+$legend_size,$PieColor[$i]);
  $legends[$i] =
    $legends[$i] . " (".number_format($A[$i],1,".",",").")";

  ImageString($im,5,$x0_legend+$legend_size+5,
    $y0_legend+$dy_legend*$i+5,$legends[$i],$black);
}
// Display and release allocated resources.
ImageGIF($im); ImageDestroy($im);
}
// MAIN PROGRAM ------------------
$inFile=$_POST["fileName"];
$x_max=$_POST["x_max"]; $y_max=$_POST["y_max"];
$x0=$_POST["x0"]; $y0=$_POST["y0"];
$dia=$_POST["dia"];
$legend_size=$_POST["legend_size"];
$x0_legend=$_POST["x0_legend"];
$y0_legend=$_POST["y0_legend"];
$in=fopen($inFile,"r") or exit("Can't open this file.");
$A=array(); $legends=array();
$Title=trim(fgets($in));
$i=-1;
while (!feof($in)) {
  $line=fgets($in);
```

```
if (strlen($line)>3) {
  $i++;
  sscanf($line, "%f %s",$A[ $i] ,$legends[$i] );
  $A[ $i] =round($A[$i] ,0) ;
  }
}
fclose($in);
generatePie($Title,$A,$legends,$x_max,$y_max,$x0,$y0,
  $legend_size,$dia,$x0_legend,$y0_legend);
?>
```

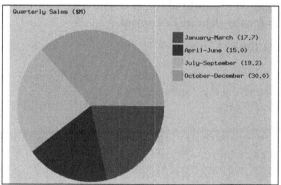

The main program is responsible for assigning some values passed from the HTML document, reading data from the data file, and passing data to function generatePie(). This code is straightforward, but note the use of the trim() function to remove return and new line characters from the end of the title string. If you don't include this step, these normally non-printable characters will be displayed as "garbage" characters at the end of the chart title text.

The data file used to generate this output is, on purpose, different from the default data, just to make sure that the application works with a user-specified number of data values. As noted previously, there is still a hard-coded limit of 12 for the maximum number of data values, because only 12 pie slice color codes are defined. You can increase the maximum number, but pie charts are not the best choice for displaying large numbers of values.

The shaded code shows how to use the number_format() function to keep a 0 after the decimal point even for a whole number

9.4   Horizontal Bar Charts

Applications other than pie charts are more difficult to implement because they require more data scaling—converting data values to pixel coordinates within the predefined image space. Past the first step of creating a graphing

space, some thought is required about what kinds of data the bar chart will
display. Assume the data values can have positive or negative values. Coding
will be a *lot* easier if you specify the minimum and maximum values, and the
values to be displayed as labels (as strings), rather than asking your sketch to
generate these values based on the contents of a data file.

Document 9.3a shows code to display hard-coded data on a horizontal
bar chart. The most general way to create the bars is to specify an upper and
lower end for each bar. If some bar values are all negative and some are all
positive, it might be useful to allow different colors for those two cases, as
has been done for the data in Document 9.3a.

Document 9.3a (Hbar1.php)

```php
<?php
Header ("Content-type: image/gif");
// define default data
$chartTitle =
  "Monthly temperature deviations from climate average";
$xLabels = array("-2.0","-1.5","-1.0","-0.5"," 0.0"," 0.5",
  " 1.0"," 1.5"," 2.0"," 2.5"," 3.0"," 3.5");
$x_MinValues = array(0,0,-0.2,-2.0,0,0,-1.1,-.5,0,0,0,0);
$x_MaxValues = array(1.3,0.9,0,0,1,0,0,0,.6,3.2,.7,.3);
$xvalue_max=3.5; $xvalue_min=-2.0; // agree with labels
$yLabels = array("January ","February ","March ",
   "April ","May ","June ",
   "July ","August ","September","October ",
   "November ","December ");
$n_x = count($xLabels); // number of x labels
$n_y = count($yLabels); // number of y labels
$max_YlabelLength=0;
for ($i=0; $i<$n_y; $i++) {
    if (strlen($yLabels[$i])>$max_YlabelLength)
$max_YlabelLength=strlen($yLabels[$i]);
}
// define image space
$x_max = 800; $y_max = 500;
// define graphing space and title/label positioning
// offsets are from (x0,y0), x+, y-
$x0 = 100; $y0 = 60; // start coordinates for graphing space
// space between x-axis labels and horizontal bars
$dx = 50; $dy = 30;
// title offsets from upper left hand corner
$x0_titleOffset = 0; $y0_titleOffset = 50;
// X label offsets
$xlabel_Xoffset=20; $xlabel_Yoffset=20;
```

```php
// Y label offsets, x-, y+
$ylabel_Yoffset=5; // x-, y+
// calculate X offset based on length of 1st label,
// 9 pix/character
$ylabel_Xoffset=$max_YlabelLength* 9+5;
// define bar size and vertical position
$bar_height = 20; // bar height
// center bar in $dy space
$bar_Yoffset=floor(($dy-$bar_height)/2);
// create image space
$im = imageCreate ($x_max, $y_max) or
  die ("Cannot create new GD image.");
$background_color = ImageColorAllocate ($im,225,225,225);
// define colors
$text_color = ImageColorAllocate ($im,0,0,0); // text color
$line_color = ImageColorAllocate ($im,0,0,0); // line color
$horizontal_line_color =
ImageColorAllocate ($im,200,200,200);
ImageSetThickness ($im,1);
// bar colors
$negative = ImageColorAllocate ($im,0,0,255);
$positive = ImageColorAllocate ($im,255,150,150);
$neutral = ImageColorAllocate ($im,100,100,100);
$title_font_size = 5; // large font for title
$title_color = ImageColorAllocate ($im,0,0,0); // black title
// outline graphing space top, left, right, bottom
ImageLine ($im, $x0, $y0, $x0+$dx* ($n_x-1), $y0, $line_color);
ImageLine ($im, $x0, $y0, $x0, $y0+$dy* ($n_y), $line_color);
ImageLine ($im, $x0+$dx* ($n_x-1), $y0,
  $x0+$dx* ($n_x-1), $y0+$dy* ($n_y), $line_color);
ImageLine ($im, $x0, $y0+$dy* ($n_y),
  $x0+$dx* ($n_x-1), $y0+$dy* ($n_y), $line_color);
// draw chart title
ImageString ($im, $title_font_size, $x0+$x0_titleOffset,
  $y0-$y0_titleOffset, $chartTitle, $title_color);
// draw Y labels and horizontal lines
for ($i=0; $i<$n_y; $i++) {
  ImageString ($im, $title_font_size, $x0-
$ylabel_Xoffset, $y0+$dy* $i+$ylabel_Yoffset, $yLabels [$i],
  $text_color);
    if ($i>0) ImageLine ($im, $x0, $y0+$dy* $i, $x0+
    ($n_x-1)* $dx, $y0+$dy* $i, $horizontal_line_color);
}
// draw bars
$xRange=$xvalue_max-$xvalue_min;
for ($i=0; $i<$n_y; $i++) {
    $x1=$x0+$dx* ($n_x-1)* ($x_MinValues [$i] -
      $xvalue_min) /$xRange;
    $x2=$x0+$dx* ($n_x-1)* (1-($xvalue_max-
```

```
        $x_MaxValues[$i] )/$xRange);


    if (($x_MinValues[$i] <=0) && ($x_MaxValues[$i] <=0))
        $color=$negative;
    elseif (($x_MinValues[$i] >=0) && ($x_MaxValues[$i] >=0))
        $color=$positive;
    else $color=$neutral;
    ImageFilledRectangle($im,$x1,$y0+$bar_Yoffset+$i*$dy,$x2,
        $y0+$bar_Yoffset+$i*$dy+$bar_height,$color);
}
// draw Y labels and vertical lines
for ($i=0; $i<$n_x; $i++) {
    ImageString($im,$title_font_size,$x0-
$xlabel_Xoffset+$i*$dx,$y0-
$xlabel_Yoffset,$xLabels[$i] ,$text_color);
    ImageLine($im,$x0+$i*$dx,$y0,$x0+$i*$dx,$y0+$dy*($n_y),
        $line_color);
}
// Create GIF image and release allocated resources.
ImageGIF($im); ImageDestroy($im);
?>
```

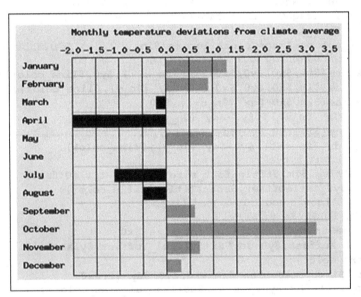

There are many lines in this code (and other code in this book) that are broken because of the page width limitations of this book, and they will have to be "unbroken" before the code will work.

The order in which lines and bars are drawn determines which lines and objects are "on top." In this code, the vertical grid lines are drawn after the bars. If you want the bars on top, change the order of operations by moving the code.

Positioning of the Y-axis labels is based on the length of the longest label—"September" for these data. The x-offset is calculated based on 9 pixels per character. The offset for the X-axis labels is set to a value of 5 pixels (to the left), but this could be changed to work like the Y-labels.

The next step is to write an HTML document that will provide input to the bar chart application and, finally, to modify the bar chart code to use data passed from HTML rather than hard-coded values. The input data required to create the bar chart is divided into two parts: one part is data-related, with values stored in an external file, and the other provides some input for changing how the data are displayed.

Document 9.3b shows the HTML interface for the horizontal bar chart application and 9.3c shows the PHP code. The data file used to create the output contains values taken from the historical temperature record for Philadelphia, PA. It is interesting to note that there may be a data error on January 6 or 7, as it seems unlikely that the high temperature for the 6th would be 11 degrees lower than the low temperature on the 7th; visual representations are valuable because they make it easy to spot these kinds of potential data problems!

Document 9.3b (HbarChart.htm)

```html
<html>
<head><title></title></head>
<body>
<h3>Create a horizontal bar chart</h3>
<form method="post" action="Hbarchart.php">
   <table border><tr><td>Data file, format:<br />title<br />
   X-axis labels<br />Y-axis labels<br />
   data<br />min max values
   </td><td><input size="50" type="text" name="fileName"
     value="Hbar.dat" />
   </td></tr></table>
   graphing space total size (pixels): X
   <input type="text" name="xSize" size="4" value="800" />
    Y <input type="text" name="ySize" size="4" value="500"
      /><br />
   Bar height (pixels):
   <input type="text" name="BarHeight" value="25"
     size="3" /><br />
   Vertical space between bars (pixels):
   <input type="text"
     name="dy" value="30" size="3" /><br />
   Horizontal space between X-axis labels (pixels):
   <input type="text" name="dx" value="50" size="3" /><br />
   <table border><tr><td>
```

```
 Positive bar color: </td><td>
   black:<input type="radio" name="positiveColor"
     value="black" size="8" />  
   blue:<input type="radio" name="positiveColor"
    value="blue" size="8" />  
   grey:<input type="radio" name="positiveColor"
     value="grey" size="8" />  
   green:<input type="radio" name="positiveColor"
     value="green" size="8" />  
   red:<input type="radio" name="positiveColor"
     value="red" size="8" checked />
</td></tr></table>
<table border><tr><td>
Negative bar color: </td><td>
    black:<input type="radio" name="negativeColor"
      value="black" size="8" />  
   blue:<input type="radio" name="negativeColor"
     value="blue" size="8" checked />  
   grey:<input type="radio" name="negativeColor"
     value="grey" size="8" />  
   green:<input type="radio" name="negativeColor"
     value="green" size="8" />  
   red: <input type="radio" name="negativeColor"
     value="red" size="8" />
</td></tr></table>
<input type="submit"
   value="Click here to generate chart." /><br />
  <input type="reset" value=
     "Click here to reset all fields." /><br />
</form></body></html>
```

Document 9.3c (HbarChart.php)

```php
<?php
function barGraph($chartTitle,$xLabels,$yLabels,$x_max,
  $y_max,$x_MinValues,$x_MaxValues,$xvalue_min,$xvalue_max,
  $dx,$dy,$bar_height,$pR,$pG,$pB,$nR,$nG,$nB,$uR,$uG,$uB,
  $bkg,$xlabel_Xoffset) {
Header ("Content-type: image/gif");
$n_x = count($xLabels); // number of x labels
$n_y = count($yLabels); // number of y labels
$max_YlabelLength=0;
for ($i=0; $i<$n_y; $i++) {
  if (strlen($yLabels[ $i] )>$max_YlabelLength)
$max_YlabelLength=strlen($yLabels[ $i] );
}
$x0 = 100; $y0 = 60; // starting coordinates for graph
// title offsets from upper left hand corner
$x0_titleOffset = 0; $y0_titleOffset = 50;
```

```
// X label offsets
$xlabel_Yoffset=20;
// Y label offsets, x-, y+
$ylabel_Yoffset=5; // x-, y+

// calculate X offset based on length of 1st label,
// 9 pix/character
$ylabel_Xoffset=$max_YlabelLength* 9+5;
//-----------------------------------
// define bar size and vertical position
$bar_Yoffset=floor(($dy-$bar_height)/2); // center bar in
$dy space
// create image space
$im = imageCreate ($x_max, $y_max) or die ("Cannot create
new GD image.");
$background_color =
ImageColorAllocate($im,$bkg[0],$bkg[1],$bkg[2]);
// define colors
$text_color = ImageColorAllocate($im,0,0,0); // text color
$line_color = ImageColorAllocate($im,0,0,0); // line color
$horizontal_line_color =
ImageColorAllocate($im,200,200,200);
ImageSetThickness($im,1);
// bar colors
$negative = ImageColorAllocate($im, $pR, $pG, $pB);
$positive = ImageColorAllocate($im, $nR, $nG, $nB);
$neutral = ImageColorAllocate($im, $uR, $uG, $uB); // - to +
$title_font_size = 5; // large font for title
$title_color = ImageColorAllocate($im,0,0,0);
// outline graphing space, top, left, right, bottom
ImageLine ($im, $x0, $y0, $x0+$dx* ($n_x-1), $y0, $line_color);
ImageLine ($im, $x0, $y0, $x0, $y0+$dy* ($n_y), $line_color);
ImageLine ($im, $x0+$dx* ($n_x-1), $y0, $x0+$dx*
   ($n_x-1), $y0+$dy* ($n_y), $line_color);
ImageLine ($im, $x0, $y0+$dy* ($n_y), $x0+$dx*
   ($n_x-1), $y0+$dy* ($n_y), $line_color);
// draw chart title
ImageString ($im, $title_font_size, $x0+$x0_titleOffset,
   $y0-$y0_titleOffset, $chartTitle, $title_color);
// draw Y labels and horizontal lines
for ($i=0; $i<$n_y; $i++) {
   ImageString ($im, $title_font_size, $x0-
$ylabel_Xoffset, $y0+$dy* $i+$ylabel_Yoffset, $yLabels[$i],
   $text_color);
   if ($i>0) ImageLine ($im, $x0, $y0+$dy* $i, $x0+
      ($n_x-1)* $dx, $y0+$dy* $i, $horizontal_line_color);
}
// draw bars
$xRange=$xvalue_max-$xvalue_min;
```

```php
for ($i=0; $i<$n_y; $i++) {
    $x1=$x0+$dx*($n_x-1)*($x_MinValues[$i] -
      $xvalue_min)/$xRange;
    $x2=$x0+$dx*($n_x-1)*(1-($xvalue_max-
      $x_MaxValues[$i])/$xRange);
    if (($x_MinValues[$i]<=0) && ($x_MaxValues[$i]<=0))
      $color=$negative;
    elseif (($x_MinValues[$i]>=0) && ($x_MaxValues[$i]>=0))
      $color=$positive;
    else $color=$neutral;
    ImageFilledRectangle($im,$x1,$y0+$bar_Yoffset+$i*$dy,$x2,
      $y0+$bar_Yoffset+$i*$dy+$bar_height,$color);
}
// draw X labels and vertical lines
for ($i=0; $i<$n_x; $i++) {
    ImageString($im,$title_font_size,
      $x0-$xlabel_Xoffset+$i*$dx,$y0-
      $xlabel_Yoffset,trim($xLabels[$i]),$text_color);
    ImageLine($im,$x0+$i*$dx,$y0,$x0+$i*$dx,$y0+$dy*($n_y),
      $line_color);
}
// Create GIF image and release allocated resources.
ImageGIF($im); ImageDestroy($im);
}
//--------- MAIN PROGRAM ------------
$inFile=$_POST["fileName"];
// read data file
$in=fopen($inFile,'r');
$chartTitle=trim(fgets($in));
$s=fgets($in); $xLabels=explode(',',$s);
for ($i=0; $i<count($xLabels); $i++) trim($xLabels[$i]);
fscanf($in, "%f %f",$xvalue_min,$xvalue_max);
$ny=-1;
while (!feof($in)) {
    $s=fgets($in);
    if (strlen($s)>3) {
      $ny++;
      sscanf($s, "%s %f %f",
        $yLabels[$ny],$x_MinValues[$ny],$x_MaxValues[$ny]);
    }
}
fclose($in);
// get data from HTML document
$positiveColor=$_POST["positiveColor"];
$negativeColor=$_POST["negativeColor"];
$neutralColor=$_POST["neutralColor"];
$colorString=$_POST["colorString"];
$bkg=explode(',',$colorString);
switch($positiveColor) {
    case "black": $pR=0;$pG=0;$pB=0;break;
    case "blue": $pR=0;$pG=0;$pB=255;break;
    case "green": $pR=0;$pG=255;$pB=0;break;
```

```php
    case "grey": $pR=100;$pG=100;$pB=100;break;
    case "red": $pR=255;$pG=0;$pB=0;break;
}
switch($negativeColor) {
    case "black": $nR=0;$nG=0;$nB=0;break;
    case "blue": $nR=0;$nG=0;$nB=255;break;
    case "green": $nR=0;$nG=255;$nB=0;break;
    case "grey": $nR=100;$nG=100;$nB=100;break;
    case "red": $nR=255;$nG=0;$nB=0;break;
}
switch($neutralColor) {
    case "black": $uR=0;$uG=0;$uB=0;break;
    case "blue": $uR=0;$uG=0;$uB=255;break;
    case "green": $uR=0;$uG=255;$uB=0;break;
    case "grey": $uR=100;$uG=100;$uB=100;break;
    case "red": $uR=255;$uG=0;$uB=0;break;
}
$x_max=$_POST["xSize"];
$y_max=$_POST["ySize"];
$bar_height=$_POST["BarHeight"];
$dx=$_POST["dx"];
$dy=$_POST["dy"];
$xLabelOffset=$_POST["xLabelOffset"];
barGraph($chartTitle,$xLabels,$yLabels,$x_max,$y_max,
    $x_MinValues,$x_MaxValues,$xvalue_min,$xvalue_max,
    $dx,$dy,$bar_height,$pR,$pG,$pB,$nR,$nG,$nB,$uR,$uG,$uB,
    $bkg,$xLabelOffset);
?>
```

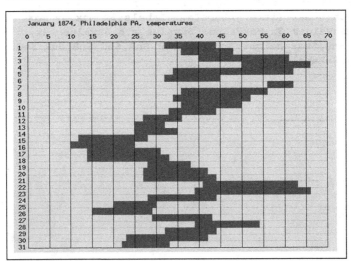

9.5 Vertical Bar Charts

Vertical bar charts are similar to horizontal bar charts. They are a little trickier to code because of the inverted y-axis (top down rather than bottom up), but let's skip the preliminary steps and go straight to the final HTML and PHP code.

Document 9.4a (VbarChart.htm)

```
<html>
<head><title></title></head>
<body>
<h3>Create a vertical bar chart</h3>
<form method="post" action="VbarChart.php">
<table border><tr><td>Data file, format:<br />
 Chart title<br />
 X-axis title<br />Y-axis title<br />
 Y-axis labels (strings, comma-separated) <br />
 Minimum/maximum allowed Y-values<br />
 X-axis labels (strings) X<sub>min</sub> X<sub>max</sub>
 <br />...<br />
 </td><td><input type="text" name="fileName" size="20"
    value="Vbar.dat" />
 </td></tr></table>
 Drawing canvas total size (pixels): X <input type="text"
    name="xCanvas" size="4" value="800" />
    Y <input type="text" name="yCanvas" size="4"
     value="500" /><br />
 Graphing space (pixels): X <input type="text" name="xRange"
value="500" size="3" />
 Y <input type="text" name="yRange" value="300"
    size="3" /><br />
 X-offset from left of canvas for start of graphing
    space (pixels):
 <input type="text" name="x0" value="100" size="3" /><br />
    Bar width (% of x-axis unit): <input type="text"
      name="barWidth" value="75" size="3" /><br />
    Background RGB color string: <input type="text"
name="colorString" value="225,225,225" size="10" /><br />
<table border><tr><td>
  Positive bar color: </td><td>
 black:<input type="radio" name="positiveColor"
    value="black" size="8" />  
 blue:<input type="radio" name="positiveColor"
    value="blue" size="8" />  
 grey:<input type="radio" name="positiveColor"
  value="grey" size="8" />  
 green:<input type="radio" name="positiveColor"
    value="green" size="8" />  
 red:<input type="radio" name="positiveColor"
    value="red" size="8" checked />
 </td></tr></table>
<table border><tr><td>
```

```
Negative bar color: </td><td>
black:<input type="radio" name="negativeColor"
    value="black" size="8" />  
blue:<input type="radio" name="negativeColor" value="blue"
    size="8" checked />  
grey:<input type="radio" name="negativeColor" value="grey"
    size="8" />  
green:<input type="radio" name="negativeColor"
    value="green" size="8" />  
red: <input type="radio" name="negativeColor" value="red"
    size="8" />
</td></tr></table>
<table border><tr><td>
 Neutral bar color: </td><td>
black:<input type="radio" name="neutralColor" value="black"
    size="8" />  
blue:<input type="radio" name="neutralColor" value="blue" \
    size="8" />  
grey:<input type="radio" name="neutralColor" value="grey"
    size="8" />  
green:<input type="radio" name="neutralColor" value="green"
    size="8" />  
red:<input type="radio" name="neutralColor" value="red"
    size="8" checked />
</td></tr></table>

<input type="submit"
    value="Click here to generate vertical bar chart." /><br />
<input type="reset" value=
"Click here to reset all fields to their original values." /><br />
</form></body></html>
```

Document 9.4b (VbarChart.php)

```php
<?php
function
drawVbar($Y_lo,$Y_hi,$yMin,$yMax,$barWidth,$barColor,
    $xTitle,$yTitle,$xLabels,$yLabels,$ChartTitle,$xCanvas,
    $yCanvas,$bgcolor,$n_x,$n_y,$xGap,$yGap,$x0) {
Header ("Content-type: image/gif");
// some constant values
$y0=50; // (x0,y0) from lower left of canvas
$ChartTitleYoffset=25;
$xTitleYoffset=25;
// some calculated values
$xTitleXoffset=$n_x* $xGap/2-strlen($xTitle)/2* 9;
$im = imageCreate ($xCanvas, $yCanvas) or
    die ("Cannot Initialize new GD image stream");
$background_color =
ImageColorAllocate($im,$bgcolor[0],$bgcolor[1],$bgcolor[2]);
```

```
$black=ImageColorAllocate($im,0,0,0);
$red=ImageColorAllocate($im,255,0,0);
$green=ImageColorAllocate($im,0,255,0);
$blue=ImageColorAllocate($im,0,0,255);
$grey=ImageColorAllocate($im,150,150,150);
// define a black and transparent dashed line for grid lines
$style = array(
   $black,$black,$black,$black,$black,
   IMG_COLOR_TRANSPARENT,IMG_COLOR_TRANSPARENT,
   IMG_COLOR_TRANSPARENT,IMG_COLOR_TRANSPARENT,
   IMG_COLOR_TRANSPARENT
);
ImageSetStyle($im,$style);
// Outline graph space
ImageSetThickness($im,2);
ImageLine($im,$x0,$yCanvas-$y0,$x0+($n_x)*$xGap,
   $yCanvas-$y0,$black);
ImageLine($im,$x0,$yCanvas-$y0-
   ($n_y-1)*$yGap,$x0+($n_x)*$xGap,$yCanvas-$y0-
   ($n_y-1)*$yGap,$black);
ImageLine($im,$x0,$yCanvas-$y0,$x0,$yCanvas-$y0-
   ($n_y-1)*$yGap,$black);
ImageLine($im,$x0+($n_x)*$xGap,$yCanvas-
$y0,$x0+($n_x)*$xGap,$yCanvas-$y0-($n_y-1)*$yGap,$black);
ImageString($im,5,$x0,$yCanvas-$y0-($n_y-1)*$yGap-
   $ChartTitleYoffset,trim($ChartTitle),$black);
// draw xTitle
ImageString($im,5,$x0+$xTitleXoffset,$yCanvas-
   $y0+$xTitleYoffset,trim($xTitle),$black);
ImageSetThickness($im,1);
// draw y labels
$offset=5+strlen($yLabels[0])*9;
for ($i=0; $i<$n_y; $i++) {
   ImageString($im,5,$x0-$offset,$yCanvas-$y0-
      $i*$yGap-8,$yLabels[$i],$black);
   ImageLine($im,$x0,$yCanvas-$y0-
      $i*$yGap,$x0+$n_x*$xGap,$yCanvas-$y0-
      $i*$yGap,IMG_COLOR_STYLED);
}
// draw yTitle
$off=($n_y-1)*$yGap/2-strlen($yTitle)/2*9;
ImageStringUp($im,5,$x0-$offset-25,$yCanvas-
   $y0-$off,trim($yTitle),$black);
// draw x labels and vertical axes
for ($i=0; $i<$n_x; $i++) {
   $off=$xGap/2-strlen($xLabels[$i])/2*9;
   ImageString($im,5,$x0+$i*$xGap+$off,$yCanvas-
      $y0+5,$xLabels[$i],$black);
   ImageLine($im,$x0+$i*$xGap,$yCanvas-
```

```
       $y0,$x0+$i* $xGap,$yCanvas-$y0-($n_y-1)* $yGap,$black);
}
// draw bars
$off=$barWidth/100* $xGap/2;
$yDataRange=$yMax-$yMin;
$yAxisRange=($n_y-1)* $yGap;
for ($i=0; $i<$n_x; $i++) {
// scaling Y-values...
    $y1=($Y_lo[$i] -$yMin)/$yDataRange* $yAxisRange;
    $y2=($yMax-$Y_hi[$i])/$yDataRange* $yAxisRange;
    ImageFilledRectangle($im,$x0+$i* $xGap+$xGap/2-
    $off,$yCanvas-$y0-$y1,$x0+$i* $xGap+$xGap/2+$off,
    $yCanvas-$y0+$y2-($n_y-1)* $yGap,$red);
}
// Release allocated resources.
ImageGIF($im); ImageDestroy($im);
}
//-------- MAIN PROGRAM ----------------
$fileName=$_POST["fileName"];
//$fileName="Vbar.dat";
$in=fopen($fileName,"r");
$xLabels=array(); $Y_lo=array(); $Y_hi=array();
$ChartTitle=fgets($in);
$xTitle=fgets($in);
$yTitle=fgets($in);
$s=fgets($in);
$yLabels=explode(',',$s);
fscanf($in,"%f %f",$xMin,$xMax);
$i=-1;
while (!feof($in)) {
  $s=fgets($in);
  if (strlen($s)>3) {
     $i++;
  sscanf($s,"%s %f %f",$xLabels[$i] ,$Y_lo[$i] ,$Y_hi[$i] );
  }
}
$n_x=$i+1; $n_y=count($yLabels);
fclose($in);
// from HTML, values to pass to PHP
$xCanvas=700; $yCanvas=400;
$xRange=450; $yRange=300;
$colorString="225,225,225"; // background color
$barWidth=80; // % of xGap
$barColor="red";
$yMin=-3; $yMax=3.5;
$x0=100; // + offset from lower left corner
// calculated values to pass to PHP
$maxYlabelLength=0;
for ($i=0; $i<$n_y; $i++) {
    $yLabels[$i] =trim($yLabels[$i] );
    if (strlen($yLabels[$i] )>$maxYlabelLength)
$maxYlabelLength=strlen($yLabels[$i] );
```

```
}
// left-pad labels with spaces, as needed.
// Don't trim() them again!
for ($i=0; $i<$n_y; $i++) {
    while (strlen($yLabels[$i])<$maxYlabelLength)
$yLabels[$i] =' '.$yLabels[$i];
}
$xGap=floor($xRange/$n_x);
$yGap=floor($yRange/$n_y);
$bkgrdColor=explode(',',$colorString);
drawVbar($Y_lo,$Y_hi,$yMin,$yMax,$barWidth,$barColor,
   $xTitle,$yTitle,$xLabels,$yLabels,$ChartTitle,$xCanvas,
   $yCanvas,$bkgrdColor,$n_x,$n_y,$xGap,$yGap,$x0);
?>
```

The HTML document specifies the input data file, which contains all the titles, labels, and data values. The minimum and maximum allowed y-values should agree with the minimum and maximum values given in the y-axis label strings. The remaining user inputs include the size of the drawing canvas and graphing space, the offset from the left of the canvas for the start of the graphing space, the bar width as a percent of the space for each x-axis item, the background color, and the bar colors. The space for each x-axis item (in pixels) is calculated in the PHP application based on the specified size of the graphing space and the number of x-values. All the size values can be changed arbitrarily and independently but, obviously, they have to make sense relative to the data being graphed.

The PHP application automatically places all the labels. The x- and y-axis values, x-values, and x- and y-axis labels are centered in their spaces, assuming 9 pixels per character. (You could add code to do the same with the chart title if you like.) The y-labels are right-justified by left-padding them with spaces so, for example, the decimal points for "0.0" and "+0.5" line up. The PHP code also shows how to create dashed lines; it is somewhat unwieldy, but it works!

```
Some random monthly data...
Month
Random data values
-3.0,-2.5,-2.0,-1.5,-1.0,-0.5, 0.0,+0.5,+1.0,+1.5,+2.0,+2.5,+3.0,+3.5
-3 3.5
Jan 1.3 1.5
Feb 0.9 1.9
Mar -0.2 1.1
Apr -2.0 -0.5
May 1 2.9
Jun -1.1 3.5
Jul -.5 1.7
Aug .6 2.2
Sep 3.0 3.5
Oct .7 1.9
Nov -2.9 0.1
Dec 0 3.2
```

Create a vertical bar chart

Data file, format: Chart title X-axis title Y-axis title Y-axis labels (strings, comma-separated) Minimum/maximum allowed Y-values X-axis labels (strings) X_{min} X_{max} ...	Vbar.dat

Drawing canvas total size (pixels): X `800`   Y `500`

Graphing space (pixels): X `500`   Y `300`

X-offset from left of canvas for start of graphing space (pixels): `100`

Bar width (% of x-axis unit): `75`

Background RGB color string: `225,225,225`

Positive bar color:	black: ○ blue: ○ grey: ○ green: ○ red: ◉

Negative bar color:	black: ○ blue: ○ grey: ○ green: ○ red: ◉

Neutral bar color:	black: ○ blue: ○ grey: ○ green: ○ red: ◉

Click here to generate vertical bar chart.

Click here to reset all fields to their original values.

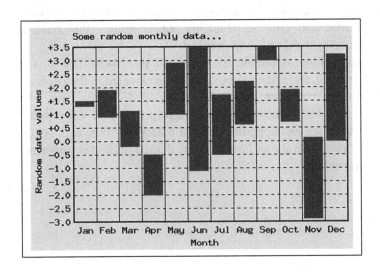

9.6 Line Graphs

Much of the code required to create a line graph is similar to that required for vertical bar charts, to the extent that titles and labels must be placed relative to a defined graphing space and data must be scaled to fit the defined x-y coordinate space. This application is designed to allow graphing up to three sets of x-y data, with the number of datasets specified in the input file. Note that, unlike vertical bar graphs, the x-axis labels are not necessarily the same as the x-values themselves.

Document 9.5a (lineGraph.htm)

```
<html>
<head><title></title></head>
<body>
<h3>Create a line graph</h3>
<form method="post" action="lineGraph.php">
<table border><tr><td>Data file, format:<br />
 Graph title<br />
 X-axis title<br />Y-axis title<br />
 X-axis labels (strings, comma-separated)<br />
 Y-axis labels (strings, comma-separated)<br />
 X<sub>min</sub> X<sub>max</sub> Y<sub>min</sub>
    Y<sub>max</sub><br />
 # of Y data sets to plot (1-3)<br />
 data: X Y1 [Y2] [Y3] <br />
 . . .
</td><td><input type="text" name="fileName" size="20"
    value="lineGraph.dat" />
</td></tr></table>
Drawing canvas total size (pixels): X <input type="text"
    name="xCanvas" size="4" value="800" />
Y <input type="text" name="yCanvas" size="4" value="500"
    /><br />
graphing space (pixels): X <input type="text"
    name="xPixelRange" value="500" size="3" />
Y <input type="text" name="yPixelRange" value="300"
    size="3" /><br />
X-offset from left for start of graphing space (pixels):
<input type="text" name="x0" value="100" size="3" /><br />
Background RGB color string: <input type="text"
 name="colorString" value="225,225,225" size="10" /><br />
<table border><tr><td>
  Y1 line color: </td><td>
 black:<input type="radio" name="Y1Color" value="black"
    size="8" />  
 blue:<input type="radio" name="Y1Color" value="blue"
```

```
      size="8" />  
  grey:<input type="radio" name="Y1Color" value="grey"
      size="8" />  
  green:<input type="radio" name="Y1Color" value="green"
      size="8" />  
  red:<input type="radio" name="Y1Color" value="red" size="8"
      checked />
</td></tr></table>
<table border><tr><td>
  Y2 line color: </td><td>
  black:<input type="radio" name="Y2Color" value="black"
      size="8" />  
  blue:<input type="radio" name="Y2Color" value="blue"
      size="8" />  
  grey:<input type="radio" name="Y2Color" value="grey"
      size="8" />  
  green:<input type="radio" name="Y2Color" value="green"
      size="8" checked />  
  red: <input type="radio" name="Y2Color" value="red"
      size="8" />
</td></tr></table>
<table border><tr><td>
  Y3 line color: </td><td>
  black:<input type="radio" name="Y3Color" value="black"
      size="8" />  
  blue:<input type="radio" name="Y3Color" value="blue"
      size="8" checked />  
  grey:<input type="radio" name="Y3Color" value="grey"
      size="8" />  
  green:<input type="radio" name="Y3Color" value="green"
      size="8" />  
  red:<input type="radio" name="Y3Color" value="red"
      size="8" />
</td></tr></table>
Symbols? Yes <input type="radio" value="Y" name="symbols"
    size="2" checked />
    No <input type="radio" value="N" name="symbols"
      size="2" />
Lines? Yes <input type="radio" value="Y" name="line"
    size="2" checked />
No <input type="radio" value="N" name="lines"
      size="2" /><br />
<input type="submit"
    value="Click here to generate line graph." /><br />
<input type="reset"
    value="Click here to reset fields to original values." /><br />
</form></body></html>
```

Document 9.5b (lineGraph.php)

```php
<?php
function drawLine ($symbol, $line, $X, $Y1, $Y2, $Y3, $c1, $c2, $c3,
   $n_Ydata, $xMin, $xMax, $yMin, $yMax, $xLabels, $yLabels,
   $ChartTitle, $xPixelRange, $yPixelRange, $xTitle, $yTitle,
   $bkgrd, $xCanvas, $yCanvas, $x0) {
Header ("Content-type: image/gif");
$y0=50; // (x0,y0) from lower left of canvas
$ChartTitleYoffset=25; $xTitleYoffset=25;
$im = imageCreate ($xCanvas, $yCanvas) or
   die ("Cannot Initialize new GD image stream");
$background_color =
ImageColorAllocate ($im, $bkgrd[0], $bkgrd[1], $bkgrd[2]);
$black=ImageColorAllocate ($im, 0, 0, 0);
$color1=ImageColorAllocate ($im, $c1[0], $c1[1], $c1[2]);
$color2=ImageColorAllocate ($im, $c2[0], $c2[1], $c2[2]);
$color3=ImageColorAllocate ($im, $c3[0], $c3[1], $c3[2]);
// define a black and transparent dashed line for grid lines
$style = array (
   $black, $black, $black, $black, $black,
   IMG_COLOR_TRANSPARENT, IMG_COLOR_TRANSPARENT,
   IMG_COLOR_TRANSPARENT, IMG_COLOR_TRANSPARENT,
   IMG_COLOR_TRANSPARENT
);
ImageSetStyle ($im, $style);
ImageSetThickness ($im, 1);
// draw xTitle
$xTitleXoffset=0;
$xTitleXoffset=$xPixelRange/2-strlen (trim ($xTitle))/2*9;
ImageString ($im, 5, $x0+$xTitleXoffset, $yCanvas-
$y0+$xTitleYoffset, trim ($xTitle), $black);
// draw x labels and vertical axes
$n_x=count ($xLabels); $xGap=$xPixelRange/($n_x-1);
for ($i=0; $i<$n_x; $i++) {
   ImageString ($im, 5, $x0+$i* $xGap, $yCanvas-
$y0+5, trim ($xLabels[$i]), $black);
   ImageLine ($im, $x0+$i* $xGap, $yCanvas-
$y0, $x0+$i* $xGap, $yCanvas-$y0-$yPixelRange, $black);
}
// draw y labels
$offset=5+strlen (trim ($yLabels[0]))* 9;
$n_y=count ($yLabels); $yGap=$yPixelRange/($n_y-1);
for ($i=0; $i<$n_y; $i++) {
   ImageString ($im, 5, $x0-$offset, $yCanvas-$y0-
      $i* $yGap-8, trim ($yLabels[$i]), $black);
   ImageLine ($im, $x0, $yCanvas-$y0-$i* $yGap, $x0+
      $xPixelRange, $yCanvas-$y0-$i* $yGap, IMG_COLOR_STYLED);
}
// draw yTitle
```

```php
$off=($n_y-1)*$yGap/2-strlen(trim($yTitle))/2*9;
ImageStringUp($im,5,$x0-$offset-25,$yCanvas-
  $y0-$off,trim($yTitle),$black);
// draw data
  $x1=($X[0]-$xMin)/($xMax-$xMin)*$xPixelRange;
  $y1_1=($Y1[0]-$yMin)/($yMax-$yMin)*$yPixelRange;
  $y1_2=($Y2[0]-$yMin)/($yMax-$yMin)*$yPixelRange;
  $y1_3=($Y3[0]-$yMin)/($yMax-$yMin)*$yPixelRange;
for ($i=1; $i<count($X); $i++) {
  $x2=($X[$i]-$xMin)/($xMax-$xMin)*$xPixelRange;
  $y2_1=($Y1[$i]-$yMin)/($yMax-$yMin)*$yPixelRange;
  if ($line=='Y') ImageLine($im,$x0+$x1,$yCanvas-
    $y0-$y1_1,$x0+$x2,$yCanvas-$y0-$y2_1,$color1);
  if ($symbol=='Y') {
    drawSymbol($im,$x0+$x1,$yCanvas-$y0-$y1_1,$color1);
    drawSymbol($im,$x0+$x2,$yCanvas-$y0-$y2_1,$color1);
  } $y1_1=$y2_1;
  if ($n_Ydata>=2) {
    $y2_2=($Y2[$i]-$yMin)/($yMax-$yMin)*$yPixelRange;
    if ($line=='Y') ImageLine($im,$x0+$x1,$yCanvas-
      $y0-$y1_2,$x0+$x2,$yCanvas-$y0-$y2_2,$color2);
    if ($symbol=='Y') {
      drawSymbol($im,$x0+$x1,$yCanvas-$y0-$y1_2,$color2);
      drawSymbol($im,$x0+$x2,$yCanvas-$y0-$y2_2,$color2);
    } $y1_2=$y2_2;
  }
   if ($n_Ydata==3) {
    $y2_3=($Y3[$i]-$yMin)/($yMax-$yMin)*$yPixelRange;
    if ($line=='Y') ImageLine($im,$x0+$x1,$yCanvas-
      $y0-$y1_3,$x0+$x2,$yCanvas-$y0-$y2_3,$color3);
    if ($symbol=='Y') {
      drawSymbol($im,$x0+$x1,$yCanvas-$y0-$y1_3,$color3);
      drawSymbol($im,$x0+$x2,$yCanvas-$y0-$y2_3,$color3);
    } $y1_3=$y2_3;
  } $x1=$x2;
}
// draw graph space boundaries
ImageSetThickness($im,2);
ImageLine($im,$x0,$yCanvas-$y0,$x0+$xPixelRange,
  $yCanvas-$y0,$black);

ImageLine($im,$x0,$yCanvas-$y0-
$yPixelRange,$x0+$xPixelRange,$yCanvas-
  $y0-$yPixelRange,$black);
ImageLine($im,$x0+$xPixelRange,$yCanvas-
  $y0,$x0+$xPixelRange,$yCanvas-$y0-$yPixelRange,$black);
ImageLine($im,$x0,$yCanvas-$y0,$x0,$yCanvas-$y0-
$yPixelRange,$black);
ImageString($im,5,$x0,$yCanvas-$y0-$yPixelRange-
  $ChartTitleYoffset,trim($ChartTitle),$black);
ImageGIF($im); ImageDestroy($im); // draw image and release
```

```
resources
}
function drawSymbol($im,$x,$y,$color) {
   Imageline($im,$x-5,$y-5,$x+5,$y+5,$color);
   ImageLine($im,$x+5,$y-5,$x-5,$y+5,$color);
}
//--------- MAIN PROGRAM ----------------
$fileName=$_POST["fileName"];
$in=fopen($fileName,"r");
$xLabels=array(); $yLabels=array();
$X=array();$Y1=array();$Y2=array();
$ChartTitle=fgets($in); // title
$xTitle=fgets($in); // x-axis label
$yTitle=fgets($in); // y-axis label
$s=fgets($in); // x value labels
$xLabels=explode(',',$s);
$s=fgets($in); // y value labels
$yLabels=explode(',',$s);
fscanf($in,"%f %f %f %f",$xMin,$xMax,$yMin,$yMax);
fscanf($in,"%u",$n_Ydata);
$i=-1;
while (!feof($in)) {
  $s=fgets($in);
  if (strlen($s)>3) {
    $i++;
    if ($n_Ydata==1) sscanf($s,"%f %f",$X[$i],$Y1[$i]);
    elseif ($n_Ydata==2) sscanf($s,"%f %f %f",
      $X[$i],$Y1[$i],$Y2[$i]);
    else sscanf($s,"%f %f %f %f",
      $X[$i],$Y1[$i],$Y2[$i],$Y3[$i]);
  }
}
fclose($in);
$colorString="225,225,225";
$bgcolor=explode(',',$colorString);
$xCanvas=800; $yCanvas=500;
$x0=100;
$xPixelRange=$_POST["xPixelRange"];
$yPixelRange=$_POST["yPixelRange"];
$Y1Color=$_POST["Y1Color"];$Y2Color=$_POST["Y2Color"];
$Y3Color=$_POST["Y3Color"];
$color1=chooseColor($Y1Color);$color2=chooseColor($Y2Color);
$color3=chooseColor($Y3Color);
$symbols=$_POST["symbols"]; $line=$_POST["line"];
drawLine($symbols,$line,$X,$Y1,$Y2,$Y3,$color1,$color3,
  $color2,$n_Ydata,$xMin,$xMax,$yMin,$yMax,$xLabels,
  $yLabels,$ChartTitle,$xPixelRange,$yPixelRange,$xTitle,
  $yTitle,$bgcolor,$xCanvas,$yCanvas,$x0);
function chooseColor($c) {
   $color=array();
```

```php
switch ($c) {
    case "red":
        $color[0] =255; $color[1] =0; $color[2] =0; break;
    case "blue":
        $color[0] =0; $color[1] =0; $color[2] =255; break;
    case "green":
        $color[0] =0; $color[1] =255; $color[2] =0; break;
    case "black":
        $color[0] =0; $color[1] =0; $color[2] =0; break;
    case "grey":
        $color[0] =150; $color[1] =150; $color[2] =150; break;
    }
    return $color;
}
?>
```

The HTML interface to lineGraph.php is similar to the bar chart interfaces; the data file includes all the data-specific information for up to three sets of data and there is additional input for defining the graph's appearance. This input includes a choice to display lines between data points, symbols at each data point, or both.

Create a line graph

Data file, format:
Graph title
X-axis title
Y-axis title
X-axis labels (strings, comma-separated)
Y-axis labels (strings, comma-separated)   lineGraph.dat
X_{min} X_{max} Y_{min} Y_{max}
# of Y data sets to plot (1-3)
data: X Y1 [Y2] [Y3]
...

Drawing canvas total size (pixels): X 800   Y 500
graphing space (pixels): X 500   Y 300
X-offset from left of canvas for start of graphing space (pixels): 100
Background RGB color string: 225,225,225

Y1 line color: black: ○   blue: ○   grey: ○   green: ○   red: ⊙
Y2 line color: black: ○   blue: ○   grey: ○   green: ⊙   red: ○
Y3 line color: black: ○   blue: ⊙   grey: ○   green: ○   red: ○
Symbols? Yes ⊙ No ○ Lines? Yes ⊙ No ○

    Click here to generate line graph.
        Click here to reset all fields to their original values.

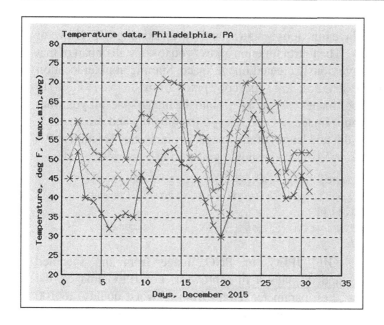

9.7 Summary of Some GD Graphics Functions

The "official" names of GD functions use all lowercase letters. However, taking advantage of the fact that PHP function names are case-insensitive, uppercase letters are used here to separate "words" in function names. Hence, `imagecreate()` is written as `ImageCreate()`. This is simply a style choice to make code a little easier to read. The variable names are just descriptive generic "place holder" names that can be changed as desired. Optional parameters are enclosed in square brackets.

9.7.1 Create and Save GD Image Space, Display Images

(resource) `ImageCreate(`*(int) $width, (int) $height)*
    Returns an image handle representing an image space of size width × height pixels.

(resource) `ImageCreateFromGIF`*(string) $filename)*
(resource) `ImageCreateFromJPEG`*(string) $filename)*
(resource) `ImageCreateFromPNG`*(string) $filename)*
`ImageCopy($im,`*(resource),$x,$y,$s_x0,$s_y0,$s_w,$s_h)*

The first three functions assign a handle to an existing GIF, JPEG, or PNG image file. The fourth function allows you to copy all or part of that image onto a previously created image space. Starting at pixel location ($x, $y) in the *(resource)* file, copy pixels from ($s_x0, $x_y0) to image pixel coordinates ($s_w, $s_h) into the image space. If you want to copy the entire image, $s_x0, $x_y0 must be 0,0 and $s_w, $s_h must be the width and length of the image, in pixels. See Document 9.6 below in Sect. 9.7.1 for code showing how to use ImageCopy().

```
ImageGIF( (resource) $image[ , (string) $filename] )
ImageJPEG( (resource) $image[ , (string) $filename,
 (int) $quality] )
ImagePNG( (resource) $image[ , (string) $filename,
 (int) $quality] )
```

Creates a GIF, JPEG, or PNG image from the specified *(resource)* and displays it in a browser. For JPEG images, the optional *$quality* parameter ranges from 0 (worst quality) to 100 (best quality), with a default value of 75. For PNG images, *$quality* is a compression level from 0 (no compression) to 9, with a default value of 6.

If the optional *$filename* parameter is used, the image will be saved as *$filename* and will not be displayed in a browser window. Both options can be exercised with two calls in the document, as shown below in Document 9.6, Sect. 9.7.3. The file type of the original image resource handle source (GIF, JPEG, or PNG) does not matter.

```
ImageDestroy( (resource) $image)
```
Frees memory associated with the image handle *$image*, after the image has been displayed on a browser page and/or saved as a file.

9.7.2 Draw Lines and Shapes

```
(int) ImageColorAllocate( (resource) $image, (int) $red,
 (int) $green, (int) $blue)
```
Returns a color identifier for the color defined by the specified RGB components. A maximum of 256 calls to ImageColorAllocate() is allowed in a single PHP application. The first call, like

```
$background_color = ImageColorAllocate($im, 200, 200,
200);
```
assigns the background color for images created with ImageCreate(). and fills the defined canvas with that color.

RGB color specifiers are base-10 integers, in the range 0–255. Often, HTML colors are expressed as hexadecimal values. For example, the hex code for a gold color is #D4A017. These RGB values can be provided as input to ImageColorAllocate() by using the hexdec() function:

```
ImageColorAllocate($im,hexdec('D4'),hexdec('A0'),
                   hexdec('17')
```

(bool) ImageSetThickness((resource) *$image*,
  (int) *$thickness*)
  Sets thickness of the line used to draw straight lines and shapes.

(bool) ImageArc(*(resource) $image, (int) $cx, (int) $cy,*
  (int) $width, (int) $height, (int) $start, (int) $end,
  (int) $color)
(bool) ImageFilledArc((resource) *$image*, (int) *$cx*,
  (int) *$cy*, (int) *$width*, (int) *$height*, (int) *$start*,
  (int) *$end*, (int) *$color*, (int) *$style*)
  Draws an arc of an ellipse or circle of size width × height pixels, centered at (c_x, c_y) coordinates from *$start* angle to *$end* angle, starting at the "three o'clock"position in conventional x-y space, outlined or fills the arc with the specified color, with the following possibilities for *$style*:

IMG_ARC_PIE draws a circular or elliptical segment
IMG_ARC_CHORD draws a triangular segment
IMG_ARC_NOFILL draws a line only around the outer edge of the segment
IMG_ARC_EDGED produces the same result as IMG_ARC_PIE.

(bool) ImageEllipse(*(resource) $image, (int) $cx,*
  (int) $cy, (int) $width, (int) $height, (int) $color)
(bool) ImageFilledEllipse(*(resource) $image,*
  (int) $cx, (int) $cy, (int) $width, (int) $height,
  (int) $color)
  Draws an ellipse (or circle) of size width × height pixels centered at the specified (c_x, c_y) coordinates, outlined or filled with the specified color.

(bool) ImageFill(*(resource) $image, (int) $x, (int) $y,*
  (int) $color)
  Floods a bounded area surrounding specified (x,y) coordinates with the specified color, where (x,y) are the coordinates of the upper left-hand corner.

(bool) ImageLine(*(resource) $image, (int) $x1,*
  (int) $y1, (int) $x2, (int) $y2, (int) $color)
    Draws a line between two specified pixel coordinates (x_1,y_1) and (x_2,y_2). A black dashed line can be created like this:

```
$black = ImageColorAllocate($image,0,0,0);
$style = Array($black,$black,$black,$black,$black,
  IMG_COLOR_TRANSPARENT, IMG_COLOR_TRANSPARENT,
  IMG_COLOR_TRANSPARENT, IMG_COLOR_TRANSPARENT,
  IMG_COLOR_TRANSPARENT);
ImageSetStyle($im, $style);
...
ImageLine($image,$x1,$y1,$x2,$x2,IMG_COLOR_STYLED);
```

    This code draws a line with black dashes 5 pixels long, and a 5-pixel "open space" between the dashes transparent to the background color. (You could assign this "open space" a different color, rather than have it be transparent.)

(bool) ImagePolygon(*(resource) $image,* (array) $points,
  (int) $n_points, (int) $color)
(bool) ImageFilledPolygon(*(resource) $image,*
  (array) $points, (int) $n_points, (int) $color)
    Draws a closed polygon using the specified array of points, outlined or filled with the specified color.

(bool) ImageRectangle(*(resource) $image, (int) $x1,*
  (int) $y1, (int) $x2, (int) $y2, (int) $color)
(bool) ImageFilledRectangle(*(resource) $image,*
  (int) $x1, (int) $y1, (int) $x2, (int) $y2, (int)
$color)
    Draws a rectangle using the two specified sets of (x,y) coordinates as opposite corners, outlined or filled with the specified color.

9.7.3 Display Text

(bool) ImageString(*(resource) $image, (int) $font,*
  (int) $x, (int) $y, (string) $string, (int) $color)
    Draws a text string horizontally starting at specified (x,y) coordinates, with a font specified from 1 (smallest) to 5 (largest). The starting coordinates are the upper left-hand corner of the first character.

(bool) ImageStringUp(*(resource) $image, (int) $font,*
  (int) $x, (int) $y, (string) $string, (int) $color)

Similar to ImageString(), but rotates the text string by –90° for drawing labels and titles on the y-axis of a graph, for example.

(bool) ImageTTFText(*(resource) $image, (int) $size, (int) $angle, (int) $x, (int) $y, (resource) $font_file, ($string) $text)*

Draws a text string using a TrueType font (.ttf) file. The font size is specified in pixels (GD1 version) or point size (GD2). (Older PHP installations may have GD1, but newer installations should have GD2.) The *$angle* at which the text is displayed, in degrees, is horizontally left-to-right for 0° and rotating counter-clockwise as the angle increases. The (x,y) coordinates specify the lower left-hand corner of the first character, but the y coordinate is the font baseline, not the bottom of a character such as g or p that extends below the baseline. (Compare with the interpretation of coordinates for ImageString() and ImageStringUp().) In order to use this function, the requested *$font_file* must be available on your computer, typically in the same directory folder as the PHP application.

Document 9.6 shows how to use a TrueType font and also how to display and save images. In this example, the GD image space is created as a GIF image, but the image is saved as a PNG file with a default compression level of 6. It worth noting that the image shown below has a file size of 20 KB with default compression and 236 KB if the compression is set to 0! It is not surprising that the compression yields such a dramatic reduction in the image file size, given that most of the image is featureless, with a single color; any compression scheme which couldn't take advantage of this fact is not worth using!

Document 9.6 (displayImage.php)

```php
<?php
Header ("Content-type: image/gif");
$TitleString =
  "Institute for Earth Science Research and Education";
$x_max = 600; $y_max = 400;
$x0=40; $y0= 40;
$im = ImageCreate($x_max,$y_max) or die
  ("Cannot Initialize new GD image stream");
$background_color = ImageColorAllocate($im, 200, 200, 200);
// define text color
$navy = ImageColorAllocate($im,0,0,150);
$src=ImageCreateFromJPEG ("IESRElogo.jpg");
```

```
ImageCopy($im,$src,$x0,$y0,0,0,126,153);
$y0=200;
ImageCopy($im,$src,$x0,$y0,50,50,126,153);
$y0=25;
ImageTTFText($im,18,0,$x0,$y0,$navy,"timesbi.ttf",
   $TitleString);
ImageGIF($im);
ImagePNG($im,"displayImage.png");
ImageDestroy($im);
?>
```

To display the entire image, you need to start at its upper left-hand corner (0,0) and you need to know its size (126×153 pixels for the image used in Document 9.6), which can be obtained from image processing software.[2] The lower image shows what happens when you display only

part of the image (by not starting at the upper left-hand corner).

The text is written in dark blue (navy) 18-point bold italic Times Roman font, using the `timesbi.ttf` file which has been copied into the \www folder where PHP applications are stored. As noted previously in this chapter, you can't determine how many pixels a TrueType font will span just by knowing the font size and counting the characters in a string because most TrueType fonts are proportionally spaced. If you really need to know, you can get that information from the `ImageTTFBbox()` function (look it up online), which returns an array whose elements include the pixel values for a "bounding box" occupied by a specified string.

---

[2]As usual, the author uses IrfanView for these tasks.

PHP from a Command Line

10

This chapter gives a brief introduction to using PHP from a command line. This capability does not require that PHP run on a server and it allows user input from the keyboard while a script is executing.

Throughout this book, the model for using PHP has been to create an HTML document to serve as an interface that passes form field values as input through the $ POST [ ] array to a PHP application running on a local or remote server. It might sometimes be useful to be able to run short PHP code examples as stand-alone applications. But, without an HTML interface to a PHP application, there is no provision for keyboard input to a server-based application that requires user input.

It is, in fact, possible to create stand-alone PHP applications that will accept keyboard input by running PHP code from a command line interface (CLI). Doing so removes the possibilities for HTML formatting of PHP output in a browser window, or for including graphics, so this is a solution that makes sense only for calculations with simple input/output requirements.

The first step toward using PHP from a local command line prompt is to find where the php.exe program resides. On a local computer, this is probably not the same folder from which you have previously executed PHP applications on your local server. On a Windows computer, assume that this file is located in C:\ PHP.

Next, create this simple PHP file with a text editor and store it as hello.php in C:\ PHP:

```php
<?php
  echo "Hello, world!";
?>
```

Here is the record of a Windows command line session to execute this file from C:\ PHP. You can type the line as shown

```
C:\PHP>php hello.php
Hello, world!
C:\PHP>
```

© Springer International Publishing AG 2017
D.R. Brooks, *Programming in HTML and PHP*, Undergraduate Topics in Computer Science, DOI 10.1007/978-3-319-56973-4_10

or you can type `php.exe hello.php`—the `.exe` extension is assumed on Windows computers.

This is a trivial PHP application, but it is important because it differs fundamentally from what has been presented in the previous chapters of this book. This PHP application will run from *any* directory that contains the `php.exe` application and its associated dynamic link library (`.dll`) file—assumed to be `C:\PHP` on this computer. This application did *not* run on a server (although it could have been)!

There are several command line options that can be used when a PHP file is executed, but they are not needed for the simple examples shown in this chapter. As always, there are many online sources of more information about using a CLI with PHP.

PHP's command line capabilities would make more sense if you can provide input to a PHP application that actually does something useful. Consider this problem:

> Write a stand-alone application that allows a user to enter an upper and lower limit and then calculates the integral of the normal probability density function,
>
> $$\text{pdf}(x) = \frac{\exp(-x^2/2)}{\sqrt{2\pi}}$$
>
> using those two limits. This function cannot be integrated analytically, so numerical integration is required. There are several ways to integrate functions numerically, but so-called Trapezoidal Rule integration will work well for this problem:
>
> $$\int_{x_a}^{x_b} \text{pdf}(x) \approx \left(\sum_{i=1}^{i=n-1} [f(x_i) + f(x_i + \Delta x)] \right) \frac{\Delta x}{2}$$

Start the code for a CLI application with this short script:

```php
<?php
  $a = $_SERVER['argv'];
  print_r($a);
?>
```

In the same way that $\$\_POST[\ ]$ contains values passed from an HTML document, the $'argv'$ element of the $\$\_SERVER[\ ]$ array contains values passed from a command line. The arguments passed to the PHP application through the $'argv'$ array include the file name of the application itself as the first element (element 0). Therefore, the lower and upper limits for the numerical integration are the second and third elements of array $\$a$, $\$a[1]$ and $\$a[2]$. Document 10.1 shows the complete code for this problem.

Document 10.1 (pdf_1.php)

```php
<?php
   $a = $_SERVER['argv'];
   print_r($a);
   $x1=$a[1]; $x2=$a[2];
   $n=200;
   $sum=0; $dx=($x2-$x1)/$n;
   for ($i=1; $i<=$n; $i++) {
      $x=$x1+($i-1)*$dx;
      $y1=exp(-$x*$x/2)/sqrt(2.*M_PI);
      $x=$x1+$i*$dx;
      $y2=exp(-$x*$x/2)/sqrt(2.*M_PI);
      $sum+=$y1+$y2;
   }
   echo "\n" . $sum*$dx/2.;
?>
```

CLI 10.1 shows a command line session that executes this code. The application expects you to provide the upper and lower integration limits after the PHP file name. No prompts are provided for this information, and it is the user's responsibility to know what needs to be entered. Note that the HTML formatting tags that have been used

```
C:\PHP>php pdf_1.php -.5 .5
Array
(
    [0] => pdf_1.php
    [1] => -.5
    [2] => .5
)

0.38292418907776
C:\PHP>
CLI 10.1
```

in previous chapters—
 to produce a line break, for example—will not work in this environment. Instead, the final echo statement in Document 10.1 contains a line feed escape character, \n.

In general, it would be more helpful to be able to provide prompts to the user about required input from within a PHP application being executed from the CLI. Document 10.2 shows another approach to evaluating the normal probability distribution function which prompts user input from the keyboard, to be entered while the script is executing.

Document 10.2 (pdf_2.php)

```php
<?php
  echo "\nGive lower and upper limits for evaluating
pdf,\nseparated by a space: ";
  fscanf(STDIN,"%f %f",$x1,$x2);
  echo $x1 . ", " . $x2;
  $n=200;
  $sum=0; $dx=($x2-$x1)/$n;
  for ($i=1; $i<=$n; $i++) {
    $x=$x1+($i-1)*$dx;
    $y1=exp(-$x*$x/2)/sqrt(2.*M_PI);
    $x=$x1+$i*$dx;
    $y2=exp(-$x*$x/2)/sqrt(2.*M_PI);
    $sum+=$y1+$y2;
  }
  echo "\n" . $sum*$dx/2.;
?>
```

```
C:\PHP>php pdf_2.php

Give lower and upper limits for evaluating pdf,
separated by a space: -3 3
-3, 3
0.99729820978444
```
CLI 10.2

Document 10.2 uses the fscanf() function. But, instead of using a user-supplied file handle as the input resource, fscanf() uses the reserved name STDIN (in uppercase letters), which identifies the keyboard as the input resource. The keyboard can be designated as the input resource for any of the other input functions that require a resource identifier, such as fgets() and fread().

It is even possible to write PHP applications that will execute either from a CLI or on a server through an HTML document. Document 10.3a provides an HTML interface and 10.3b is a PHP application that will work either on a server or as a stand-alone CLI application.

Document 10.3a (pdf_3.htm)

```html
<html>
<head>
<title>Integrate the normal probability density
function</title>
</head>
<body>
```

```
<h3>Evaluate the normal probability density function</h3>
<form method="post" action="pdf_3.php">
x1:  <input type="text" name="x1" value="-0.5" /><br />
x2:  <input type="text" name="x2" value=".5"  /><br />
<input type="submit" value="Click to evaluate." />
</form>
</body>
</html>
```

Document 10.3b (pdf_3.php)

```
<?php
  if ($_SERVER['argc'] > 0) {
    $a = $_SERVER['argv'];
    print_r($a);
    $x1=$a[1]; $x2=$a[2];
  }
  else {
    $x1=$_POST['x1'];
    $x2=$_POST['x2'];
    echo $x1 . ", " . $x2 . "<br />";
  }
  $n=200;
  $sum=0; $dx=($x2-$x1)/$n;
  for ($i=1; $i<=$n; $i++) {
    $x=$x1+($i-1)*$dx;
    $y1=exp(-$x*$x/2)/sqrt(2.*M_PI);
    $x=$x1+$i*$dx;
    $y2=exp(-$x*$x/2)/sqrt(2.*M_PI);
    $sum+=$y1+$y2;
  }
  echo $sum*$dx/2.;
?>
```

When Document 10.3b is run from a server, the output looks like this:

```
-0.5, .5
0.38292418907776
```

When Document 10.3b is run from a CLI, the output looks like it did for CLI 10.2.

In Document 10.3b, the 'argc' element of $_SERVER[] contains the number of command line input values passed to the script when it is executed in a CLI. If this value is 0, then the alternate path is executed to retrieve the values passed from Document 11.3a.

The capabilities introduced in this chapter for passing arguments from a command line and accepting user input typed at a keyboard should be very familiar to C programmers, an observation that most readers of this book may find totally irrelevant. There is no doubt that a text-based CLI is primitive by the standards of today's graphical user interfaces (GUIs), but it still has its place for some kinds of applications. Whether you find using a CLI for some PHP applications useful or a giant leap backwards into the long-gone and best forgotten days of text-based computing may depend on your previous programming experience and quite possibly your age!

For proficient programmers, the low resource requirements and pro-gramming overhead of CLI code are attractive advantages for some kinds of applications. For casual programmers, the arguments favoring the use of a CLI are less compelling. However, it is worth remembering that when PHP scripts run from a CLI, they are completely portable because they do not require a server. On a Windows computer you can store such applications on a USB drive along with the php.exe application and its .dll file. Here are the contents of a directory on a USB thumb drive that allows running the PHP applications presented in this chapter from a command prompt on any (Windows) computer.

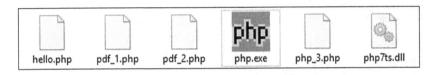

hello.php   pdf_1.php   pdf_2.php   php.exe   php_3.php   php7ts.dll

When you develop your own PHP applications, it may be worth con-sidering whether they can or should be made CLI-compatible, considering the input and output limitations.

Appendices

A.1 List of Code Examples

(continued)

© Springer International Publishing AG 2017
D.R. Brooks, *Programming in HTML and PHP*, Undergraduate Topics
in Computer Science, DOI 10.1007/978-3-319-56973-4

(continued)

Document and name		Page
8.1	formatTest.php	154
8.2	siteFile.php	159
8.3	displayVariables.php	160
8.4	splitString.php	162
8.5	stringCompare.php	164
8.6	ExplodeArray.php	170
8.7	varDump.php	171
8.8	arrayList.php	171
8.9	windspd.php	173
8.10a	getMass.htm	175
8.10b	getMass.php	178
8.11	bmp_info.php	181
8.12	bmp_read.php	183
8.13	bmp_grayscale.php	186
8.14	bmp_hidetext.php	188
8.15	DateTimeConversions.php	191
9.1	graphingSpace.php	194
9.2a	pie2.php	198
9.2b	pieChart.htm	200
9.2c	pieChart.php	201
9.3a	Hbar1.php	204
9.3b	HbarChart.htm	207
9.3c	HbarChart.php	208
9.4a	VbarChart.htm	213
9.4b	VbarChart.php	214
9.5a	lineGraph.htm	219
9.5b	lineGraph.php	221
9.6	displayImage.php	229
10.1	pdf_1.php	233
10.2	pdf_2.php	234
10.3a	pdf_3.htm	234
10.3b	pdf_3.php	235

A.2 Displaying Special Characters

There are many characters that cannot be entered directly into an HTML document from the keyboard. HTML defines so-called "escape sequences" as a way to embed non-keyboard characters, including from PHP scripts. Each character can be entered either as a numerical code or by using a mnemonic name. Only the names will be shown here. The following list provides some commonly used characters that may be useful for science and engineering applications. The list is a *very* small subset of characters supported by various browsers. In cases where special character names follow a predictable pattern (for the Greek alphabet, for example), just one example is given. (See notes at the end of the list.) There is no guarantee that the escape sequence names will be recognized or that characters will be displayed properly in all browsers or, when printed, by all printers.

&alpha;	α	lowercase Greek alpha[*]
&asymp;	≈	mathematics "approximately equal to" symbol
&aacute;	á	lowercase "a" with acute accent[**]
&acirc;	â	lowercase "a" with circumflex[**]
&aelig;	æ	lowercase "ae" ligature (Æ for uppercase)
&agrave;	à	lowercase "a" with grave accent[**]
&aring;	å	lowercase "a" with ring[**]
&auml;	ä	lowercase "a" with umlaut[**]
&bull;	·	small "bullet" symbol (to indicate multiplication, for example)
&ccedil;	ç	lowercase "c" with cedilla[**]
&cent;	¢	cent symbol
&cong;	≅	mathematics "approximately equal to" symbol
&copy;	©	copyright symbol
&deg;	°	degree (as with temperature)
&dagger;	†	dagger symbol
&Dagger;	‡	double dagger symbol
&divide;	÷	mathematics "divide by" symbol
&euro;	€	Euro currency
&frac12;	½	fraction notation for 1/2
&frac14;	¼	fraction notation for 1/4
&frac34;	¾	fraction notation for 3/4
&ge;	≥	mathematics "greater than or equal to" symbol
&gt;	>	mathematics "greater than" symbol (to avoid conflict with angle bracket in HTML tags)

(continued)

&hellip;	...	horizontal ellipsis
&infin;	∞	mathematics "infinity" symbol
&int;	∫	mathematics "integral" symbol
&iques;	¿	inverted question mark
&ldquo;	"	left double quote ("smart quote")
&lsquo;	'	left single quote ("smart quote")
&le;	≤	mathematics "less than or equal to" symbol
&lt;	<	mathematics "less than" symbol (to avoid conflict with angle bracket in HTML tags)
&micro;	μ	micron
&ne;	≠	mathematics "not equal to" symbol
		forced space
&ntilde;	ñ	lowercase n with tilde[**]
&oelig;	œ	lowercase "oe" ligature (Œ for uppercase)
&para;	¶	paragraph symbol
&plusmn;	±	mathematics "plus-minus" symbol
&pound;	£	British pound sterling
&prop;	∝	mathematics "proportional to" symbol
&quot;	"	quote symbol (e.g., for inserting quote marks in quote-delimited text string)
&radic;	√	mathematics "square root" symbol
&rdquo;	"	right double quote ("smart quote")
&rsquo;	'	right single quote ("smart quote")
&reg;	®	product registration symbol
&sect;	§	section symbol
&szlig;	ß	"sz" ligature (lowercase only)
&times;	×	mathematics "times " ("multiply by") symbol
&trade;	™	trademark symbol

[*]Other Greek letters can be displayed by spelling the name of the letter. If the name starts with an uppercase character the corresponding uppercase Greek letter is displayed. For example, γ displays γ and Γ displays Γ

[**]Other modified letters follow the same pattern. Start the name with an uppercase or lowercase letter to display a modified uppercase or lowercase character

A.3 ASCII Character Codes

The first 127 ASCII character codes are standardized and the remaining characters are system-dependent; the values shown are for Windows-based PCs. These characters can be displayed from a Windows computer keyboard by pressing and holding the Alt key and pressing the corresponding base-10 (Dec) code on the numerical keypad ("locked" with the NumLock key).

Dec	Hex		Dec	Hex		Dec	Hex	
0	0	(1)	32	20	(2)	63	3F	?
1	1	☺	33	21	!	64	40	@
2	2	●	34	22	"	65	41	A
3	3	♥	35	23	#	66	42	B
4	4	♦	36	24	$	67	43	C
5	5	♠	37	25	%	68	44	D
6	6	♠	38	26	&	69	45	E
7	7	•	39	27	'	70	46	F
8	8	◘	40	28	(	71	47	G
9	9	○	41	29	)	72	48	H
10	A	◙	42	2A	*	73	49	I
11	B	♂	43	2B	+	74	4A	J
12	C	♀	44	2C	,	75	4B	K
13	D	♪	45	2D	-	76	4C	L
14	E	♫	46	2E	.	77	4D	M
15	F	☼	47	2F	/	78	4E	N
16	10	►	48	30	0	79	4F	O
17	11	◄	49	31	1	80	50	P
18	12	↕	50	32	2	81	51	Q
19	13	‼	51	33	3	82	52	P
20	14	¶	52	34	4	83	53	S
21	15	§	53	35	5	84	54	T
22	16	▬	54	36	6	85	55	U
23	17	↨	55	37	7	86	56	V
24	18	↑	56	38	8	87	57	W
25	19	↓	57	39	9	88	58	X
26	1A	→	58	3A	:	89	59	Y
27	1B	←	59	3B	;	90	5A	Z
28	1C	∟	60	3C	<	91	5B	[
29	1D	↔	61	3D	=	92	5C	\
30	1E	▲	62	3E	>	93	5D	]
31	1F	▼						

Dec	Hex		Dec	Hex		Dec	Hex	
94	5E	^	134	86	å	175	AF	»
95	5F	_	135	87	ç	176	B0	
96	60	`	136	88	ê	177	B1	
97	61	a	137	89	ë	178	B2	
98	62	b	138	8A	è	179	B3	
99	63	c	139	8B	ï	180	B4	┤
100	64	d	140	8C	î	181	B5	╡
101	65	e	141	8D	ì	182	B6	╢
102	66	f	142	8E	Ä	183	B7	╖
103	67	g	143	8F	Å	184	B8	╕
104	68	h	144	90	É	185	B9	╣
105	69	i	145	91	æ	186	BA	║
106	6A	j	146	92	Æ	187	BB	╗
107	6B	k	147	93	ô	188	BC	╝
108	6C	l	148	94	ö	189	BD	╜
109	6D	m	149	95	ò	190	BE	╛
110	6E	n	150	96	û	191	BF	┐
111	6F	o	151	97	ù	192	CO	└
112	70	p	152	98	ÿ	193	C1	┴
113	71	q	153	99	Ö	194	C2	┬
114	72	r	154	9A	Ü	195	C3	├
115	73	s	155	9B	¢	196	C4	─
116	74	t	156	9C	£	197	C5	┼
117	75	u	157	9D	¥	198	C6	╞
118	76	v	158	9E	Pts	199	C7	╟
119	77	w	159	9F	ƒ	200	C8	╚
120	78	x	160	A0	á	201	C9	╔
121	79	y	161	A1	í	202	CA	╩
122	7A	z	162	A2	ó	203	CB	╦
123	7B	{	163	A3	ú	204	CC	╠
124	7C			164	A4	ñ	205	CD	═
125	7D			165	A5	Ñ	206	CE	╬
126	7E	}	166	A6	ª	207	CF	
127	7F	⌂	167	A7	º	208	D0	╨
128	80[3]	Ç	168	A8	¿	209	D1	╤
129	81	ü	169	A9	⌐	210	D2	
130	82	é	170	AA	¬	211	D3	╥
131	83	â	171	AB	½	212	D4	╘
132	84	ä	172	AC	¼	213	D5	╒
133	85	à	173	AD	¡			
Dec	Hex		174	AE	«			

Dec	Hex		Dec	Hex	
214	D6		235	EB	δ
215	D7		236	EC	∞
216	D8		237	ED	φ
217	D9		238	EE	ε
218	DA		239	EF	$\cap$
219	DB		240	F0	$\equiv$
220	DC		241	F1	$\pm$
221	DD		242	F2	$\geq$
222	DE		243	F3	$\leq$
223	DF		244	F4	$\lceil$
224	E0	α	245	F5	$\rfloor$
225	E1	β	246	F6	$\div$
226	E2	Γ	247	F7	$\approx$
227	E3	π	248	F8	$\circ$
228	E4	Σ	249	F9	$\cdot$
229	E5	σ	250	FA	$\cdot$
230	E6	μ	251	FB	$\sqrt{}$
231	E7	τ	252	FC	^{n}
232	E8	Φ	253	FD	^{2}
233	E9	Θ	254	FE	$\blacksquare$
234	EA	Ω	255	FF	(4)

[1] ASCII 0 is a null character.

[2] ASCII 32 is a space (as produced by pressing the space bar on your keyboard).

[3] Because the Euro did not exist when the ASCII character sequence was standardized, its symbol, €, does not have a representation in the standard sequence (although it is available as a special character for many fonts in Microsoft Word, for example). On some European computer systems, it may take the place of Ç, the character for ASCII code 128.

[4] ASCII 255 is a blank character.

A.4 Strategies for Solving Computational Problems

There are two basic skills you must develop while learning to write programs in any language, including PHP. Obviously, you must learn the details of the programming language you are using. But, it is equally important to develop a consistent strategy for solving computational problems that is *independent* of the language you are using.

This strategy requires five steps:

1. Define the problem.
2. Outline a solution.
3. Design an algorithm.
4. Convert the algorithm into program code.
5. Verify the operation of the program.

Step 1 Define the problem.

Real-world computing problems need to be defined carefully. It is often the case that properly defining a problem in terms of the tools that are available is a giant step toward solving that problem. This step involves making sure you understand the problem and can state it clearly in your own words. It is not possible to solve a problem that you can't explain to yourself! And, until you can do this, there is no point proceeding to Steps 2–5.

Step 2 Outline a solution.

This is an informal but very important step. You should focus first on understanding the information needed to solve the problem and then on the nature of the output produced as a result of solving the problem. You need to be sure you understand whatever processing steps or mathematical calculations are required.

It is often difficult to think about solving problems in the straightforward and linear way that is required in order to write a successful computer program:

input → calculations or other processing → output

However, you should have these steps clearly in mind before proceeding to Step 3.

Step 3 Design an algorithm.

This step is critical to writing successful programs. It may sometimes be combined with Step 2 whenever the conceptual knowledge required to solve a problem is already at hand. In a programming context, an algorithm consists of specific steps that must be followed in sequence to attain a clearly defined goal. This may seem obvious, but a common problem for beginning programmers is that the code they write imposes an "algorithm" that does not make sense because it does not proceed in a logical step-by-step fashion. When this happens, conceptual and organizational difficulties are inextricably intertwined with language-specific code problems. Worst case: the program may "work" without obvious errors, but it will not produce the desired result. It can then become very difficult to isolate and solve problems.

For this step, it is helpful to design algorithms with a generic set of commands that do not depend on the syntax of a particular programming language, as described below.

Step 4 Convert the algorithm into program code.

In the early stages of learning a new programming language, this is the most difficult step. But, if you have completed Step 3, then you can focus *just* on programming language details and not on the problem itself.

Step 5 Verify the operation of the program.

This step is often overlooked. Beginning programmers are often so overjoyed when a program "works" and produces outputs without any obvious errors that they assume the answers must be right. This is a dangerous assumption! PHP is a relatively forgiving languages in the sense that calculations will appear to work even when they are wrong. For example, mistyping and using the name of a PHP variable on the left-hand side of an assignment statement (writing `texas` when you meant `taxes`, for example) will not produce an error message, because variable names don't need to be "declared" ahead of time.

Sometimes it is easy to verify the operation of a program by checking calculations by hand or with a calculator. But, for many scientific and engineering calculations, wrong answers will look as reasonable as right answers. Even the most elegantly and cleverly written program has no value if it does not produce correct answers under *all* applicable conditions. It is up to you to define those conditions and test your results.

The algorithm development step, Step 3 in the problem-solving process described above, is critical to writing successful programs. It can best be undertaken using what is called a pseudocode language. Pseudocode instructions encompass the range of actions a program can take, but those instructions don't have to follow the syntax rules of a specific language. An algorithm written in pseudocode consists of a series of syntax-free "action commands" which, when translated into the syntax of a specific language, will produce the desired result.

Here is a list of pseudocode commands, given in alphabetical order. If you are reading this section before having actually written any programs, some of the terminology may be unfamiliar. But, the good news is that this relatively short list of commands includes at least conceptually all the actions PHP needs to take for the kinds of problems described in this book.

ASSIGN or CALCULATE

Set a variable equal to a value, another variable, or an expression. See also the **INCREMENT** and **INITIALIZE** commands.

CALL

Invoke a subprogram (see **FUNCTION**). This command describes information flow between a subprogram and the point in your pseudocode from which the **CALL** is invoked. It is especially important to differentiate between input to and output from a function. The ability to modularize a program by creating functions is an essential element of modern programming languages.

CHOOSE

This command defines actions that can be taken based on selecting one value from a restricted list of possibilities—a selection from a pull-down HTML menu of choices, for example. The choice-dependent action might be some simple calculations or a **CALL** to a **FUNCTION**.

CLOSE

Close an open external file.

DEFINE

This pseudocode command provides a mechanism for defining the variables and user-defined data objects such as arrays that your program will need. In scientific and engineering calculations, it is important to identify physical definitions and units when you define variables.

FUNCTION

This command marks the start of a separate code module, with the flow of information to and from the module specified through the **CALL** command. Initially, you should specify the input to and output from a function. Later, as your pseudocode develops, you can return to the function and define the internal calculations. Remember that in PHP (and many other languages) variables defined "locally" inside a function are visible *only* inside that function.

IF... THEN... ELSE...

If something is true, then take a specified action. If it is false, then do something else. The **ELSE...** branch is optional, as there may not be an "else" action when the "if" isn't true. This sequence of actions can be extended:

IF... THEN..., ELSE IF... THEN... ..., ELSE...

INCREMENT (or DECREMENT)

This is a special kind of assignment statement used to indicate operations such as $x = x + 1$. This operation makes no algebraic sense, but has a very specific interpretation in programming languages. It is often used inside loop structures to count the number of times actions inside the loop have been performed.

INITIALIZE

This is a special kind of assignment command used to take into account the fact that variables should be given values before they are appear on the right side of an **ASSIGN**ment operator. This command can often be combined with the **DEFINE** command.

LOOP {conditions}... END LOOP

Execute instructions repeatedly until (or as long as) certain conditions are met. In some situations, count-controlled loops are appropriate when it is possible to determine how many times instructions should be executed. In other situations, pre-test or post-test conditional loops are appropriate. With pre-test loops, instructions inside the loop may never be executed, depending on the values of variables prior to the start of the loop. With post-test loops, instructions inside the loop will always be executed at least once, with terminating conditions tested at the end of the loop rather than at the beginning.

OPEN

Open an external file for reading or writing.

READ

Pass information to a program. In an HTML/PHP environment, the source of information is values entered in a form field or read from a data file.

WRITE or *DISPLAY*

Generate output. Displayed data include values calculated or graphed in a PHP application. For graphics applications, you can use this pseudocode command to provide details about what you wish to graph and how you want it to look.

This set of commands can be modified and extended as convenient for a particular programming environment, in order to take into account language-specific capabilities while deferring concerns about implementation details. For example, when working with HTML/PHP applications, it might be appropriate to add commands such as *READ CHECKBOX* and *CHOOSE RADIO*, to provide more specific references to handling these two HTML structures.

Large or complex programming problems may require several iterations through pseudocode. The first step might be just to define input and output. The next step might include the processing steps: defining local variables, decision points, and repetitive calculations. Finally, the details of each required calculation can be given. At this point, translation of pseudocode to actual code should be straightforward if you understand the syntax of the language you are using. If you have problems with language syntax, at least it will be possible to focus just on those details, separate from implementing the algorithm you have designed.

Here is a trivially simple calculation that illustrates how to use pseudocode: Given a radius, calculate the area and circumference of a circle.

DEFINE radius (cm), area (cm^2), circumference (cm)
READ radius
CALCULATE area= π•radius^2, circumference = 2π•radius
DISPLAY area, circumference

In this case, the coding steps are trivial, but this is often not the case. Here is an example that could have been used to design the code for Document 7.8:

Calculate the position of an Earth-orbiting object in its orbit as a function of time.

(HTML user interface to define inputs)
DEFINE/ASSIGN
  semimajor axis a (km)
  eccentricity e (dimensionless, from 0 to <1)
  # of time steps n

(PHP application: See Section 7.5.4 for required equations)
READ input values from HTML document
CALCULATE
  orbital period τ, seconds
  time step dt = τ/n
LOOP (count through n time steps)
  CALCULATE
    mean anomaly M from t and τ
  ASSIGN
    initial guess for eccentric anomaly E = M
  CALL function getE() to calculate eccentric anomaly from initial E,
    M, and e
  CALCULATE f from E and e
  DISPLAY t. M, F
END LOOP
FUNCTION getE(recursive function to return eccentric anomaly E)
  INPUT: M, e, and initial guess for E
  OUTPUT: final value of E

This pseudocode outlines all the steps required to solve this problem, but
without the syntax-specific implementation details. The input requirements
are defined and a function is invoked to calculate the eccentric anomaly
from mean anomaly, eccentricity, and an initial guess for the eccentric
anomaly.

At this point in the problem solution, the specific steps required inside
function getE() are "to be determined." (The equations in Sect. 7.5.4 provide what you need to know to implement the details of this function.) You
can always temporarily insert code to return a "dummy" value from functions to make sure the rest of your code is working. For this problem,
returning M as a placeholder for E would be a reasonable choice.

Exercises

1. Introducing HTML
2. HTML Document Basics

1-2.1. Create a simple Web page for yourself and store it on the computer you are using with this book. It is not necessary (and not even necessarily a good idea!) to put this Web page online. If you are using this book as a course text, your instructor may tell you where to post your work.

Add some content to your Web page. This could be a short biographical sketch or something less personal. Use some of the HTML elements described in these chapters. Experiment with setting different colors and font sizes. Include at least one image—preferably one you create yourself. Be sure to display the source of the image if it is not your own. Do not use commercial images unless you can demonstrate that you have permission to use them.

Create a style sheet file for your Web page. Save this as a `.css` file. Modify your Web page so that it uses this style sheet. Create at least one other Web page that shares this style. The contents of this second page don't matter, but there must be enough content to demonstrate that the style is being implemented.

1-2.2. Here's how to create an internal link, essentially a "bookmark" to a specified point in a document:

```
<a href="#section1">Link to Section 1.</a>
...
<a name="section1">Start of Section 1.</a>
... {text of Section 1.}
```

The # sign appearing in the value of the `href` attribute indicates that this is an internal document link. The `<a name="...">` ... `</a>` tags typically surround a section heading, or perhaps the first few words in a section. (See Sect. 2.3.)

Create a document with a table of contents linked to several sections. At the start and end of each section, include a link back to the table of contents. The sections don't have to be long, as the purpose of this exercise is just to learn how to create internal document links.

© Springer International Publishing AG 2017
D.R. Brooks, *Programming in HTML and PHP*, Undergraduate Topics in Computer Science, DOI 10.1007/978-3-319-56973-4

1-2.3. Create an HTML document that contains at least two clickable images that are linked to other HTML documents. In Microsoft Word, for example, you can use the "WordArt" feature to create graphics images that explain the link, as with these examples.

My Pictures

My Pets

1-2.4. Create an HTML document that displays this heading and HTML code:

Here is some HTML code...

```
<html>
<head>
<title>Displaying HTML code in a document</title>
</head>
<body>
Here is an HTML document.
</body>
</html>
```

All the HTML tags, including their left and right angle brackets, should be displayed in red font. Note that this is *not* an HTML code listing. It is a display of the contents of an HTML document. Hint: Review Document 2.1 and its explanation.

3. HTML Tables, Forms, Lists, and Frames

3.1. Create a table containing a personnel evaluation form. The first column should contain a statement, such as "Gets along well with others." The second column should contain four radio buttons containing choices like "Never," "Sometimes," "Often," and "Always." The table should have at least two performance statements. Provide appropriate instructions for filling in the form and submitting it using mailto: to the creator of the form.

Name:				
Gets along well with others	Never ○	Sometimes ○	Often ○	Always ○
Work quality	Terrible ○	Mediocre ○	Good ○	Excellent ○
Please fill out this form and press this button to send it				

(NOTE: It is possible that mailto: simply won't work at all with your computer system.)

3.2. Using Table 2.1 as a guide, create an HTML document and table that displays the 16 standard HTML colors and their hex codes. The color names should be displayed in their color against an appropriate background color, or you can use the color names as the background with names in white or black.

3.3. Using Table 2.2 as a guide, create a table that displays results of assigning specific and generic font families to text. For example, display an example in serif and Times fonts.

3.4. Display a list of names. Clicking on a name should open a window that displays information about that person.

Opening a new window has not been covered in the text. This is done with the `window.open()` method of the HTML window object; you can find more about the syntax online. Here is some code to get you started.

Creating the table:

```
<html><head>
<title>List of Professors</title>
</head><body>
<table border>
<tr><th>Biographical sketch for...<br />
(click in name box)</th></tr>
<tr>
   <td onclick ="window.open('ProfWonderful.htm',
    'ProfWonderful', 'alwaysRaised=yes,toolbar=no,width=600,
    scrollbars=yes');">
    Professor Wonderful, Super University</td>
</tr>
</table>
</body>
</html>
```

The HTML document for Professor Wonderful:

```
<head>
<title>Professor Wonderful</title>
<!--
-<link href="WindowStyle.css" rel="stylesheet"
type="text/css" />
-->
</head>
<body>
<b><i>Professor I. M. Wonderful, PhD</i></b><br />
  Enter biographical stuff about Professor Wonderful.
</body>
</html>
```

4. Creating a PHP Environment
5. Introduction to PHP

Some of these exercises can be done with separate HTML and PHP files, as in Document 4.5, or as a combined HTML/PHP application, as in Document 4.6. For some exercises you may need to look ahead to the math constants and functions in Tables 7.2 and 7.3 in Chap. 7.

4-5.1 Set up a PHP environment on the computer you will use with this book. If you are using your own personal computer, install an Apache server. Copy Documents 4.1-4.3 and make sure they work in your PHP environment.

4-5.2 Using Document 4.5 as a guide, write an HTML/PHP application to convert a temperature in degrees Fahrenheit to degrees Celsius and Kelvins 0K is absolute zero. The conversion from Fahrenheit to Celsius is $T_C = 5(T_F - 32)/9$. The conversion from T_C to Kelvins is $K = T_C + 273.15$.

4-5.3 Using Document 4.4 as a guide, create your own data file and write code to read and display its contents and save the output in a `.csv` file. Make sure you can open and graph the output file in a spreadsheet, similar to Fig. 4.1. The data file can be much smaller than the example used in Document 4.4 and there need be only one set of y-values for each x-value.

4-5.4 Enter air temperature in degrees Fahrenheit and the wind speed V in miles per hour. Calculate and display the windchill temperature according to:

$$T_{WC} = (0.279V^{1/2} + 0.550 - 0.0203V)(T - 91.4) + 91.4$$

where T must be less than 91.4 °F and $V \geq 4$ mph. Include code to test the input values for T and V and display an appropriate message if they are out of range.

4-5.5 The Body Mass Index (BMI) provides a way to characterize normal weights for human adult bodies as a function of height. It is defined as:

$$BMI = w/h^2$$

where w is mass in kilograms (2.2046 kg mass per pound weight) and h is height in meters (1 in. = .0254 m).

Write an application that asks for the user's weight in *pounds* and height in *feet and inches*, and then calculates and displays the BMI. An adult BMI of 25 or over is generally regarded as overweight; the interpretation for children, teens, and highly trained athletes is different.

4-5.6 Prompt the user to enter the month n, date d, and year. Calculate and display the day of the year n, from 1 to 365 or 366, depending on whether the year is a leap year. The formula is

$$n = INT(275\,m/9) - k \bullet INT[(m + 9)/12] + d - 30$$

where INT() means "the truncated (not rounded) integer value of" and $k = 1$ for a leap year and $k = 2$ otherwise. Note that INT is just mathematical "shorthand" for the desired result, not a PHP math function.

To check your code, perform the reverse calculation that converts the day of the year n to its corresponding month and day.

$$n < 32: \quad m = 1 \text{ and } d = n$$
$$\text{otherwise:} \quad m = INT[9(k + n)/275 + 0.98]$$
$$d = n - INT(275m/9) + k \cdot INT[(m + 9)/12] + 30$$

A year is a leap year if it is evenly divisible by 4 and, if it is a centurial year, it is evenly divisible by 400; that is, 2000 was a leap year, but 1900 was not. Provide results for several inputs, including the first and last days of leap and non-leap years, and February 28 or 29 and March 1.

4-5.7 Atmospheric pressure decreases with elevation. When barometric pressure is given in weather reports, it is always referenced to sea level. (Otherwise it wouldn't be possible to draw weather maps showing the movement of air masses.) Scientists often need to know the actual pressure, the "station pressure," at a site. An approximate conversion from sea level pressure to station pressure is:

$$P_{station} = P_{sea\,level} - h/9.2$$

where pressures are in millibars and h is site elevation in meters. The author uses this formula:

$$P_{station} = P_{sea\,level} \bullet exp(-0.119h - 0.0013h^2)$$

where h is the elevation in kilometers. Write an application that calculates and displays elevation and pressure calculated from these two formulas.

These formulas are reasonably accurate at elevations of a few hundred meters, but less accurate at higher elevations. For example, Mauna Loa Observatory in Hawaii is at an elevation of about 3400 meters and its average station pressure is about 680 mbar. Both these formulas give lower values.

In the United States, barometric pressure is reported in units of inches of mercury. Almost everywhere else in the world, the units are millibars (hectopascals). Values for standard atmospheric conditions at sea level are 1013.25 millibars or 29.921 inches of mercury. Because these two units have such different values associated with them, your code can determine the units in which the pressure was entered. If the sea level pressure value entered is less than 40, assume the units are inches of mercury and convert that value to millibars:

$$p_{millibars} = p_{inches\ of\ mercury} \cdot (1013.25/29.921)$$

As an example, look at an online weather report for Denver, Colorado, USA, often called the "mile high city" because its elevation is about 5300 ft (1.6 km). The barometric pressure will be reported as a value typically just a little above 1000 millibars, just as it is at sea level. Use your PHP application to calculate the actual barometric pressure in Denver under standard atmospheric conditions.

4-5.8 Cardiac output is defined as the volume of blood pumped by the heart per minute:

$$cardiac\ output = stroke\ volume\ (milliliters) \times heart\ rate\ (beats\ per\ minute)$$

A typical resting rate is 60 ml and 70 bpm. During exercise, the stroke volume can double and the heart rate might rise to 200 bpm. During deep sleep these values might fall to 45 ml and 45 bpm.

Write an application that calculates and displays cardiac output for user-supplied values of stroke volume and heart rate.

4-5.9 Blood pressure is a fundamental indicator of overall general health. It is measured in units of millimeters of mercury and reported as the systolic pressure—the pressure created when your heart is pumping—over the diastolic pressure—the pressure when your heart is at rest between beats. The mean arterial pressure is defined as 1/3 times the systolic blood pressure plus 2/3 times the diastolic blood pressure.

A good blood pressure reading for adults is 120/80. A consistently measured resting value of 140/90 is considered high, and a condition that should be treated.

Write an application that accepts as input the systolic and diastolic blood pressure, displays a message based on the systolic and diastolic values, and calculates and displays the mean arterial pressure.

For example, if the blood pressure readings are 140/90, then the message could urge the user to seek treatment. (There may be other appropriate messages for intermediate values. Consult a health care professional!)

4-5.10 A cylindrical liquid storage tank of radius R and length L lies on its side, with its straight sides parallel to the ground. In order to determine how much liquid remains in the tank, a dip stick over the centerline of the tank is used to measure the height of the liquid in the tank. The volume is L · A, where A is the area of a partial circle of radius R with a cap cut off horizontally at height H from the bottom of the circle:

$$A = R^2 \cos^{-1}[(R-H)/R] - (R-H)(2RH-H^2)^{1/2}$$

where $\cos^{-1}(x)$ is the inverse cosine (arccosine) of x.

Write an application that accepts input values for R, L, and H and then calculates and displays the volume of liquid in the tank.

4-5.11 Paleontologists have discovered several sets of dinosaur footprints preserved in ancient river beds. Is it possible to deduce from these footprints the speed at which dinosaurs walked or ran? The two pieces of information that can be determined directly from the footprints are the length of the dinosaur's foot and the length of its stride, which is defined as the distance between the beginning of a footprint made by one foot and the beginning of the next footprint made by that same foot.

Because of the dynamic similarities in animal motion, an approximate linear relationship between relative stride and dimensionless speed applies to modern bipedal and quarupedal animals as diverse and differently shaped as humans, ostriches, camels, and dogs[1]:

$$s = 0.8 + 1.33v$$

Relative stride s is defined as the ratio of stride length to leg length, s = S/L. Dimensionless speed is defined as the speed divided by the square root of leg length times the gravitational acceleration g, $v = V/(Lg)^{1/2}$. Although it might seem that gravitational acceleration shouldn't influence an animal's speed on level ground, this isn't true, as gravity influences the up and down motions of the body required even for walking.

Leg length from ground to hip joint for dinosaurs of a known species can be determined from fossils. However, even when the dinosaur species responsible for a set of tracks is unknown, its leg length can be estimated by multiplying the footprint length by 4. (Try this for humans.)

---

[1]See R. McNeill Alexander, *Dynamics of Dinosaurs & Other Extinct Giants*. Columbia University Press, New York, 1989.

Write an application to calculate the speed of a dinosaur based on measurements of its footprint and stride length. Use metric units. Test your calculations for a footprint 0.6 m long and a stride length of 3.3 m (a BIG dinosaur!).

Extra credit: Is it possible to determine whether the dinosaur was walking or running? Using data for human strides—walking or running— you should be able to speculate about the answer to this question.

4-5.12 Create a table with a form into which a user enters total credit hours and grade points for 8 semesters. The code should calculate the GPA for each semester:

GPA = (grade points)/(credit hours)

where an A gives 4 credit points, a B gives 3 credit points, etc. The last line in the form should be the cumulative GPA:

cumulative GPA = (cumulative grade points)/(cumulative credit hours)

4-5.13 The wavelengths of the Balmer series of lines in the hydrogen spectrum are given by

$$\lambda = 364.6n^2/(n^2-4) \text{ nanometers}$$

Write a script that generates and displays the first 10 wavelengths in the Balmer series.

4-5.14 Create an HTML/PHP application to calculate costs for ordering several items. (Include at least three items). The first column in the HTML document contains a brief description of each item. The second column contains the price for one item. The `<input>` fields in these two columns should be marked as `readonly`. The third column contains a field in which the user enters the number of items to order. This information is passed to the PHP application that calculates the extended price for each item, and the total amount for the entire order, including sales tax and shipping; make up your own rules for calculating shipping and sales tax.

The PHP application should re-create the HTML table with all the calculated values filled in. Once the PHP output is displayed, you should be able to copy and paste it into a word processing document.

4-5.15 The original population of a certain animal is 1,000,000. Assume that at the beginning of each year, the population increases by 3%. By the end of that year, 6% of the total population (including the births at the beginning of the year) dies. Write a script that calculates and displays the population at the end of each year until the population at the end of the year falls to 75% or less of its original value. Although, in principle, you can figure out how many years this will take, don't do that. Use a conditional loop.

4-5.16 PHP makes it easy to access the values of HTML `<input>` fields. Write an HTML/PHP application that includes `radio` fields in the HTML document for which the values are the days of the week. The PHP part of the application should display the value of the selected day. (NOTE: Document 6.12 shows how to access the values of `checkbox` fields, which requires the use of arrays because multiple values can be selected.)

4-5.17 Create an HTML/PHP application that converts values from one units system to another. For example, 1 foot = 0.3048 m. Use at least three `type="radio"` input fields to hold the quantities (length, speed, etc.) and their "from" and "to" units.

4-5.18 Snell's law of refraction relates the angle of incidence Θ_i of a beam of light to the angle of refraction Θ_r of the beam as it enters a different medium:

$$n_i \sin(\Theta_i) = n_r \sin(\Theta_r)$$

The table gives the refractive index for four materials. Assuming that the incident material is always air, create a table that shows incident angles from $10°$ to $90°$ in steps of $10°$. The angle of refraction corresponding to an incident angle of $90°$ is the angle beyond which light incident from within the refracting material is reflected back into that medium, rather than exiting into air.

Material	Index of refraction
Air	1.00
Water	1.33
Glass	1.50
Diamond	2.42

4-5.19 In a materials testing experiment, samples are given random doses of radiation R every hour. The maximum total radiation exposure R_{max} is specified and the experiment is stopped if the next radiation dose will cause R_{max} to be exceeded. The units for the radiation do not matter for this problem.

Write an HTML/PHP application that accepts as input R_{max} and the minimum and maximum individual doses. The PHP application should then generate a table summarizing the random doses delivered to the sample. It could look something like this:

Maximum cumulative radiation = 1000		
Maximum individual dose = 200		
Dose	Amount	Cumulative
1	144	144
2	200	344
3	73	417
4	59	476
5	168	644
6	119	763
7	99	862
8	177	not delivered

4-5.20 A circuit containing an inductance of L henrys and a capacitance of C farads has a resonant frequency f given by:

$$f = \frac{1}{2\pi\sqrt{LC}}\,Hz$$

Write an HTML/PHP application that allows the user to input a range of inductances and capacitances along with a "step size" for each component, and generates a table containing the resonant frequency for each LC pair of values.

For example, the output could generate a table for inductances in the range from 20 to 100 µh in steps of 20 µh and capacitances from 100 to 1000 µf in steps of 100 µf. It does not make any difference which of these components are the rows in the table and which are the columns as long as they are labelled appropriately.

4-5.21 Section 7.5.2 described how to calculate a monthly repayment schedule. The user specifies the loan amount, the annual interest rate, and the duration of the loan in years.

For n loan payments, where n is the number of years times 12, the monthly payment P for a loan amount A at annual interest rate r (expressed as a decimal fraction, not a percent) is

$$P = (A \cdot r/12)/[1-1/(1+r/12)^{n}]$$

At the end of the loan repayment schedule, display the total amount received in loan payments.

Suppose you were thinking about lending this money yourself. The alternative is to deposit the money in an interest-bearing account. What APY (annual percent yield) would that account have to pay in order for you to have the same amount of money at the end of y years as you would have received from the loan repayments?

If you don't reinvest the loan payments as you receive them, calculate the APY from:

$$A_{final} = A_{start} \cdot (1 + r_{APY})^y$$

If you immediately reinvest each loan payment in an account paying an annual rate R (presumably lower than rate r) then at the end of y years (n months) that account will hold

$$A_{final} = A_{start} \cdot [(1 + R/12)^n - 1]/(R/12)$$

Here is an example. The monthly payments for a two-year, 8% loan of $200,000 are $9045.46. The total amount paid is 24 × $9045.46 = $217,091. The APY for an account with an initial deposit of $200,000 that would yield this amount is $(A_{final}/A_{start})^{(1/y)} - 1 = 4.19\%$. Suppose you reinvest the monthly payments as you receive them at 4%, compounded monthly. When the loan is repaid, you will have a total of $225,620, which is equivalent to an APY of 6.21% on a 2-year investment of the $200,000.

		Payment	Balance	Reinvestment
			200000.00	Rate = 4%
Payment #	1	9045.46	192287.88	9045.46
	2	9045.46	184524.34	18121.07
	3	9045.46	176709.04	27226.93
	4	9045.46	168841.64	36363.14
	5	9045.46	160921.79	45529.81
	6	9045.46	152949.15	54727.04
	7	9045.46	144923.35	63954.92
	8	9045.46	136844.05	73213.56
	9	9045.46	128710.88	82503.06
	10	9045.46	120523.50	91823.53
	11	9045.46	112281.53	101175.07
	12	9045.46	103984.61	110557.78
	13	9045.46	95632.39	119971.76
	14	9045.46	87224.48	129417.13
	15	9045.46	78760.52	138893.98

	16	9045.46	70240.13	148402.41
	17	9045.46	61662.94	157942.55
	18	9045.46	53028.57	167514.48
	19	9045.46	44336.63	177118.32
	20	9045.46	35586.75	186754.17
	21	9045.46	26778.54	196422.14
	22	9045.46	17911.60	206122.34
	23	9045.46	8985.55	215854.88
	24	9045.46	0.00	225619.85
Total Income		217091.00		225619.85
Return		4.19%		6.21%

6. Arrays

6.1. Use the rand() function to create 10,000 randomly distributed integers in the range [0,2] and count the occurrences of 0, 1, and 2. (Store the number of occurrences in an array.) Show results from several trials. Do the results look reasonable? rand(n,m) is *supposed* to generate values between n and m, inclusive, and this code should serve as a test to check whether this is true.

6.2. For 10,000 rolls of two dice, how many times would you expect to see "snake eyes" (two 1s) or "box cars" (two 6s), or 7s? Store results of the 10,000 rolls in an array. Use your results to validate the mathematically determined probability of each of these outcomes.

6.3. Write code that finds the maximum, minimum, mean, standard deviation, and median of numerical values in an array.

$$\text{mean} = \Sigma x_i / n$$

$$(\text{standard deviation})^2 = [\Sigma x_i^2 - (\Sigma x_i)^2 / n] / (n - 1)$$

where the x_i's are the elements of the array, n is the number of elements, and "Σ" means "sum from 1 through n." You can use the max() and min() functions for finding the maximum and minimum values.

The array must be sorted in ascending or descending order to find the median. For an array with an odd number of elements, the median is the middle value. For an array with an even number of elements, the median is the average of the two middle elements. You can use rand() to generate the array elements, with the understanding that the standard deviation calculation doesn't really apply to an array of uniformly distributed values.

6.4. Write a script that copies the elements of an array into a new array, in reverse order.

6.5. Consider a data collection system consisting of 10 reporting stations. Each station is supposed to report data once per month. An array holds reports as they come in, not necessarily in any particular order. Write a script that organizes these

ID	Report for month #
1	3
10	2
1	7
9	6
9	8
...	

data reports into a table for which the left-hand column is the station ID, the next 12 columns are months filled with an X if the station has reported and blank if not, and the rightmost column is the total number of months for which the station reported data.

6.6. A bored postal employee is playing with a row of mailboxes. Initially, all the boxes are closed. Then, starting with the second box, the employee opens every second box. Then, starting with the third box, the employee opens every third box if it's closed and closes it if it's open. Then starting with the fourth box,... and so forth. When the employee gets to the end of the line of mailboxes, which ones are still closed? Use an array of 1s (closed) and 0s (open) to represent the state of the boxes. A row of 40 or so boxes are sufficient to see the pattern.

6.7. A table consists of two columns of numerical values. The first column gives values of an independent variable X and the second column gives values of the corresponding dependent variable Y. Write a script that will calculate a Y values for an X value between the minimum and maximum tabulated values by linearly interpolating between the X values. For a value of x that lies between x_1 and x_2,

X	Y
5.0	5.9
10.0	6.6
15.0	7.1
20.0	8.3
25.0	10.0
30.0	12.2

$$y = y_1 + (y_2 - y_1)\frac{(x - x_1)}{(x_2 - x_1)}$$

Using the data supplied, be sure to test your results for X = 5 and X = 30. Also, your code should not allow extrapolation of Y values for X values lying outside the tabulated values.

6.8. Suppose a card deck is represented by the integers from 1 to 52. Write a script that will shuffle this deck; that is, it will randomly reorder values from 1 to 52. It is OK to swap cards more than once and that a card can be swapped with itself. To make this a little easier, you might want to define a

keyed array starting at an index of 1 rather than 0. Read through the 52 cards
in the deck and swap each card with another card in the deck:

```
temp = card(i)
index = random number, 1–52
card(i) = card(index)
card(index) = temp
```

6.9. The game of Life provides a simple model of how organisms are born,
survive, and die. It is played on a two-dimensional board with m rows and n
columns. The game is started by establishing an initial distribution of
organisms in a small region of the board. The distribution of the next
generation of the population is determined according to these rules:

(1)   A new organism will appear in the next generation in any empty square with
      exactly three living neighbors.

(2)   An organism with only one neighbor will die from loneliness in the next
      generation and an organism in a square surrounded by more than three
      neighbors will die from overcrowding in the next generation.

(3)   An organism with two or three neighbors will survive into the next generation.

Write a script to play this game. A 20 × 20
board is large enough. Produce output for several
generations using at both of the two initial

------	---X--
--XXX–	----X-
---X---	--XXX–

population distributions shown here, where an X indicates that an organism
occupies that square.

Assume that any organism occupying a row or column at the edge of the
game board simply disappears in the next generation. That is, the rules for
the game apply only to (m − 1) × (n − 1) squares on the board.

You must create an intermediate board configuration that marks births and
deaths for the next generation. This is necessary because organisms don't die
immediately when you detect that they have less than two or more than three
neighbors. They stay there until all the rules have been applied to all squares
on the board for the current generation. Similarly, new organisms aren't born
until the start of the next generation, so they can't count as neighbors during
the current generation.

6.10. Automata can be thought of as artificial life forms that, with the aid of
a set of rules for reproducing themselves, appear to be self-organizing.
These rules can lead to surprising patterns, related to fractal theory. One
well-known pattern is the Sierpinski triangle, shown here.

```
Generation  0------------------------*-----------------------
Generation  1-----------------------*-*----------------------
Generation  2----------------------*---*---------------------
Generation  3---------------------*-*-*-*--------------------
Generation  4--------------------*-------*-------------------
Generation  5-------------------*-*-----*-*------------------
Generation  6------------------*---*---*---*-----------------
Generation  7-----------------*-*-*-*-*-*-*-*----------------
Generation  8----------------*---------------*---------------
Generation  9---------------*-*-------------*-*--------------
Generation 10--------------*---*-----------*---*-------------
Generation 11-------------*-*-*-*---------*-*-*-*------------
Generation 12------------*-------*-------*-------*-----------
Generation 13-----------*-*-----*-*-----*-*-----*-*----------
Generation 14----------*---*---*---*---*---*---*---*---------
Generation 15---------*-*-*-*-*-*-*-*-*-*-*-*-*-*-*-*--------
Generation 16--------*-----------------------------*-------
Generation 17------*-*-----------------------------*-*-----
Generation 18----*---*-----------------------------*---*----
Generation 19---*-*-*-*---------------------------*-*-*-*---
Generation 20--*-------*-------------------------*-------*--
```

In order for the elements to line up, use `echo` to set a monospaced font like Courier.

The pattern starts out with a single "life form" (an asterisk) in the middle of the array. This array has 45 elements. The propagation rules are:

For cell i, if cell i-1 is occupied and cells i and i+1 are not, or if cell i-1 is empty and cell i+1 is occupied, then an organism will appear in cell i in the next generation. Otherwise the cell will be empty.

Write code that reproduces the output shown. HINT: Initialize the array to 0 or 1 (false or true), depending on whether it is populated or not. You can't apply the rules to the array itself to determine the distribution of organisms in the next generation. You need to copy the organism distribution array at the start of each generation and test the propagation rules as applied to that copy, in order to update the organism distribution array.

6.11. Given an array A, calculate the symmetrical n-point running average of the values. For this exercise, n should be an odd number. Suppose n = 7. Sum the first 7 elements of A, take the average, and assign it to the 4th element of the running average array. (The first three elements are undefined.) Starting at the 5th element, add element 8 to the sum and subtract element 1. Take the average and assign it to the 5th element of the running average array. Suppose there are 100 elements in A. Continue to calculate the running average until the 97th element of A. The final 7-point average is the average of elements 94-100 and there are no values in the running average array past element 97. This code requires some careful planning because PHP array elements start at index 0, not 1.

"Symmetrical" running averages use future and past data points. As described, these are also unweighted averages in the sense that all past, present, and future values are given equal weight. The point of running averages is to show trends by smoothing out noise that may be present in data. For real-time data where future values aren't known (stock market prices, for example), you would have to calculate a "backward" average using past and present data only.

6.12. A terrain map is stored in digital form as integers in a two-dimensional array. Write a script to examine the array and find high and low spots in the terrain. The criterion for a high or low spot will be a value a specified amount above or below the average of the eight surrounding values. For the purposes of

```
Look for differences
> 4.000
8004972    +-------
9899376    |  H
9296364    |L
4265615    |L
6970387    |        L
```

this exercise, assume the terrain values are values 0–9. Print the original array and, next to it, an array that has high and low spots marked with H and L. A 20 × 20 array is large enough. Part of an array is shown here. Outline the borders of the output array as shown in the example and do the calculations only for the interior 19 × 19 terrain values. You can either use a random number generator to create the original array or manually create some more meaningful pattern such as a "mountain range" or "valley."

6.13. The designer of a new computer chip is concerned about operating temperatures within the chip. Tests show that passive heat sinks attached to each side of the rectangular chip can maintain each edge of the chip at a specified temperature. The four edges can be at different temperatures, which allows designing the board so that the most

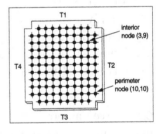

temperature-sensitive components can be located near the coolest edge. Write a script to determine the temperature distribution within the chip.

One way to solve this problem is to divide the rectangular area into a two-dimensional grid, as shown in the sketch (using a 10×11 grid). Initialize the nodes at each edge to the specified temperatures. Initialize the interior nodes to some other value; a good choice would be the average of all the edge temperatures. Then, using an iterative loop, recalculate the temperature of each interior node as the average of the temperatures of the four surrounding nodes. Terminate the iteration when the difference between the current and recalculated temperatures for every node is less than some specified small amount; $0.1°$ might be reasonable for board temperatures near or above room temperature. This approach means that every time you create a new iterated array, you will have to copy its contents into a separate array so you can compare its contents with the next generated of the iterated array.

7. Functions

7.1. Write and test three functions that will calculate the following quantities for two three-component arrays:

sum or difference: $A + B = \sum_{i=1}^{i=3}(Ai + Bi) \quad A - B = \sum_{i=1}^{i=3}(Ai - Bi)$

scalar (dot) product: $A \cdot B = \sum_{i=1}^{i=3}(AiBi)$

vector (cross) product:

$$A \times B = AyBz - ByAz, AzBx - BzAx, AxBy - BxAy$$

(Sums, differences, and scalar products will work for n-component arrays, too.)

7.2. Consider a system of linear equations with three unknowns:

$a_1x + b_1y + c_1z = d_1$

$a_2x + b_2y + c_2z = d_2$

$a_3x + b_3y + c_3z = d_3$

Cramer's Rule can be used to solve for x, y, and z:

$x = D_1/D \quad y = D_2/D \quad z = D_3/D$

where D is the determinant for the system:

$D = a_1b_2c_3 + b_1c_2a_3 + c_1b_3a_2 - a_3b_2c_1 - b_3c_2a_1 - c_3b_1a_2$

D_1, D_2 and D_3 are found by substituting the constants d_1, d_2, and d_3 for the coefficients in column 1, 2, and 3, respectively:

$$D_1 = a_1 b_2 c_3 + b_1 c_2 a_3 + c_1 b_3 d_2 - d_3 b_2 c_1 - b_3 c_2 d_1 - c_3 b_1 d_2$$
$$D_2 = a_1 d_2 c_3 + d_1 c_2 a_3 + c_1 d_3 a_2 - a_3 d_2 c_1 - d_3 c_2 a_1 - c_3 d_1 a_2$$
$$D_3 = a_1 b_2 d_3 + b_1 d_2 a_3 + d_1 b_3 a_2 - a_3 b_2 d_1 - b_3 d_2 a_1 - d_3 b_1 a_2$$

Write a function for solving three linear equations with three unknowns. It is possible for the value of D to be 0, in which case the system of equations has no solution. Your code should test for this possibility and provide an appropriate message. Include your solution for this system of equations:

$$3x + 4y + 2z = -1$$
$$5x + 7y + z = 2$$
$$5x + 9y + 3z = 3$$

7.3. Simulation studies in science and engineering often require random numbers drawn from a normal (Gaussian, "bell-shaped") distribution rather than from a uniform distribution. By definition, a set of normally distributed numbers should have a mean of 0 and a standard deviation of 1. The Box-Muller transform generates pairs of independent *normally* distributed random numbers, Z_1 and Z_2, given a source of *uniformly* distributed random numbers, U_1 and U_2, on the interval [0,1] inclusive.

$$Z_1 = \cos(2\pi U_2)\sqrt{-2lnU_1} \qquad Z_2 = \sin(2\pi U_2)\sqrt{-2lnU_1}$$

PHP's random number function generates uniformly distributed integer values in the range $[n_1, n_2]$, inclusive. You can use these equations to generate real numbers in the [0,1] range by dividing large integers:

```
rand(0,100000)/100000.
```

(If you forget the decimal point, which is required to do real number division in this expression, you will almost always get a value of 0.) Because $ln(0)$ is undefined, your code should check every value of U_1 to make sure it is not 0. If it is, replace U_1 with some arbitrary very small value. This should happen only rarely if the range of integers specified in `rand()` is large, so it will not bias the statistics of even a fairly small sample. If `rand(0,n)/n` returns a value of 1, $ln(1) = 0$, but this will cause no problem.

Calculate 1000 normally distributed numbers in the range from 0 to 1. Remember that when you use a `for...` loop for this calculation, each trip through the loop generates two numbers. Use the code you wrote for Exercise 6.3 to calculate the statistics for these numbers to see if they look (approximately?) normally distributed (mean = 0, standard deviation = 1).

7.4. Convert your code from Exercise 7.3 to a function that returns a normally distributed array of numbers (not necessarily in the range 0-1). Then use your code from Exercise 6.3 to calculate the statistics for the array.

7.5. Two quantities a and b are in the Golden Ratio if $(a + b)/a = a/b \approx$ 1.618, where a is the larger value. Write a modified version of Document 7.4 that demonstrates the relationship between Fibonacci numbers and the Golden Ratio. (Look at the ratio F_n/F_{n-1} as n becomes large.) It is easy to find a lot of information online about the Golden Ratio in art, architecture, and nature.

7.6. An incompressible fluid flows at speed v_1 through a cylindrical pipe with cross-sectional area A_1. The pipe then narrows gradually to area A_2. The mass flowing the pipe must remain constant, so the velocity v_2 of the fluid in the smaller pipe is given by the equation of continuity:

$$A_1 v_1 = A_2 v_2$$

Write and test a function that accepts as input two pipe diameters and v_1 and returns v_2. Assuming water (1000 kg/m^3) is the liquid flowing through the pipes, also return the mass per second flowing through the pipes.

7.7. The root mean square (rms) speed of gas molecules v_{rms} is given by

$$Vrms = \sqrt{3kT/m}$$

where k is Boltzmann's constant, 1.38×10^{-23} J/K, T is temperature in Kelvins, and mass m is in kilograms. Express mass in terms of the atomic weight of the gas times the mass of one atomic mass unit, 1.660×10^{-27} kg. The average speed v_{avg} of gas molecules is approximately related to rms speed by $v_{rms} \approx 1.09\ v_{avg}$.

Write and test a function that returns v_{rms} and v_{avg} for a specified gas and temperature, for example, oxygen molecules at 25°C. An oxygen molecule (O_2) has a mass of 32 atomic mas units. $0\ °C = 273.15$ K.

7.8. Using Exercise 4-5.7 as a starting point, rewrite the code to put the required pressure calculations and conversions into functions.

7.9. Write and test a function that, given the (x,y) coordinates of two points in a plane, returns the shortest distance between the two points, the (x,y) coordinates of a point halfway between the two points along a straight line joining the points, and the slope of the straight line joining the points.

7.10. The Julian day system is used in astronomical calculations to overcome the complexities inherent in the modern civil calendar system. These problems occur because the length of a solar year is not an even number of calendar days. (One solar year is *approximately* 365.25 days).

Every day is assigned a unique, consecutively numbered Julian day starting at January 1, -4712, 12:00:00 UTC. Julian days begin at noon at the Greenwich Observatory near London, so all nighttime astronomical observations there would have the same Julian Date. For example, midnight at the start of Greenwich calendar day January 1, 1998, or January 1.0, 1998, is JD 2450814.5 and Greenwich noon, January 1.5, 1998, is JD 2450815.0.

For a specified month m, day d, and year y in the modern Gregorian calendar[2], the corresponding JD is given by this algorithm:

1. If m > 2, leave y and m unchanged. If m equals 1 or 2, replace y by y-1 and m by m+12.
2. Calculate A=<y/100> and B = 2 − A + <A/4>. (<...> expressions mean "the truncated integer value of." You can use the floor() function to evaluate these <...> expressions.)
3. Then,

$$JD = \, <365.25(y+4716)> \, + \, <30.6001(m+1)> \, + d + B - 1524.5$$

4. Convert hours, minutes, and seconds into a day fraction and add it to JD. (24 hours/day, 1440 minutes/day, 86400 seconds/day.)

To convert JD back to the corresponding Gregorian calendar date:

1. Add 0.5 to JD. Let z be the integer part and f the decimal part of the result. If z < 2299161, A=z. Otherwise:

$$\alpha = \, <((z-1867216.25)/36524.25 >$$
$$A = z + 1 + \alpha - <\alpha/4>$$

2. $B = A + 1524$
$$C = \, <(B-122.1)/365.25 >$$
$$D = \, <365.25C >$$
$$E = \, <(B-D)/30.6001 >$$
$$d = B - D - <30.6001E > \, + f$$
m = E−1 if E < 14 or E − 13 if E = 14 or 15
y = C−4716 if m < 2 or C−4715 if m = 1or 2

Write and test two functions, one of which converts a calendar date and time to JD and the other of which converts JD back to the calendar

| Calendar Date: 2016/6/21 17:30:30 |
| Julian Date: 2457561.2295139 |
| Calendar Date: 2016/6/21 17:30:30 |

---

[2]The Gregorian calendar is the modern "Western" civil calendar in almost universal use today, replacing the Julian Calendar in most of Europe after its inception in 1582. (Some countries delayed changing to this calendar.)

date. (You must convert the day as a decimal fraction to integer hours, minutes, and seconds.)

7.11. Assume that the probability of a randomly selected individual in a target population having a disease is PD. Suppose there is a test for this disease, but the test is not perfect. There are two possible outcomes reported from the test:

1. Test is positive (disease is present?).
2. Test is negative (no disease is present?).

Because the test is imperfect, if the individual has the disease, result 1 is returned for only PWD (test positive, with disease) percent of the tests. That is, only PWD percent of all individuals who actually have the disease will test positive for the disease. If the individual does not have the disease, result 2 is returned only NND (test negative, no disease) percent of the time. That is, only NND percent of all individuals who do not have the disease will test negative for the disease.

Bayesian inference can be used to answer two important questions:

1. Given a positive test result, what is the chance that I really do have the disease?
2. Given a negative test result, what is the chance that I have the disease anyhow?

Define the following variables (assuming PWD and NND are expressed as values between 0 and 1 rather than as percentages):

PND = positive test result, but with no disease = $(1 - NND)$

NWD = negative test result, but with disease = $(1 - PWD)$

$P\_has\_disease$ = person has disease, given a positive test result

$= (\# \text{ of true positives})/(\# \text{ true positives} + \# \text{ false positives})$

$= (PWD \cdot PD)/[PWD \cdot PD + PND \cdot (1 - PD)]$

Probability that a person does not have the disease, given a positive test result = $1 - P\_has\_disease$

$N\_has\_disease$ = person has disease, given a negative test result

$= (\# \text{ false negatives})/(\# \text{ false negatives} + \# \text{ true negatives})$

$= (NWD \cdot PD)/[NWD \cdot PD + NND \cdot (1-PD)]$

The probability that a person has the disease even though the test result is negative is called a Type II error. The probability that a person does not have the disease even though the test result is positive is called a Type I error. From a treatment point of view, Type II errors are perhaps more serious because treatment will not be offered. However, it is also possible that treating for a disease that does not actually exist, as a result of a Type I error, may also have serious consequences.

As an example, consider a rare disease for which PD=.001, PWD=0.99 and NND=0.95. Then the probability that a person has the disease, given a positive test result is:

P_has_disease $= (0.99 \cdot 0.001)/(0.99 \cdot 0.001 + 0.05 \cdot 0.999) = 0.019$

and for a negative test result:

N_has_disease $= 0.01 \cdot 0.001)/(0.01 \cdot 0.001 + 0.95 \cdot 0.999) = 0.0000105$

The somewhat surprising result that the probability of having this disease is very small despite a positive result from a test that *appears* to be highly accurate is explained qualitatively by the fact that there are many more people without the disease (999 out of 1000) than there are with the disease. In such a population, approximately 50 people will test positive for the disease even though they don't have it. Approximately 1 person will test positive for the disease when they have it, so (actual positives)/(all positive test results) $\sim 1/51 \sim 0.02$.

The very small probability of having the disease even with a negative test result is explained by the fact that 999 out of 1000 people don't have the disease and almost all of these people get negative test results.

Write am HTML/PHP application that displays results from the indicated calculations. Include user-defined functions if you think they clarify the calculations. What happens when the tested disease is found in 50% of the population? What happens for both disease situations when the positive and/or negative tests are much less reliable, say 50%?

7.12. A recursive algorithm for generating Fibonacci numbers is given in Sect. 6.5. Here is a variation that defines the totally obscure and completely useless "Brooks function" for positive values of n:

$B_n = 1$, n=1 or 2
$B_n = 3$, n=3
$B_n = (0.5B_{n-1} + 0.75B_{n-2})/B_{n-3}$

Give results for at least n=1, 2, 3, 4, 5, and 20. You *must* use a recursive function to calculate values of the Brooks function.

EXTRA CREDIT: Invent a new recursively defined function that is actually good for something.

7.13. Consider this HTML interface that defines the calculations for permutations and combinations of n distinct objects taken m at a time, with and without allowing repetitions. For permutations, the same objects in a different order constitute a distinct permutation. That is, for the example shown, CA is different from AC. For combinations, the same objects in a different order do not constitute a distinct combination. That is, CA is equivalent to AC. Hence, there are 6 permutations of CAT, but only 3 combinations.

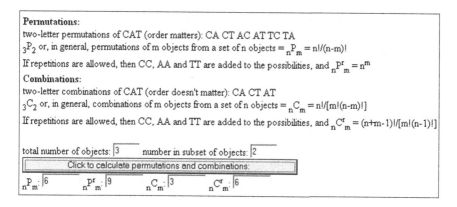

Write an HTML/PHP application to calculate these permutations and combinations. (You don't have to include all the explanatory text in your HTML document.) Write user-defined functions for each calculation.

7.14. Rewrite the solution to Exercise 6.3 with a user-defined function that accepts as input an array and returns the minimum, maximum, mean, median, and standard deviation of the values in the array. Note that to find the median, the values need to be sorted in ascending or descending order.

7.15. Consider a string that contains a date and time in a 12-hour AM/PM tab- or space-delimited format, like these two examples:

```
10 17 2010 9   29 35 AM
10 17 2010 13 30 00 PM
```

Write a PHP function that will read such strings and create a new string in which the date and time are given in a 24-hour format, like this, 09/17/2010 09:29:35, using these substitutions:

If (AM/PM is AM) and (hour $\leq$ 11) the hour is unchanged.
If (AM/PM is PM) and (hour = 12) the hour is 12 (unchanged).
If (AM/PM is PM) and (hour < 12) the hour is hour + 12.
If (AM/PM is AM) and (hour = 12) the hour is 0.

Single-digit values 0–9, such as 9 for 9 o'clock am, must be displayed with a leading 0—09 rather than 9.

7.16. Insolation is defined as the incoming solar radiation S_o falling on a horizontal surface at Earth's surface under "clear sky" conditions (no clouds). Around noon on a clear summer day at mid latitudes, S_o is roughly 1000 W/m^2.

The presence of clouds reduces the insolation by an amount which varies in very complicated ways with the amount and type of cloud cover. Here is one simple model for approximating the reduction in insolation as a result of cloud cover.[3]

$$S = S_o \cdot \left(1 - 0.75n^{3.4}\right)$$

where n is the fraction of cloud cover ranging from 0 (clear) to 1 (overcast). Integrated over a day, such a model might be useful for approximating total daily incoming solar radiation.

The clear sky insolation can be approximated if you know the value at solar noon. Solar noon is within several minutes of, but not the same as, clock noon, depending on time of year and longitude.

Given the clear sky solar noon insolation, the clear sky insolation at other times can be modeled as a "pinched cosine" curve:

$$S_o(t) = S_o(noon) \cdot \cos[\pi(t_{noon} - t)/t_{halfday}]^{\beta}$$

where t is time relative to solar noon, $t_{half\ day}$ is the time from sunrise or sunset to solar noon, and β has a value around 1.2.

Write a PHP application (with or without an HTML interface) that calculates insolation at half-hour or shorter intervals (relative to solar noon) and sums up those values, assuming $S_o(noon) = 1000$ W/m^2, to approximate total solar energy received during the day. There are 1440 minutes in a day. Be sure your code rejects negative insolation values from the daily sum.

(a) Show results for several cloud amounts from 0 to 1.
(b) Write some data to a .csv output file and graph the results in a spreadsheet.

Although user-defined functions aren't actually required for a reasonable solution to this problem, it makes sense to use them to "compartmentalize" the various calculations.

7.17. The value of equipment used in manufacturing and other businesses declines as the equipment ages. Businesses must recover the cost of "durable" equipment by depreciating its value over an assumed useful

---

[3]At the time this book was written, a version of this model could be found at shodor.org/ os411/courses/_master/tools/calculators/solarrad/.

lifetime of n years. At the end of n years, the equipment may have either no value or some small salvage value. Depreciation can be computed three ways:

1. *Straight-line depreciation.* The value of an asset minus its salvage value depreciates by the same amount each year over its useful life of n years.

2. *Double-declining depreciation.* Each year, the original value of an asset minus the previously declared depreciation is diminished by 2/n. (This method does not depend on an assumed salvage value.)

3. *Sum-of-digits depreciation.* Add the integers from 1 through n. For year i, the depreciation allowed is the original value of the asset minus its salvage value, times (n − i) + 1, divided by the sum of the digits.

Write an HTML document that allows the user to enter the original value of an asset, the number of years over which the depreciation will be taken, and its salvage value at the end of the depreciation period. Then write a PHP application that will use these values to print out a depreciation table showing the results for each depreciation method. Here is a sample table.

The code that generated this table used `echo` statements and the `round ()` function to generate the output, because that was a little easier to do while the code was being developed. You can gain more control over the output by, for example, having 100 print as 100.00, using `printf()` with appropriate format specifiers.

Original value	$1000					
Salvage value	$100					
Lifetime (years)	7					
Year	Straight line	Asset value	Double declining	Asset value	Sum of digits	Asset value
1	128.57	871.43	285.71	714.29	225	775
2	128.57	742.86	204.08	510.2	192.86	582.14
3	128.57	614.29	145.77	364.43	160.71	421.43
4	128.57	485.71	104.12	260.31	128.57	292.86
5	128.57	357.14	74.37	185.93	96.43	196.43
6	128.57	228.57	53.12	132.81	64.29	132.14
7	128.57	100	37.95	94.86	32.14	100

Businesses often like to "front load" the depreciation of an asset in order to realize the maximum tax deduction in the year that the funds were actually spent for the equipment. For this reason, they would likely not choose the straight line method even though it is the simplest of the three.

8. Files, Input/Output, and Strings

8.1. Write a PHP application that will read a text file and count the number of occurrences of each letter in the file. (Use the `fgetc()` function to read one character at a time from the file.) Upper- and lowercase letters should be counted as the same character. Store the results in an array with 26 upper- or lowercase character keys and display the contents of the array when all characters have been read from the file.

8.2. Create a data file containing an unspecified number of values between 0 and 100. Define an array with letter grades as keys:

```
$a = array("A" => 90, "B" => 80, ...);
```

This array defines cutoff points for each letter grade.

Define another array with the same character keys. The elements of this array should be initialized to 0. Then, when you read through your data file, increment the appropriate grade "box" by 1. (This could be done with multiple if... statements, for example.) When you are finished, display the keys and contents of the second array in a table that shows the number of A's, B's, etc.; for example:

```
A 3
B 7
C 5
D 2
F 1
```

This is just another version of the histogram problem, but the boxes are named by the keys of $a, and the limits for letter grades can easily be changed.

8.3. Create a file of names and densities of various materials. Write an HTML/PHP application that will read this file and display all materials and densities for which the density is greater than or less than some value specified in the HTML document. (Use a radio button to select greater or less than.)

8.4. Define a "heat wave" as a condition for which the maximum temperature exceeds 90°F on any three consecutive days. Write a PHP application that will read and display a file of daily maximum high temperatures, including in your output an appropriate message when a heat wave is in progress.

Note that you can define a heat wave only retroactively, because the heat wave is known to be occurring only on the third day. This means that you must store data from at least the two previous days before you can display an appropriate message for the heat wave days.

Here is a sample data file with appropriate output:

```
07/01/2006 89
07/02/2006 90 heat wave day 1
07/03/2006 93 heat wave day 2
07/04/2006 92 heat wave day 3
07/05/2006 94 heat wave day 4
07/06/2006 89
07/08/2006 91 heat wave day 1
07/09/2006 90 heat wave day 2
07/10/2006 92 heat wave day 3
07/11/2006 89
07/12/2006 87
```

9. PHP Graphics

For some of these exercises, it is much easier to save an output file and do the graphing in a spreadsheet. Although you might want to use a spreadsheet to check your work that, of course, is not the point of these exercises!

9.1. Using Document 6.13 as a starting point, display the contents of the histogram as a horizontal or vertical bar chart.

9.2. Modify the vertical bar graph application (Documents 12.7a and 12.7b) so that it can display two bars, side-by-side, for each x-axis label. The bars should be different colors and a label identifying the purpose of each bar should be displayed somewhere in the graphing space.

9.3. The distribution of wind directions recorded over a specified period is typically summarized in a wind rose diagram. Wind directions are often classified according to 16 named 22.5-degree categories:

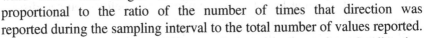

N, NNE, NE, ENE, E, ESE, SE, SSE,
S, SSW, SW, WSW, W, WNW, NW, NNW

The graphic shows a very simple 16-point wind rose. The length of each arm is proportional to the ratio of the number of times that direction was reported during the sampling interval to the total number of values reported.

Wind directions are measured from due north and represent the direction from which the wind is *coming*. Thus, a NE wind is a wind coming out of the northeast and blowing *toward* the southwest. (Which wind direction is missing in the sketch?)

Write a PHP application that reads a collection of wind direction data, expressed as one of the 16 compass point identifiers, and generates a 16-point wind rose. You can "hard code" the wind directions, but it might be easier to store them in a separate file so you can change the data without editing your PHP script. You don't need to provide an HTML interface.

Extra credit:

(1) Alternatively, wind directions can be rounded to the nearest 10 degrees, in which case there would be 36 points in the wind rose. Write your code so that the 16-point 22.5-degree wind rose can easily be changed to a 36-point (10-degree) wind rose. In that case, the data file should contain wind directions in degrees rather than compass point identifiers. The code required to implement these changes should be accessed as a result of specifying the number of arms as 36 rather than 16. In this case, you should probably provide an HTML interface to tell the PHP application what kind of data to expect.

(2) The circles at the tips of the wind rose arrows are OK and easy to draw, but actual arrow points would look a lot nicer. Add code to draw properly oriented filled triangles for arrow points.

9.4. The table gives data recorded with a sun photometer—an instrument that measures wavelength-dependent radiation coming directly from the sun. The first column is the voltage V, the second is the "dark voltage" V_0 when there is no sunlight incident on the instrument, and the third is the relative air mass m—a measure of the amount of atmosphere between the instrument and the sun; m=1 when the sun is directly overhead.

0.582	0.003	8.2398
0.681	0.003	7.0438
0.746	0.003	6.2972
0.799	0.003	5.6974
0.849	0.003	5.1569
0.896	0.003	4.7228
0.931	0.003	4.4054
0.962	0.003	4.1332
1.006	0.003	3.7906
1.037	0.003	3.5338
1.068	0.003	3.2936
1.091	0.003	3.0758
1.121	0.003	2.8257
1.158	0.003	2.6090
1.176	0.003	2.4870
1.203	0.003	2.3003
1.223	0.003	2.1956
1.24	0.003	2.1043
1.25	0.003	1.9784
1.272	0.003	1.8467

For data collected under suitable conditions, $ln(V - V_0)$ plotted against m should be a straight line. Generate a line graph to display these data. Display values of $ln(V - V_0)$ with symbols. Write code to generate a least-squares linear regression analysis and plot the resulting solid line on the graph. Display the regression equation in the form y = a + bx, and the correlation coefficient r^2 on the graph. Here are the equations for the regression analysis:

$$a = [(\Sigma y_i)(\Sigma x_i^2) - (\Sigma x_i)(\Sigma x_i y_i)/[n\Sigma x_i^2 - (\Sigma x_i)^2]$$
$$b = [n\Sigma x_i y_i - (\Sigma x_i)(\Sigma y_i)]/[n\Sigma x_i^2 - (\Sigma_i)^2]$$
$$s_{y,x}^2 = (\Sigma y_i^2 - a\Sigma y_i - b\Sigma x_i y_i)/(n-2)$$
$$s^2 = [\Sigma x_i^2 - (\Sigma x_i)^2/n]/(n-1) \quad r^2 = 1 - s_{y,x}^2/s_y^2$$

9.5. Using Exercise 6.11 as a starting point, create a line graph that displays the original data with symbols and the running average as a solid line.

9.6. An electrical circuit contains a DC voltage source, a capacitor C, an inductor L, and a resistor R in series with a switch. The switch is closed at time t=0 and current starts to flow, oscillating with time. What is the charge on the capacitor as a function of time?
For $4L/C - R^2 > 0$, the solution is:

$$q(t) = CV\left[1 - \exp(-\frac{Rt}{2L})\cos\left(\frac{t\sqrt{4L/C - R^2}}{2L}\right)\right]$$

The equilibrium charge as t → ∞ is CV coulombs. Reasonable values to test are:

$V = 100$ volts, $L = 0.02$ henrys, $R = 25$ ohms, $C = 0.000001$ farads

For these values, q is very near equilibrium after about 10 ms.
Calculate charge as a function of time and graph the results.

9.7. Using Exercise 6.7 as a starting point, graph the tabulated X and Y values, connected by solid lines. Graph the interpolated point with a "+" character. If you want a bigger or different symbol, you will have to "draw" it.

9.8. Using Sect. 7.5.4 as a starting point, add code to Document 7.8 to graph the position of an Earth-orbiting object as a function of time. Assume the orbit starts at perigee at coordinates $(0, r_p)$ and proceeds counterclockwise. Draw the orbit path using as many time intervals as you need to generate a reasonably smooth curve for the orbit. Then put a small circle at coordinates for each of the time steps chosen for the original problem.

In addition to the equations given in Sect. 7.5.4, you will also need

$$p = a \bullet \left(1 - e^2\right)$$
$$r_{perigree} = a \bullet (1 - e)$$
$$r_{apogee} = a \bullet (1 + e)$$
$$r_x = \cos(f) \bullet p/[1 + e \bullet \cos(f)]$$
$$r_y = \cos(f) \bullet p/[1 + e \bullet \cos(f)]$$

9.9. Write a PHP application that will reproduce the telephone keypad image shown here. The keypads are filled ellipses of size 75 × 75 pixels. ImageString() was used to draw the letters at the top of the keypads; the "1", "*", and "#" keypads usually don't have text at the top. The text size was specified as 5, the largest allowed value. (Remember that text size for ImageString() is just a relative value rather than an actual point size or a size in pixels.)

ImageTTFText() was used to draw the larger numbers in the keypads using TrueType fonts, which can be scaled to much larger sizes than is possible for text drawn with ImageString(). The code used to produce this image gets its font information from an arial.ttf font file. To use any .ttf font, find the file on your computer and copy it into the directory where you store your PHP applications. (On Windows computers, font files should be in the `C:\WINDOWS\Fonts\` directory.) The desired font size will need to be specified either in pixels or (more likely) point size, depending on which version of the GD library you are using—you can quickly figure this out just by trying some size values and observing the results.

10. PHP from a Command Line

Any application with basic input/output requirements is a reasonable candidate for rewriting as a command line interface (CLI) application—Exercise 4-5.6 is just one typical example.

Algorithm Index

The examples and exercises in this book include algorithms for a variety of computational problems. Here is a list, with page numbers.

© Springer International Publishing AG 2017
D.R. Brooks, *Programming in HTML and PHP*, Undergraduate Topics in Computer Science, DOI 10.1007/978-3-319-56973-4

Topic Index

In the topic index, symbols are "alphabetized" according to the ordering assigned by a spreadsheet. File extensions starting with a period (.), special characters starting with a & symbol, escape characters starting with a backslash (\), file access permissions enclosed in single or double quotes (' or "), tags enclosed in angle brackets (<...>) or data type references enclosed in parentheses ((...)) are indexed alphabetically as though those non-letter characters were not present.

© Springer International Publishing AG 2017
D.R. Brooks, *Programming in HTML and PHP*, Undergraduate Topics in Computer Science, DOI 10.1007/978-3-319-56973-4

Printed in the United States
By Bookmasters